AF430634

THE LOST PARADISE

A FAMILY'S UNFORGETTABLE ODYSSEY THROUGH RUSSIA, PERSIA, AND GERMANY

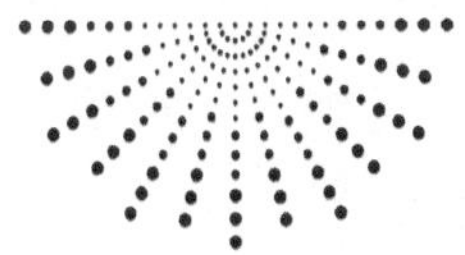

YUNES PAYANDEH

Copyright © 2024 by Yunes Payandeh

All rights reserved.

No part of this book may be reproduced in any form or by any electronic or mechanical means, including information storage and retrieval systems, without written permission from the author, except for the use of brief quotations in a book review.

To Gisela, the light of my life, my rock.
To Minou & Kambiz, whose laughter is my favorite sound.

~

And to all my dear family members from the past, present and future.

CONTENTS

Nalchik
Grozny
Vladikavkaz
Makhachkala
Aktau
Ustyurt National Preserve
Kutaisi
CAUCASUS
GEORGIA
Derbent
Caspian Sea
Tbilisi
Marneuli
LESSER CAUCASUS
Gora Bazardyuzyu
Kars
Gyumri
Ganja
Sumqayit
Baku
ARMENIA
AZERBAIJAN
Krasnovodsk
Great Ararat
Balkanabat
Van
Khvoy
Tabriz
Ardabil
Urmia
Azadshahr
RESHTEH-YE KUHHA-YE ALBORZ
Gorgan
Duhok
Zanjan
Mosul
Qazvin
Erbil
Karaj
Tehran
Semnan
Sulaymaniyah
I
Kirkuk
Sanandaj
R
Hamadan
A
Qom
N
Samarra
Z
Kermanshah
A
Arak
I
Al Bour
G
A
Baghdad
R
N
Al-Aziziyah
O
Karbala
S
Isfahan
IRAN
Al-Hillah
Kut
Dezful
M
Yazd
Najaf
O
U
Al Amarah
N
T
Ahvaz
A
Kuh-e Dena
I
Nasiriyah
N
S
Basra
Abadan
Umm Qasr
Shiraz

INTRODUCTION

IN THE NAME OF GOD, THE GRACIOUS AND MERCIFUL

The Hadj Bey family was an old and famous Persian family from North Azerbaijan province. In the early 1800s, following the annexation of northern Azerbaijan and other areas of Persia by Russia, these territories were separated from their motherland, Persia. The family name was changed to the Russian spelling, Hadj Bekoff, but the family's Persian identity remained intact.

My father, M. Taghi Khalilbey, left his noble family in Persia at about sixteen years old and moved to Baku in Azerbaijan. There, he learned Russian from his uncle and began a commercial apprenticeship. Later, he married my mother, Sara, one of six daughters of the oil baron, Hadj Bekoff.

During the Russian Revolution, my grandfather passed away. As the situation became increasingly dangerous, my parents, along with my grandmother and aunts, fled to Tabriz, Persia, leaving their wealth behind. However, my industrious father established a dairy factory and became well-known and wealthy due to the high demand for his famous Liqvan sheep's cheese!

My parents were determined to give their children a better future than the privileged life they had in Baku. As the fourth of nine siblings, I followed in the footsteps of my older brothers and went to Germany to study civil engineering. At the end of my studies, and without my parents' knowledge, I boldly married a pretty German girl named Gisela, who came from a background similar to my own.

In 1966, a major turning point occurred when I returned to Persia with my wife. We lived there for about ten years, experiencing many challenges until we were expelled by the Islamic Revolutionists, much like our ancestors before us, and we returned to Germany once again.

This book portrays my early years in Germany, followed by my life with Gisela in Tabriz, where we navigated different customs and culture until the Islamic Revolution. It tells the story of the descendants of Hadj Aga Bekoff, the oil baron, and his son, Haj Bekoff, our grandfather from Baku, which is now the capital of the Republic of Azerbaijan.

The book also explores the forced migration of our ancestors from their homeland to Persia during the Russian Revolution and the compelling story of Leo Ramsauer's granddaughter, who was expelled from East Prussia to West Germany during World War II, and her subsequent life in Persia until the Revolution.

MY BIRTH IN TABRIZ, PERSIA 1943

"I am neither of the East nor of the West, no boundaries exist within my breast."

— *RUMI*

The sky was blue, the air pure and fresh, and the sun shone brightly, warming the magnificent plains of Liqvan. A faint gust of desert wind rustled through the silver-green leaves of tall birch trees, whispering across cool meadows and fields of melons, tomatoes, eggplants, and other bounties of nature. The fields were still damp with dew from the night, and here and there, a few drops fell from the fruit trees. A wonderful aroma emanated from the grass and trees. Birds swooped down, almost touching the fragrant meadows, before soaring high above the towering birch trees. Flocks of sheep grazed lazily in the distance. It was a typical gorgeous summer day in July 1943.

My father was in Liqvan on business. The village, located about 40 kilometers east of Tabriz, the capital of East Azerbaijan

Province, is a beautiful, typical Persian village nestled in the foothills of the Sahand mountains. The lush meadows, rolling hills, and flowing streams are a delight to the eyes and soul.

Agriculture and animal husbandry were the primary sources of income for the villagers. The landscape was untouched and pure, as it had been for hundreds of years. Far from the noise of civilization, there was no electricity, telephone service, or even tap water. Nothing disturbed this oasis of peace. Sheep breeding had been practiced here for generations, primarily due to the high quality of the milk. My father had been buying milk from this village for years and had become well-known for producing renowned cheese throughout the country, providing our family with financial security.

Over time, a strong business relationship and friendship developed between the farmers and my father. Friendship was particularly important to us; it wasn't always easy to build, but once established, it was based on great trust. Problems were solved together without involving third parties, and decisions were made simply on trust. A promise was kept and breaking it would have been a great offense.

The villagers lived simple, honest lives. Their homes had no form of security—they left their houses open from the time they went to the fields early in the morning until they returned in the evening. Nothing was ever stolen. It was not in their nature to lie, be violent, or envy others. These patient, God-fearing people lived and worked in harmony with nature. Over the years, I observed and studied their way of life. I watched how a simple piece of bread was eaten with relish at meals, chewed slowly to savor the taste of the wheat they had sown, harvested, ground, and baked themselves, connecting them to the earth.

From spring to autumn, the farmers waited patiently for their harvest, which they nurtured like a child in the womb and finally harvested in the fall. God's gifts—milk, yogurt, cream, cheese, golden honey, luscious seedless grapes, herbs, vegetables, and fruits

—were all enjoyed by these good-natured and faithful people, who appreciated these gifts from the Almighty. Gratitude was second nature to them, evident in their treatment of nature, people, and animals. There was a respectful attitude towards each other; their cattle and all animals were treated with care. They were united with nature, and I often saw the farmers holding a piece of wood, a flower, or even a single leaf carefully in their hands. The village didn't have its own school, so the students—boys in gray and girls in colorful costumes—walked along the river to a neighboring village a few kilometers away to attend school.

My father visited the village every year at the beginning of summer to negotiate the price of milk for cheese production. For him, this was a time of vacation and recreation, as he loved the clean and healthy environment and appreciated the enchanting nature of the place.

The village elders and farmers would fix the price for milk for the whole year. Afterward, the farmers delivered the milk to our cheese preparation facility in the village. The finished cheese was ripened in large canisters in brine and then delivered to our stores in Tabriz and Tehran. In the capital, we had a thriving business, and our food store, "Magaseh – Iran," was famous for quality cheese, butter, and other dairy products from Liqvan, Azerbaijan. My father had worked for years to perfect these products, and everyone had confidence in his abilities.

~

I WAS BORN on July 7, 1943. My father was informed of my arrival by the village elders, who congratulated him and said a prayer of thanks together. After that, my father rushed back to Tabriz.

Our family was rich in children. I was the seventh of ten: four older brothers, two older sisters, and two younger brothers, along with one younger sister. We were all about three years apart in age, with each child breastfed for two years before the next pregnancy began. The first-born child, a son, had unfortunately died in infancy, likely due to medical or hygienic conditions of the time. I believe our parents decided to have many children for this reason.

Our father was born in Khameneh, a small village near Tabriz that had about 1,000 inhabitants at the time. His ancestors had connections with Europeans long ago—some emigrated to Russia or Azerbaijan in the Caucasus, some traded with Europe, and others went to Moscow to study and eventually became famous merchants in Hamburg, Germany.

Father left home at a very young age and went to Baku, today's capital of the Republic of Azerbaijan, located on the Caspian Sea. It was easy to cross the sea by boat from Anzali, a port on the Persian side of the Caspian Sea, to reach the European side. He did a commercial apprenticeship in Baku with his uncle, a well-known and respected businessman, while learning Russian.

I was four years old in Tabriz.

BAKU - CAPITAL OF THE REPUBLIC OF AZERBAIJAN

The Hadj Bekoff family was one of the oldest and most renowned Persian families, with business connections stretching from Moscow through Persia to India. According to legend, the Persian King Nasir al-din Shah once visited their estate and stayed overnight as their guest.

Our mother was the daughter of a Persian-born oil baron in Baku. She had grown up surrounded by the finer things in life. Her grandfather, Hadj Agha Bekoff, was a wealthy and well-known figure in Baku. After his death, his son, Haj Bekoff, took over the family business. In addition to the oil industry, Haj Bekoff established a chain of small stores selling modern foodstuffs in the city, becoming a prosperous businessman.

Through these business connections, my father's uncle introduced him to Haj Bekoff, a respected merchant with a strong reputation, with whom my father became well acquainted. This introduction eventually led to my father meeting Haj Bekoff's daughter. When my father asked for her hand in marriage, the baron gladly gave his blessing. The wedding took place in 1918, marked by an elaborate celebration. For weeks, food was distributed to dockworkers, mainly Persian emigrants, and to the poor. The entire family, from Russia and the Caucasus, gathered for the occasion, and the next few years were indeed happy ones for the newlyweds.

Mother often shared stories of her trips to Moscow and other Russian cities, where she enjoyed opera, theater, and circus performances. When they started their family, the birth of their first child, a boy, and then a girl, fulfilled their wishes, and Mother's happiness seemed complete. It was a fulfilling life; Father had many plans, and Mother enjoyed a carefree life caring for her children.

However, this happiness was short-lived. Dark clouds loomed over the Hadj Bekoff family—not the usual thunderstorms that occasionally swept over Baku, causing the girls to hide behind heavy curtains in fear, but the growing threat of the Russian Revolution, which was gaining strength in distant Moscow.

Mom and Dad at their engagement ceremony in Baku.

Mom and Dad on their wedding day in Baku.

From left: Firuze, Dad, Rahim, and Mother in Tabriz.

THE RUSSIAN REVOLUTION

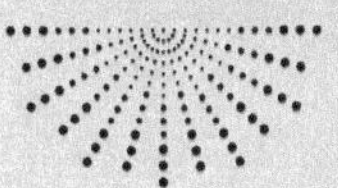

On March 15, 1917, the 300-year rule of the Romanov dynasty ended with the abdication of Nicholas II. He and his family were exiled to Siberia, where they were later brutally murdered, including their sick son, the heir to the throne. The brief period of freedom from monarchist rule lasted only about half a year, as the Bolsheviks launched the October Revolution later that same year.

The Russian Civil War, which began in 1917, ended in 1920 with the Bolsheviks' victory, ultimately leading to the establishment of the USSR in 1922. Meanwhile, on May 28, 1918, the Azerbaijan Democratic Republic (AXC) was proclaimed and recognized de facto by the international community as a subject of international law. This secular, pro-Western state, with a strong legislature, enjoyed 23 months of freedom before being conquered by the Bolsheviks. The national government went into exile, first to Poland, then Germany, and later to Turkey.

The oil fields of Baku were a significant target during the Russian Revolution. In 1893, the USA accounted for 51% of the world's oil production, while Russia contributed 46%. By 1898, Baku had overtaken the US as the leading oil-producing region.

After the Bolsheviks marched into Baku, they looted homes and stores belonging to the wealthy, including our family's. The Red Army soon arrived, and the expropriation of the oil fields completed their takeover. Amid the ensuing chaos, angry workers rioted in Baku, debtors killed creditors, and the newly formed District Committee, composed of criminals and opportunists, took the law into their own hands. Innocent people were killed, the Baku prison was stormed, and criminals were set free. It was a dangerous and catastrophic situation that threatened the very lives of our close-knit family.

Many fled across the Aras River to Persia to survive the chaos. Our family was fortunate in having loyal workers and servants who protected us from attacks, though we were constantly worried about our relatives—my mother's sister and her husband, a chemist, who lived in Moscow, and another relative who lived in Makhachkala, the capital of Dagestan on the Caspian Sea. The reach of the new regime seemed to have no boundaries.

The news from Moscow was dire. It was uncertain whether the Red Army had gained full control or if the Liberals had succeeded. After a few difficult weeks, it became clear that the Red Army was firmly in control, and the USSR was born. An ultimatum was issued to Persians without Russian citizenship: either leave the country and return to Persia or become Russian citizens and live under socialist rule according to Lenin's teachings. Our family, like many others, had to make this difficult choice.

By the early 1800s, the regions now known as Azerbaijan, Georgia, Armenia, Dagestan, and other territories of the Caucasus were, still part of present-day Iran. After long wars between Persia and Russia, the Treaty of Gulistan in 1813 and the Treaty of Turkmenchay in 1828 resulted in Iran losing its possessions in the Caucasus and being confined to its current borders along the Aras River. This river, flowing from Mount Ararat to the Caspian Sea, thus divided Azerbaijan.

Although our ancestors fell under Russian rule, they managed to preserve their Persian identity. However, all citizens within Russian borders were forced to live under the Communist regime.

Haj Bekoff died suddenly of pneumonia, perhaps weakened by a sense of the troubles that lay ahead for our family. After his death, my grandmother became the head of the family, and the responsibility of making decisions fell upon her shoulders. As she had no brothers, there were no men to carry on the family title.

4
OLD BAKU

Old Baku was once known as the gateway to the Orient. As a port, it provided an accessible route for Europeans to reach Russia. Baku, a city with a maze of narrow streets and old houses, was historically a fortress. Many of its walls and towers, reinforced after the Russian conquest in 1806, have stood since early Persian times. Notable landmarks include the world-famous palace of the Khans of Shirvan and the Virgin Tower, dating back to the 11th century. Baku was a bustling hub of activity and trade, serving as the starting point for caravans embarking on arduous journeys across the Steppes. The city was remarkably well-developed for its time, with horse-drawn trams, wide avenues, and flourishing institutions such as its university, opera, and theaters.

A special delight was sitting in one of the beautiful restaurants along the Caspian Sea promenade, enjoying the famous caviar. A visit to the bustling bazaar of Baku was a must, as was seeing the beautiful mosque. Many famous Europeans had second residences there.

In 1873, Robert Nobel, the eldest brother of Ludwig and Alfred Nobel, founded the Nobel Brothers Petroleum Company in Baku, one of the largest oil companies of that time. The millionaire oil barons, including Christians, Jews, and Muslims, could afford to build villas in the neo-gothic style. These modern palaces, designed by famous European architects, projected a dreamlike quality. In the northern part of Baku, these villas belonged to rich and famous personalities from Europe and beyond, each more beautiful than the last.

Writers, artists, and merchants from around the world gathered in cosmopolitan Baku, where there was a high demand for newspapers, books, and art. Operettas were sung with passion, and the haunting notes of music filled the air. Baku was widely acknowledged as a multicultural city, and even its mayor from 1898-1902 was a German named Nikolaus von der Nonne.

My mother was born and raised in this rich cultural environment, but she knew little of Persia. Tabriz was foreign to her, a place known only by name, though conversations with visiting merchants gave her some ideas of fabled Persia. Little did she dream that she would one day live there! To leave one's native environment voluntarily to emigrate to a foreign country, especially without knowing what the future held, would have been unthinkable at that time.

In the meantime, my mother had her second child, a girl. Under normal circumstances, my parents would have been a happier couple, but fate intervened and played a different tune. My grandmother, Lady Haj Bekoff, was forced to decide how to proceed. My father advised her that the sooner they emigrated to Persia, the better. If they waited too long, they might not receive an exit permit, which would worsen the situation considerably. It was imperative to make a swift decision, so after a few days of anxious deliberation, the fateful choice was made.

Everyone, except for two sisters who lived with their families in Moscow and Dagestan, agreed to leave. My father quickly took action. He notified his acquaintances and business partners in Tabriz and Rasht of his decision and organized the trip by ship to avoid unnecessary hardships. It was a tremendous responsibility.

Our family did not know Persia at all, but as my father was born there, he was familiar with the ways of his countrymen. He knew that the family would face challenges in their new environment.

One evening, my grandmother sat alone on the veranda of her house, lost in thought. She reflected on the past—on beautiful times, on her father, her husband, and the relatives and friends she would soon leave behind. Like a movie, these memories flashed before her eyes. A maid, who had stayed with the family, announced that a gentleman had arrived and wished to speak to the lady of the house. Grandmother allowed him to enter.

A middle-aged man wearing a dark Kazakh uniform stood before her. He was well-groomed, with gray hair and an extremely long mustache. He greeted her politely and explained that he had known her husband well. The late Hadj Bekoff had come to his aid many times, and he owed him a substantial debt. He went on to say that he had always fought for justice and freedom, and now that workers and peasants were free from their masters, he wanted to help the family as a way of repaying his debt. He was aware of how soldiers might treat a wealthy family and wanted to protect them if possible.

My grandmother was touched and grateful that some people still had a conscience in such cruel times. She knew that trying to recover the debt owed to her late husband would be futile, as the money was now worthless. So, she thanked the man and forgave the debt without even asking how much it was. The mysterious man was relieved and left without another word. We would soon discover the depth of his gratitude.

OUR MYSTERIOUS VISITOR obtained the necessary papers for the move, including permits and passes that allowed us to take our household items to Persia. We were fortunate that the women's precious trousseaus were included. He also provided the exit papers, enabling us to organize everything in time, which was extraordinary. He took care of the passports and ensured that any investigations into the family were not intrusive. In this way, a little peace was restored to our daily life. Now that we were under the protection of the Communist Party, we could leave the country at any time, and the family was left alone for a while.

However, this cherished peace did not last long, as the full extent of the catastrophe gradually became clear to us all. Within two years, the family had lost everything: our entire property, our happy existence, which had been built over several centuries by capable and steadfast men and women and passed on to generations, and especially the loss of the head of the family, Grandfather, and our home. My grandmother held onto the hope that within a few months, everything would calm down, and with the return of law and order, the family might be able to return.

In the meantime, extensive preparations were made. Many precious items that were not allowed to be taken were carefully hidden or buried. Jewels, porcelain, gold, silverware, coins, and other valuables were secreted away. After long, tearful deliberations, the final plan was carried out. Night after night, under cover of darkness, massive wooden boxes packed with heirlooms were buried in the large gardens. Even the walls, ceilings, and niches of the house concealed valuables, and we wondered whether we would ever see them again. One of the aunts took a significant risk by packing her pure gold dishes among the cheap ones she wanted to keep with her. Others hid gold and jewels in oil canisters, while pearl necklaces were sewn into the soles of shoes.

At last, the remainder of our belongings were packed for transport to Persia, with the hope that they would safely cross the border. These measures were taken as a means of making a new start and sustaining us for some time in the foreign country. My mother cleverly hid some of her diamonds and precious stones in a tube of toothpaste, desperately hoping to save something from her jewelry collection. Our household goods and furniture were packed by experienced men, and incredibly, the manifest was approved. We knew that this was only possible because of the careful organization by my grandfather's debtor, the mysterious man with the long mustache. We wondered about the high position he must have held in the Party to allow us to escape with so many household and luxury items.

My father had shipped a large quantity of cement in sealed canisters to Dagestan a few months earlier. Fortunately, the cargo was diverted to Rasht in Persia before the political upheaval in Azerbaijan. He had planned to build a dignified house for the Haj Bekoff family, should the cargo arrive safely in Tabriz. He was concerned about the first impressions his young wife's family would have of his homeland. Having been away from his homeland for more than 20 years, he did not know much about it himself. He had not seen his own family for many years and missed them deeply. However, his brother still lived in Khameneh, his birthplace, and his only sister lived in Tabriz. He had not heard from his other relatives for a long time.

My grandmother, Lady Haj Bekoff, who we called
Abatshi.

Dad with his uncle in Baku discussing business.

Left to right: Our carriage driver, Dad, my aunt Khorshid, Mom, my oldest brother Rahim, and the maid at the house in Baku, Russia.

5

EXPULSION

We finally departed on a gloomy and sad autumn day. With fully loaded carts, my mother with two children, grandmother, three sisters with their husbands and children, and my father formed a long column with carriages and horses, heading to the port of Baku. The house, along with the remnants of our belongings, was left in the care of the staff. Before leaving, my mother made one last round of farewells, saying goodbye to the walls, ceilings, cupboards, carpets, and even the curtains. She ventured into the large hall, gazing out through the window over the beautiful gardens and the blue sea beyond. She had spent many happy times with her father, watching the ships sail by. It was so hard for her to leave this place, filled with memories of charming weddings, Nowruz festivities, and even sorrowful funeral services. Whispering a tearful prayer for her late father, she sorrowfully left the house, possibly forever. Our family, now torn apart, was expelled from the life we had known.

At the border we had some luck. Our aunt made it through with her special, beloved dishes, which went unnoticed. But when my mother's handbag was examined, she turned red in the face and began to tremble.

The inspector became suspicious and asked what she was carrying. For the first time in her life, my mother had to lie, and she felt deeply embarrassed. Searching her heart for help, she prayed to her favorite saint, Imam Hossain. Without hesitation, she smoothly explained that, as a Muslim, she was ashamed to have a man go through her private belongings. The inspector, showing pity and understanding, let her pass. A terrible moment for the family had been overcome by deception, though it was for a good cause.

After an exhausting journey, the families finally arrived in Tabriz. It quickly became clear to my mother that life in Persia was going to be hard and difficult, and so it proved to be.

Left: My Dad in Moscow Right: My Grandmother
Abadji and daughter Kanom Aziz.

Left to Right: Mother's youngest sister Khadije, Mom, my oldest brother Rahim and oldest sister Firuzeh.

A NEW BEGINNING IN TABRIZ, PERSIA

In Tabriz, Father rented a few small houses next to each other in a safe part of town. Each house had a square courtyard, with two-room apartments on three sides and a shared kitchen and toilet near the entrance on the fourth side. The women quickly furnished the apartments as best they could and were immensely grateful that their belongings had arrived safely and that they had a roof over their heads.

I often noticed that in difficult times, family and friends tend to band together closely, which helped us overcome unpleasant moments. They cooked together, and the women did their best with the limited resources available. In the beginning, life was very difficult for the family. There were no acquaintances or relatives nearby, and the locals were deeply religious and not always welcoming. The circumstances and conditions were very different from what we had known in Baku. However, Father, aware of these challenges, did everything possible to make our lives more bearable, especially considering the lifestyle we had left behind.

He admired the perseverance and patience of the people in Tabriz, who, despite their misfortunes, gracefully accepted their fate. Mother was a devout person who believed not only in God's will but also in the role of fate. She was convinced that bad events were not without reason but were harbingers of good things to come, which helped her endure many trials. For her, religion was a source of faith, and with that faith in God and His goodness, she did her best to understand the people of Tabriz, though it was not easy. Many other immigrants from Azerbaijan were very skeptical, but Mother made efforts to embrace the different customs of the country and integrate with Father's family and relatives, though this took time and patience.

Father began rebuilding his business. As a skilled merchant, he quickly realized that food was always a good investment. However, many other necessities were lacking in the country. Due to the Russian Revolution, the price of cement had skyrocketed, so it was fortunate that he had sent a shipment to Rasht many months earlier. With the new, exorbitant price of cement, his sales made him financially secure, and with the help of Mother's diamonds, he was able to start afresh. He bought the small houses that had been previously rented and began preparations to build our new home.

The house we grew up in must have been designed by an architect because the technical details were quite sophisticated for those times, and the designers and bricklayers were well-educated. Our new home was ahead of its time and featured many modern designs and comfortable amenities. I always wanted to ask my father about them, but somehow, I never got around to it. There are things in life that, despite our best intentions, never happen.

DEATH OF A FIRST CHILD

While Father was building and renovating the family home, my eldest brother fell seriously ill. Vaccinations and preventative medicines for many diseases were in their infancy at that time, and the doctors could do little for our brother, who was only six years old. He simply withered like a flower and died in the arms of our grieving mother. Losing their first child, a beautiful boy, so unexpectedly and quickly, was a heavy blow to her. Overwhelmed by grief, she found no pleasure in anything and lost her faith in God. In a short time, she had experienced immense losses: the death of her father, the loss of her home, her relatives, and much of her fortune. She had moved to a foreign country, lived with the bare necessities, and then lost her dearly beloved son. Father, desperate in his own grief, tried to hasten the construction of the house to keep Mother occupied and distract her troubled mind.

In the desert, people relied on underground channels called "qanats" to conduct water from distant mountains. There was a severe shortage of water in the summer, especially clean drinking water. If not for these qanats, which brought water down into large catchment basins, the problems would have been insurmountable.

Public cisterns, known as "ab anbars," were technically constructed to supply fresh water to the city year-round. These cisterns were large, vaulted chambers set in the ground, lined with water-resistant mortar, and covered with domes. A staircase led down into the cistern, with steps that reached deep, no matter how far the water level dropped. However, it was nearly impossible for anyone to reach them on foot during the winter to fetch water, no matter how necessary it might have been. Some fortunate houses, like ours, had their own cistern regularly supplied with water.

In our yard, there was a huge underground water basin, large enough to climb into for cleaning. It was a room about 3 x 4 meters in size, with a vaulted roof 3 meters high, and a pond was placed above the vault to equalize the pressure. It took almost all night to fill the cistern with water, and after a few days, the water would become clear. We would then pump it out by hand, filter it, and boil it before consuming it.

Mother made it her mission to ensure clean water was available for everyone using the ab anbar. A very experienced person, called a "mirab," who knew a great deal about the area's underground water sources, was consulted. Under his guidance, a specific location was chosen where he believed a good water vein could be found. Father purchased the land, and the construction of the well began.

It was an incredibly challenging task. Water needed to be accessed at a depth of about 30 meters, so a pit had to be dug until the groundwater was reached. The mirab started by digging a circular pit around himself, about one meter in diameter. As he dug, he sank deeper and deeper into the pit, singing old songs to himself. At a certain depth, he could no longer be seen or heard, and from that point on, he communicated with those above using signals. The work continued in this manner, following a steady rhythm.

After a few months, they reached the groundwater, but the digging continued as far as possible—the deeper, the better. Once the water in the pit reached a significant height, it was necessary to secure and line the bottom of the well and the damp walls with brick. Stairs were built to reach the surface, typically constructed with natural stone, lime, and a plaster mixture. The tried-and-true techniques of centuries past were employed. The staircase, built with a slight angle, resembled a tunnel leading to the outside, surrounded by a solid wall.

As the ab anbar took shape, Mother gradually began to recover her old self.

Mom and Dad

8

A MIRACLE WILL HAPPEN

Work on our ab anbar was almost complete, and it was hoped to be fully operational within a matter of days. However, one afternoon, an accident occurred. On the last section of the tunnel, which was nearly at street level, part of the ceiling collapsed, burying two workers underneath. When Mother learned of the disaster, she—uncaring for decorum and unveiled—ran to the scene, bitterly complaining to God.

"In the name of Imam Hossain, this was built for the poor! For the Shiites, he is the greatest martyr of all time!" she cried out. "Blood is flowing, and innocent workers perish in the process—how is this possible?" Overcome with grief and anger, she swore to God, "If either of the two buried should have even a nosebleed, I will never speak the name of Imam Hossain again."

The onlookers were stunned and whispered among themselves in amazement. For the first time, the foreign lady, the Mohajer (immigrant) from Baku, who knew Imam Hossain and spoke so confidentially with God, was weeping with them. My fearless Mother calmed the crowd as the frantic digging continued to reach the buried workers.

She reassured them, saying confidently, "Don't worry,

everything will be fine, and nothing bad will happen. I assure you; no one will die because this is not our well; it belongs to Imam Hossain, and the water is his. You are all his guests, so he will not abandon us." Then, with a shift in tone, she implored, "I don't want water from him if innocent people are killed in the process." She turned directly to Imam Hossain and begged him for help. (Years later, I was told that she was in an extraordinary state, completely unaware of what had happened.)

After much distress and anxiety, a helper finally cried out with tears of relief, "We have both workers! Here they are, exhausted but unharmed! By holding their hands on the handle of their shovel, they created a small pocket of fresh air. It was surely a miracle that saved their lives."

Through this incident, the family, especially Mother, earned the recognition and respect of the locals in our district. They now had a safe and clean water source. Mother's faith was so strengthened by this event that she maintained a deep connection with her master, Imam Hossain, until the end of her life. The completed ab anbar brought her a sense of fulfillment and restored her by allowing her to care for others after the tragic death of her child. Indeed, a miracle had happened.

MEANWHILE, Mother's favorite sister moved to Tabriz from Moscow. She had married a chemist named Mirza Hamid, who had studied in Moscow. "Mirza" was a title, similar to that of a consul today. He worked as an engineer in a well-known leather factory in Tabriz and was planning to build a factory of his own. He looked very dashing in his black Cossack uniform, especially when riding his black Arabian horse. Mother was pleased that her sister and her husband had joined them, as it strengthened the family ties. Mirza Hamid was a respected figure in Moscow and well-known in professional circles. The upper class of Tabriz also knew him, which was beneficial for his many plans for the future.

Without delay, he bought a large plot of land in the southeast of Tabriz, which had once been a plantation with magnificent pomegranate and walnut trees. Azerbaijan (on the Persian side) was renowned for its wonderful fruit trees and indigenous plants. Almost everything ripened there, except for citrus fruits due to the cold, snowy winters. In the northeast, near the Caspian Sea, where snow was scarce, citrus fruits thrived. The grapes of Azerbaijan were particularly famous, and I knew dozens of varieties, each differing in color, size, and taste. The most renowned was the Shiraz grape.

We always referred to Mirza Hamid simply as Uncle, and I call him Uncle throughout this book. Like my father, he too started building his own house and planned to construct his leather factory right next to it. Despite delays, both the house and the large factory, which employed about 200 workers, were completed within about a year. We often visited their home and were spoiled by our aunt and uncle. As I grew older, I spent more time with Uncle in the factory, where he proudly showed me how leather was treated and manufactured using machinery built by him and his employees.

He was constantly expanding and modernizing his factory. He even converted sections of it into a large, modern fruit and vegetable garden. Cows, sheep, and various poultry were also kept and bred there, making it possible to meet the daily needs of the family and many employees with fresh meat, dairy products, eggs, fruits, and vegetables. For the experienced farmers, he built houses on the property so they could continue managing their daily lives in familiar surroundings, and he ensured their children received an education.

Years later, I met the son of one of these farmers in Bandar Abbas on the Persian Gulf while I was working there. He still remembered my name and told me that his father had worked for my uncle, and that all three of his children had studied with the help of Mirza Hamid.

Uncle also built a huge swimming pool, which I remember well because we children spent many happy days splashing about in the cool water. It was no easy task at that time to build a functioning swimming pool with limited building materials, but he did it, nonetheless!

My mother and her sister, Khnom Aziz (wife of Hamid Aga)

Mirza Hamid, the Chemist

9

OUR HOUSE IN TABRIZ

Our house was a large, 2.5-story, north-facing building with a yellowish brick facade. It had a courtyard on the south side and a large rectangular water basin, about 4 meters by 8 meters, situated in the middle of the garden. Flowerbeds with beautiful flowers and shrubs lined both sides of the basin. A high, pyramid-shaped stone staircase with a wrought-iron bellringer led through a landing to the large hallway, which connected to the second floor. From the hallway, there were large reception rooms on both sides. The room on the right provided access to the private area of the master bedroom and the entrance to the annex. Opposite, a wide staircase led to the upper floor, which housed about nine rooms—ample space for a large family. The high ceilings and wooden windows with three-part glazing were harmoniously arranged, and the building materials were a mix of wood, clay, and terracotta bricks.

The combination of thick walls, generous ceiling height, and the north/south layout proved ideal for the cold winters and warm summers of Tabriz. The walls were extremely thick, and the windowsills, about 1 meter deep, were often used as benches. On warm summer days, these benches, with their view of the colorful garden, became popular spots to sit. Years later, during my studies in Germany, I often wondered how my father knew so much about building. As far as I know, no architect was hired to build the house. There was only an old, experienced foreman named Kalba Bager, whom I still remember with his bearded, kind face. He built the house with the help of local workers.

The basement was divided into functional rooms. One room, used for bread storage, had a large wooden pallet about 5 meters by 5 meters suspended from the ceiling vault by strong chains. On warm summer days, we children used the half-meter-high board as a swing. Another room stored charcoal and equipment. Other rooms were for storing food such as rice, flour, cooking oil, pickled vegetables, or fruits, all placed in large terracotta containers on wooden stands. When I think back now, many years later, I can't believe how simple, healthy, clean, and beautiful life was in those days, and how much has changed in such a short time.

Tabriz is an old city with a rich history. It has been besieged, invaded, and occupied several times. Located in the northwest of Persia, close to the Turkish border and the former Soviet Union, Tabriz was strategically significant. (The northern part of what is now the Republic of Azerbaijan, with its capital Baku, is part of Europe.) The city was invaded multiple times by Russians, Ottomans, and other marauders. To protect themselves, the citizens built houses with high outer walls in narrow alleys. These alleys, often several kilometers long and about 1.5 to 2 meters wide, could only be accessed by foot, horse, or donkey. The alleys frequently intersected, making it easy for strangers to get lost.

Several earthquakes over the years destroyed many of Tabriz's historical monuments, such as the Citadel fortress, Arg-e-Alishah, Masjed-e Kabud (the Blue Mosque), and the town hall, whose tower housed a German clock that has since been preserved and can still be seen today.

Our house was also built in one of these narrow alleys, and we could reach the city center and the bazaar by foot in about 30 minutes. Father walked to and from his office every day. He was an early riser and would be up at 5 a.m. After his morning prayers, he usually occupied himself with the flowers and plants in the yard or the winter garden before heading to work. At 6 a.m., we children were awakened, and the maids turned on the samovar.

Boiling water in the samovar was not easy. First, the charcoal was lit and made to glow, then placed into the middle of the samovar's cylindrical built-in fireplace. The heat from the glowing charcoal made the cylinder hot, heating the water until it boiled. The water remained hot for hours. When the fire in the samovar was smoke and vapor-free, it was carried into the house and placed on a table near the window next to the dining table. The table was then set with an embroidered tablecloth, splendid crystal glasses, and all kinds of sweets, oriental pastries, jams, and tea. This spot in the living room was the most popular and cozy corner, which we all enjoyed immensely.

After breakfast, around 7:30, Father would go to the office. He ate lunch at noon every day, except on Fridays (our Sunday). On Fridays, his favorite dishes were prepared, usually by Mother. Father's usual lunch was chelow kabab, a national rice dish with meat and grilled tomatoes, which is especially tasty when served in a restaurant that specializes in it. In most Islamic countries, Friday is a day of rest, unlike Sunday in other parts of the world.

Next to our house was a smaller building that housed our staff. It was a one-story structure with round columns supporting a large, covered terrace. The facade was trimmed with beautiful bricks and secured with a fine wrought-iron railing. During the warm summer days, we often played on this terrace, and at night, we slept there under the clear sky, with bright stars seemingly close enough to touch.

Opposite, on the other side of the yard, stood another building of similar size. It had several fireplaces, and this was where the cooking was done. There were many galvanized copper cooking pots of various sizes, some so large that we could even hide in them!

An open fireplace, heated with wood, was ready for cooking day and night.

One room was dedicated solely to baking bread. The hearth of the oven was a large terracotta container, similar to a cylinder-shaped flowerpot, with a diameter of about 1 meter and a depth of 2 meters, bricked into the floor. Firewood was burned at the bottom of the cylinder to heat it, and when the terracotta walls were hot, the oven was ready for baking. Two bakers sat around this fireplace, called a "tandoor," and stuck the rolled-out lavash dough onto the hot walls of the tandoor using a flat, pillow-shaped plate. The thin lavash bread—as thin as pizza dough but about a meter long—baked quickly. The bakers, mostly women, arrived before sunrise, around 4 a.m., after their morning prayers. They baked hundreds of thin, crispy, and delicious lavash bread throughout the day, filling the air with the wonderful smell of freshly baked bread. In the evening, the bread was stacked on wooden pallets and carried to the cellar, where it was stored on hanging wooden boards. It took about two weeks to complete the baking, and the cellar was filled with bread.

The preparation of such a large quantity of dough was a story in itself! In an adjoining room of the kitchen, the terrazzo floor was scrubbed clean, and a large plastic sheet was spread out. The dough, made with flour, salt, water, and yeast, was then mixed on the sheet. The baker, dressed in a clean white coat that made him look more like a surgeon, wore new rubber boots and walked back and forth on the dough for hours, as kneading such quantities by hand was impossible. Mother supervised closely, and we laughed at the amusing sight, comparing it to the funny black-and-white films of Laurel & Hardy or Charlie Chaplin, which were popular at the time.

As I grew older, I realized that the bread was not only for us but also for our neighbors, who, during the snowy winter months, could not walk to the baker on the main street and often had no money. Evening after evening, the front door was left ajar for an hour so that neighbors, or those in need, could help themselves in peace, without being recognized.

This practice also extended to other essential foodstuffs, such as rice. Northern Persia, near the Caspian Sea, is known for its rice cultivation. The Caspian Sea, covering 37,100 square kilometers, is one of the largest lakes on Earth and is famous for its caviar. The region's large tea plantations supply the tea consumed throughout the day. In addition to juicy, aromatic citrus fruits, many other fruits thrive there, thanks to the mild, humid, and rainy climate. The high mountains, dense forests, and numerous rivers give this part of the country a unique image, quite different from what one might expect on the Persian plateau. Rice, along with bread, is a staple food in Persia and is prepared quite differently from that in East Asia.

Dad hosted many guests at our home in Tabriz. As is tradition in Persia, we always offered a large platter of fruit, bowls of nuts, and chai (Persian tea). The tall double frame doors were beautifully handcrafted and acted as a divider between different rooms.

A snapshot of my brother Parwiz (right), me (middle), Yaghoub
(left) in our school uniforms with our younger siblings, sister
Manije (right front) and Ayoub in Tabriz.

My older brother Parwiz with my dear sister Ferangis dressed in
their school uniforms in Tabriz.

10

TEA IS ALWAYS PRESENT

ea and sugar were delivered in large wooden boxes directly from wholesalers. Although it may seem unusual to store tea and sugar in bulk, it was necessary in those days. Pre-packed sugar cubes didn't exist—sugar was delivered in large blocks and had to be skillfully chopped into pieces. The different varieties were then mixed, sifted, packed again in boxes, and stored. Black tea is ubiquitous in Persia and is an indispensable companion throughout the day. It is drunk on all occasions and is an integral part of social life, though it is not considered a thirst quencher. Tea is not served in cups or large mugs, but in small, fine glasses. The samovar, quietly simmering, serves as a constant reminder of its history and its readiness to offer refreshment. Whether for quiet leisure or sociable chit-chat, a strong tea in small glasses invigorates both body and soul and is always welcome. Various types of sugar are served with tea, such as white candy-like pieces that taste of rose water, or rock candy sugar cooked with saffron, giving it a bright yellow color.

It is not uncommon for a glass of tea to inspire thoughts of a little snack. Crunchy almonds coated in sugar, caramel brittle with or without nuts, and baklava—always a favorite—make teatime especially popular. Fleshy, soft, and highly aromatic Persian dates are also a healthy snack to enjoy with tea.

Tea was prepared in a large porcelain pot, with boiling water poured over the leaves and then placed on the samovar to steep, but not boil. The strong tea brew was diluted with more hot water from the samovar as desired. At home, fresh tea was prepared and served several times a day. Our daily consumption must have been quite high because every evening a wonderful big tin (which still came from Baku) was refilled with tea for the next day.

In our rooms, we had wood stoves that required a great deal of firewood—too much to carry from the store. So, trees in the forest were selected, felled, and cut into manageable lengths for the loggers to work with. With the help of twenty donkeys, we managed to haul them home. Of course, the forests belonged to a large landowner who billed Father later. The wood was offloaded and stacked in the middle of the garden, creating a large mountain for us children to climb and play on. Sometimes, we got scratches, fractures, or even a few dislocated joints! However, the fun was so great that we hardly noticed the pain. Besides, we knew a bone healer—Kurd Khawar was her name. This kind woman had extensive knowledge of human bone structure and provided excellent treatment when accidents happened. With a bowl of warm water, she skillfully set dislocated joints and made bandages with heated natural resin, comparable to today's plaster casts. I was one of her regular customers, and often one of my younger brothers was there before me!

The woodcutters arrived very early in the morning to cut the trunks into one-meter lengths. But before they started work, Mother served them breakfast. A large tray was set out for everyone with fresh bread, butter, cheese, eggs, homemade jam, tea, and hot milk. I doubt any of them expected to be spoiled like that. After this hearty breakfast, they were ready to work.

Groaning and singing in rhythm, the workers cut the tree trunks into logs, which were then stacked in the cellar. We watched this interesting spectacle for weeks, enjoying the sweet smell of freshly cut wood.

Many people could not afford wood because it was too expensive, so they used coal instead. Father took care of it and stored extra charcoal. It took at least two weeks to deliver and store the coal. After delivery, it was washed in large quantities and stored in the cellar. The coal dust and residues from the washing process were formed into fist-sized balls and used as firelighters.

At that time, there was a very economical and pleasant heating system called the "korsi." It was a low, rectangular wooden table (about 60 cm high) placed in the middle of the room and covered with a large blanket. The undersides of the korsi table were heated with glowing coal. Families would sit on soft cushions on the floor, or even on the korsi blanket itself, enjoying the pleasant warmth radiating from the smokeless, glowing coal placed under the korsi using a mangal (a portable flat stove made of cast iron). This setup provided warmth for those sitting close by, though the rest of the room would remain freezing! The larger the family, the larger the korsi, and it was a central part of winter life. However, in our house, there was no korsi. Father was against it because he believed the coal was better used for helping our needy neighbors.

Tabriz had four distinct seasons. Spring was mild, summer warm and dry, and autumn pleasantly cool until the cold winter arrived. As winter approached, the weather became more severe, and supplies such as cooking oil and meat had to be stored. Vegetable oil and margarine did not exist in those days. We bought our cooking oil from Kermanshah, a city in the province of Kurdistan. Additionally, butter from our own dairy was melted in large quantities and brought to a boil. The liquid butter was then poured into large terracotta jars and stored, preserving it for a long time.

Qaradag, a village that belonged to my father, supplied us with live sheep. As children, we were tasked with feeding and playing with them, which we enjoyed immensely. However, the day soon came when the sheep were to be slaughtered, and we were very sad to see them go. Our pleading and crying didn't help, and one by one, the animals were slaughtered. As a reward, the fur and offal were given to the local butcher. Then the meat processing began. It was first roasted, then preserved according to certain procedures, and finally stored. The entire process took all day, and by evening, nothing remained of the six large sheep.

Tea was always present!

11

PERSIAN CUISINE

*P*ersian cuisine is versatile, varied, and healthy, with individual ingredients and food courses skillfully coordinated in taste, color, and consistency. The food smells wonderfully pleasant, stimulating the appetite. Vegetables supply all the necessary building blocks of life—protein, carbohydrates, fats, vitamins, minerals, and trace elements—while rice and cereals are the staples. Abundant herbs and fragrant spices are essential in any true Persian menu. Although Persian cooking is not spicy, each ingredient is used to retain its natural aroma.

In composing dishes, special attention is given to balancing cold and warm elements, as each has its own effect and value, stimulating the digestive organs and contributing to our physical and mental well-being. This is why strict attention is paid to the proportions of warm and cold elements in the ingredients. These practices have evolved into tradition over time, though precise measurements are not always emphasized.

Warm elements are believed to raise blood pressure, while cold elements are thought to lower it. For example, cabbage and garlic are considered cold foods, whereas honey, cinnamon, and dates are seen as warm. Mother stored as much as possible of these healthy ingredients—herbs, spices, vegetables, and fruits—for the winter. Without refrigerators or freezers, and with no canned foods as we have today, people were very self-sufficient.

When the tomatoes ripened, large quantities were delivered to the house for processing. Tomato paste, a key ingredient, was made in large batches, with everything done naturally using the hot sun of Tabriz and the patience and diligence of the experienced women in the kitchen. Herbs were also processed in large quantities depending on the season; after cleaning and washing, they were sorted, chopped, and dried in a room on the upper floor, where white cloths covered the floor, and the herbs were laid out to dry. This process lasted for weeks, filling the house with wonderful fragrances. The dry and warm summer air made the scent pleasant but not overpowering. Even now, the sweet fragrance lingers in my memory.

Juices were also an important part of our kitchen, providing healthy and refreshing drinks on hot summer days, made from fresh fruit and herbs. Vinegar, wine vinegar, lemon, pomegranate, and tomato juice were used in cooking, with each juice preserved according to age-old methods. The production of each juice was different and special, reflecting the importance of food in life rather than merely producing a commodity. Without supermarkets, making vinegar and wine vinegar took significant time and effort. Unripe, sour grapes were harvested in large quantities from our own or neighboring plantations, selected for taste and variety, and brought home in large woven baskets on mules. The juicing method was similar to winemaking, with part of the juice placed in large jars and left in the garden to ripen in the sun. This special wine vinegar was unique to our region and, as far as I know, was unknown in the West. It was considered very healthy, especially for conditions like gout and rheumatism, and played an important role in Persian cuisine. Regular vinegar was made from the leftover grape remnants.

Green, red, purple, and yellow grapes were harvested, all

deliciously sour and fresh. When the workers arrived with the pressing machine, our mother watched closely to ensure everything was clean and neat. Even the grape residues were used, formed into small balls and dried for use as flavor enhancers or in medicines during winter. Vegetables were also preserved for winter, some pickled in vinegar or brine—such as eggplant, cucumbers, peppers, cabbage, and green unripe tomatoes—while others were dried. Cherries, strawberries, apricots, figs, and green unripe walnuts were turned into delicious jams and marmalades, stored in large quantities in the pantry. It was customary to send some of these homemade preserves to relatives and friends as a way of showcasing one's cooking skills. For example, our aunt's young vine leaves were soaked in salt water, seasoned, and used to prepare dolmas, which were very popular, as they are now in the West. My sister's strawberry jam is unsurpassed in taste and aroma—I just wish I had her recipe!

12

WINTER IN TABRIZ

*M*any fruits were dried both for cooking and consumption, including raisins, apricots, dates, figs, sour cherries, and plums. The seeds from watermelons and honeydew melons, which we ate every day in the summer after nap time, were not discarded but dried and roasted for snacking on long winter nights. Honeydew melons were eaten with the main meal; soft and sweet varieties paired with spicy dishes, while firm, aromatic varieties complemented sweet dishes. Some fruits, such as apples, pears, and plums, were stored in wooden boxes among hay, keeping them fresh for months. Grapes were tied to their stems with string and hung from ceilings in dry, airy rooms, remaining juicy and fresh almost until the end of winter. Entering a room filled with grape chains hanging in rows of beautiful bright colors was particularly appetizing. During the bright autumn sun, they shone like diamonds! The clean, dry air allowed one to identify the scent of different fruits and where each was stored. Sadly, I have never experienced this again.

When the first wind from the mountains swept over Tabriz and the leaves changed color, winter was just around the corner. In our home, the pantries were filled under the direction of our mother, while father took care of the garden. The large lemon trees, about three meters high, were re-potted with fresh soil in the fall. Other plants and flowers were also winterized, being repotted with fertilizer and bird droppings added to the new soil before they were carried to the warm, humid winter quarters in the cellar.

The thick outer walls of the house, made of brick and a lime-gypsum mixture, warmed up during the day and cooled down at night, creating natural air circulation. From October, Tabriz became cooler and the days shorter. Cold winds drove sand and dust from the southern mountains into the city, making the season uncomfortable until the autumn rains arrived, clearing the air.

By November, the first snowfall came. The house roofs, flat and covered with terracotta slabs, were walkable terrace-shaped spaces where many people slept on warm summer nights. In winter, these roofs had to be cleared of snow, which was shoveled into the yard or the alley, eventually piling up like small mountains in the narrow alleys. To reach school, we had to navigate these snow mountains, making the winter months hard and difficult.

On evenings when we had a few hours of electricity, we would listen to the radio after dinner. However, strong interference from the Soviet Union made it difficult to understand the station, so at 7:30 p.m., we all went to bed. Mother often stayed up, listening to Radio Baku or Moscow, her only connection to her motherland. While listening to Radio Baku, she would become sad, thinking of her past and silently crying. It wasn't until many years later, when I experienced homesickness myself, that I could empathize with my mother's sadness. Homesickness is hard to bear and indescribable, understood only by those who have felt it. We had no other electrical appliances, not even a telephone. Some evenings, my brother would read novels to us, and I still remember the stories well, like *The Count of Monte Cristo, Duma,* or *Robinson Crusoe.* Reading aloud kept us entertained during those long winter nights.

As the snow set in, Tabriz became very cold and quiet, with most people staying indoors. Some stores in the bazaar opened around noon, but traffic was minimal. Buses only stopped at the request of passengers, and horse-drawn carriages struggled in the snow and ice, especially in the narrow streets, making staying at home the most sensible option.

Our pantry became our salvation, invaluable not just for us, but also for others who could help themselves from our winter stores. Every evening around 7 p.m., our heavy front door was closed and locked, but until then, it remained open for anyone to take what they needed from the supplies in the basement. Even as a child, it was comforting to know that no one in our neighborhood would starve or need to beg in the dark alleys.

Every morning, the milkman brought us fresh milk in the same canister and measuring cup, filling our pot to the brim. We fetched the rest of the staples, such as bread, butter, cheese, and honey, from the cellar. Remarkably, there was practically no waste or garbage at that time. The garbage man came once a month, but there was little to collect because vegetable scraps, potato peels, and fruit waste were given to the chickens and sheep, while leftover food was fed to dogs and cats. Paper bags from stores were returned for reuse, and old laundry was used as fuel. There were no ready-made clothes to buy; sweaters, stockings, hats, and gloves were crocheted and knitted at home, filling the long winter days. You can imagine how eagerly everyone looked forward to spring!

13

NOWRUZ – THE PERSIAN NEW YEAR FESTIVAL

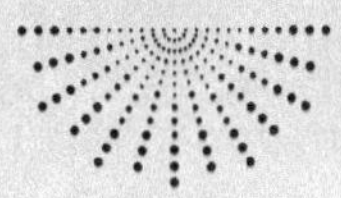

"Beauty surrounds us, but usually we need to walk in a garden to know it."

— RUMI

The month of March marks the beginning of spring, specifically on the 20th or, in some years, the 21st, which also coincides with the Persian New Year Festival. This celebration occurs around the same time as Easter in the Christian world. It may come as a surprise to learn that the roots of this festival are closely interwoven with Christian traditions, a result of Persia's rich tapestry of cultures and peoples. These include Armenians, Syrians, Azaris in the northwest, Kurds in the northeast, as well as Turkmen, Gilek, Tajik, and Afghan communities in the central highlands. The Parsis, from whom the country derives its name, are found in the south, along with the Lor, Baluch, and Persian Arabs, among others. As a result, a variety of languages, cultures, and religions have been practiced in Persia.

The Jewish presence in Persia dates back to around 700 B.C., making it home to the second-largest Jewish community after Israel. Many Jewish sanctuaries are located in Persia. Over 2,500 years ago, Cyrus the Great liberated the Jews and granted them full religious freedom, leading many to settle in Persia. The Jewish mausoleum of Esther, the wife of Xerxes, and Mordecai in Hamadan is one of the numerous Jewish sanctuaries in the country.

Armenians have also long lived alongside Persians, and the present-day Republic of Armenia was part of the Persian Empire until the early 1800s. One of the most important Armenian sanctuaries is Karakilisa, the Black Church and Tomb of St. Tadeo, located in the Chaldean Mountains about 25 km from the Turkish border, northwest of Tabriz. Each year, Armenian believers from around the world gather there. The Armenian Apostolic Cathedral in Isfahan is one of the most beautiful and significant in the Orient.

Before the advent of Islam, the Zoroastrian religion thrived in Persia and is still practiced today, particularly in Yazd and the surrounding areas where numerous fire temples are found. The Ismaili (Mullahs), whose leader and Imam is known to many as Aga Khan, originate from Mahallat, a city in central Persia. Although most Ismailis now live abroad, a few remain scattered throughout the country. Sunnis predominantly live in the north and south of the country.

All these peoples and religious communities have lived peacefully together for a long time, practicing their religions and speaking their own languages. The official language of the country is Farsi (Persian), which is taught in schools. A brief overview from Wikipedia can provide further insight into the country's history.

Persian transcription:

"Nowruz is such a tradition. Literally translated means New Day. The words RUZ, or ROJ in Iranian languages, which stands for day, go back to the Ru-Inoiran Rauca (pronounced: Rautscha), which in turn comes from the Ur-ind European, Luck, from which also the, Luc in Russian, Licht in German, Leukos in Greek, Lux in Latin and Luy in Armenian, have arisen. In Old Iranian Avestic, Raocah was used for light and for new, Nava. It is celebrated as the greatest festival in all Persian-speaking people around the world and within Aryan peoples. It was banned in Turkey and Syria for decades. Since 1994, Nowruz has been officially considered an Old Turkic festival. Since the last century, Nowruz has spread widely throughout Iran, Turkey, Iraq, Syria, and all of Central Asia. Moreover, today people celebrate Nowruz in Russia, and in the Balkans. Each country has its own spelling and pronunciation of Nowruz."

Preparations for Nowruz would begin months before spring arrived, with new clothes being one of the most important aspects of this celebration. In our house, it was a very festive occasion. We selected fabrics for underwear, shirts, and suits well in advance, allowing the tailor enough time to complete the work. Shoes were ordered from the cobbler, as there were no ready-made shoes available. The women and girls had their own tailor to create their fancy clothes. By the time of the feast, our clothes were ready, and both rich and poor celebrated alike, having saved throughout the year. All civil servants and workers received a 13th-month bonus, always paid in time for Nowruz preparations.

New Year cleaning was a crucial task, done thoroughly to ensure the house shone from the basement to the roof before the feast began. Rooms were repainted, curtains and carpets cleaned, and mattresses and bedding renewed. Silverware sparkled, and the cooking pots were re-galvanized. Everything gleamed! The large water basin was drained, repainted, and refilled with fresh water. The yard was cleaned, and the garden replanted with colorful flowers and plants. Alleys and doorways were cleared of snow and ice in time for the festival, and with the sun's warmth, the snow melted quickly. The weather always changed abruptly, and as far as I can remember, it suddenly became spring-like warm. Mother and her staff, several women who were always with us, began making the final preparations for the feast, as many things still needed to be done.

Dyeing eggs, a custom also common in the Christian world for Easter, has been an important tradition at our Nowruz feast for thousands of years. Our mother wrapped eggs in special colorful fabrics, sewed them shut, and then cooked them. After cooling, the fabrics were removed, revealing beautifully patterned eggs that were admired by everyone—a process passed down from Mother's happy days in Baku. A day before the Nowruz feast, the table was set with the seven symbols that begin with the letter 'S': Apple (Seeb) as a sign of beauty and health; Vinegar (Serke) representing the incorruptible; Hyacinth (Sonbol) symbolizing the arrival of spring; Coin (Sekae) for prosperity and wealth; Silver tray (Sineh) as a sign of soil stability; Spice from the vinegar tree (Somag) symbolizing the color of the rising sun; and Garlic (Syr) for health and healing. These symbols were tastefully placed on the table with love and patience. The holy book, the Quran, along with a mirror, goldfish in water, sabzi (greens), sweets, and colored eggs, were also placed on the feast table.

When Earth, in its orbit around the sun, reached a specific point, spring began, marking the change of the year. This event could happen during the day or night; I have experienced the change of the year at midnight and in the early morning. The beginning of spring was recorded in the new calendar so that everyone could plan accordingly. Decades later, as the country modernized, these traditions evolved. Many people began planning their annual vacations or travel during this time, perhaps not only to escape the hustle and bustle but also to reunite with their families for the celebration.

During the New Year, we all stood around the Nowruz table as Father recited the New Year's prayer, wishing us all a healthy year ahead, along with good wishes for people around the world. Then, congratulations, hugs, and kisses were exchanged, and new banknotes and coins were distributed. At this special moment, people remembered those who were absent, prayed for the sick and wished them a speedy recovery, and honored the deceased.

The celebrations continued for a week. It was also traditional for the older generation to distribute new banknotes to the children and gold or silver coins to adults, if affordable. We often received new banknotes in different denominations and some gold coins during the festive days, which allowed us to afford some additional items until the end of the summer vacation.

Spring in Tabriz was always beautiful, with a blue sky and dry air. The days gradually became longer and warmer, and nature awoke in one swift motion. Trees blossomed, and meadows suddenly became vibrant with colors, resembling a large Persian carpet. The dry and pleasantly warm air carried the fragrance of flowers. In spring, it did not rain often, so the blossoms of plants and trees lasted for months. Every garden had fruit trees, and almost all kinds of fruit flourished there, such as apples, cherries, pears, peaches, apricots, plums, nectarines, pomegranates, and various berries, nuts, and grapes. The land was fertile, with many fruit plantations and richly cultivated fields, making winter long forgotten.

On the first day of the New Year, all our relatives, important businessmen, acquaintances, and neighbors visited us. Close relatives stayed for dinner, and some even stayed for a few days. Visitors were served tea, cake, and later, fruit. After a short visit, they would say goodbye and move on to visit others. It was a continuous coming and going until late in the evening when the last guest said goodnight.

Our cousins often stayed with us until the 13th of Farvardin, the first month of the Persian calendar, which is an official holiday. This day is celebrated in a special way, with families moving to the open air for a picnic in the forest or meadow, usually by a river or stream. A large carpet is spread on the ground, and the family spends the whole day there, enjoying plenty of food and drink, local games, music, and dance. The sabzi is sprinkled into flowing water, sending millions of wheat germs to distant areas while also providing food for many animals.

14

THE SECOND WORLD WAR

During World War II, Iran was occupied by the USSR and Great Britain. British and Soviet troops took over neutral Persia on August 24, 1941. As the Germans advanced as far as Moscow and America entered the war, the Allies devised a cruel plan that led to the occupation of the country and the seizure of the Trans-Iranian Railway to supply Russia with weapons and food. This precious food, desperately needed by the local population, was diverted to the Russian front, causing widespread famine.

At that time, Reza Shah, the first king of the Pahlavi dynasty, had constructed the 2,000 km-long Trans-Iranian Railway, stretching from the Persian Gulf to the north of the country, with the help of a German engineer under extremely difficult financial conditions. The project began in 1927 and, after years of hard work, was completed in 1938—a true technical feat, as it involved penetrating mountains with complex tunnels and crossing wild rivers with bridges of immense spans and heights, almost unprecedented for that time. The Allies demanded that Iran sever its relationship with Germany and expel all Germans from the country. Although Iran declared itself neutral at the beginning of

World War II and expelled all German diplomats, engineers, and technicians, the British invaded from the south across the Persian Gulf, while the Russians came in from the north, occupying the country. The king was forced to abdicate in favor of his son, Reza Shah.

Reza Shah went into exile, eventually ending up in South Africa. His journey took him from Isfahan to Bushehr, a port on the Persian Gulf, where the British provided an old cargo ship—lacking all comforts—forcing him to endure unbearable 40-degree heat. From there, he traveled to India and then to South Africa. In the Persian Gulf, the inexperienced Persian Navy was bombed and destroyed by the British Air Force, sinking all the ships. Meanwhile, in the north, the Red Army invaded and occupied all of Azerbaijan, practically handing it over to the Soviets.

The country was in a critical situation, without a king or a functioning government. However, thanks to the quick action of the Prime Minister and the young Crown Prince, Mohammed Reza Pahlavi, and without the knowledge of the Allies, the Crown Prince was sworn in by Parliament and duly appointed as King of Persia. Although the country was able to reassert its sovereignty, the harsh reality was that the Allies were in control.

Foreigners took over all ministries, effectively controlling the country's destiny. Silos of wheat, rice, and sugar were confiscated, and textile factories were seized, with everything needed for the Russian front, leaving the population to suffer from famine.

In Tabriz, Iranian communists, with the help of the Soviets, established their own communist government, declaring all national laws invalid and initiating a new social order based on the Soviet model. The Democratic Republic of Azerbaijan was declared independent from Iran. With Europe and the Far East engulfed in war, no one was interested in the fate of the people in my homeland. We were left as abandoned orphans, forced to fend for ourselves.

About twenty years after leaving Tabriz, my family

encountered the Russians once again. After so much time, Mother had almost forgotten her old homeland of Baku and the relatives who had stayed behind, but now old wounds were being reopened. Russian soldiers patrolled everywhere once more. Masses of workers and peasants, incited by Soviet agents, tried to adapt to Communist ideology and Soviet ways. The big landowners and the wealthy were arrested, given a short trial, and executed, with the owner of Liqvan village being the first victim. I readily admit that in our country, apart from kings, princes, and governors, many feudal kingdoms and landowners have existed over the centuries. These rulers commandeered everything that rightfully belonged to the people, who had always been abused, exploited, and kept under a heavy yoke. Although the sides had changed, the suffering continued, just in a different guise.

A few days after our arrival, Father was arrested. He had owned some villages but had sold the stone mine in Karadagh and given the land to the farmers while selling other villages as well.

Our last name used to be Khalil Beigi. Father had changed it because "Beig" or "Bey" is a sign of Persian nobility. Father's seventh ancestor, Khalil Bey, was a Sardar, a noble and a general of the highest rank, who was assassinated over two hundred years ago. When word of Father's arrest spread, our family, along with loyal peasants, merchants from the bazaar, neighbors, and acquaintances, besieged the Tabriz prison and managed to free him, as he commanded great respect. What a relief! Our uncle, a factory owner, had also been a target of the marksmen, but was protected by his own workers and farmers who lived with him, so he fortunately came to no harm.

The leftist and pro-Soviet government began a radical social upheaval, starting with the introduction of the Azari (Turkish) language as the official language of the region, replacing Persian. Azari is similar to the Turkic language, but quite different from Persian, much like the difference between English and German. Both in the north, now the Republic of Azerbaijan, and in the south, on the Persian side, this language is still spoken. We had learned to read and write only Persian in school. My parents didn't know Farsi when they first arrived in the country. Although Persians were in the minority, the country was called Persia until 1935, when the official name was changed to Iran, meaning "Land of the Aryans."

The term Iran, in its broader sense, refers to a larger region encompassing territories of Afghanistan, Tajikistan, Azerbaijan, Iraq, Uzbekistan, Turkmenistan, parts of Turkey, and Pakistan, known as the Iranian Highlands. But the new rulers changed everything. A separate police force and army were formed. Newspapers were published in Azari and the language was spoken on the radio. School books and education were also changed accordingly. Ministries were created following the Soviet model. Exports and imports were banned, so goods or food could not be shipped outside Azerbaijan, bringing Father's business to a standstill. Russian soldiers patrolled everywhere, keeping the country under their control. The region had now become an occupied police state. Night after night, drunken Russian soldiers roamed the area, searching for girls and knocking on doors until they found what they were seeking. It was the worst imaginable scenario in an Islamic city like Tabriz that had a thousand years of history and culture. Infidels and foreign occupiers demanded local daughters to service them, and quite often, their brutally murdered bodies were found in some alleyway in Tabriz. The Russians had gone too far.

~

MOTHER WAS DEEPLY worried as summer was coming to an end, and the cellar and pantry were empty, with no provisions for the winter. She discussed the situation with Father, who wanted a list of the most necessary items. Arriving at his office, he inquired with the farmers about the wheat and other grain in the village, and how it would be distributed. The farmers agreed to bring this question to the village committee. The answer came quickly because they realized the dire situation and how the locals would suffer in the winter. In the spirit of communism, the village committee decided to help provide the families with everything needed from Liqvan.

The peasants, now landowners and masters in their own right, took swift action. After a few weeks, the village elder informed my father that the Ministry of the Interior and the Party headquarters had agreed with the Soviet Committee to provide the families with wheat to get them through the winter. This must have been the best news for Mother. The wheat, which was usually sent to the front despite the locals starving, was now permitted to be delivered to us! The farmers assured us they would lead the operation themselves, so Father gave them the address of the miller for direct delivery.

Two of my cousins were working in a match factory at that time. Both were born in Baku and could speak Russian. They were also blond, so they were accepted as comrades of the Committee and were able to make decisions. Additionally, they received larger rations of food. At last, the grandchildren of Haj Bekoff were able to experience some benefits from the Russian revolution, even after their lives had been so brutally disrupted by it.

Days went by despite numerous incidents and difficulties, as the war continued to rage in Europe. Eventually, thanks to the Persian Railway and supplies, the Germans were pushed back. In the middle of winter, the withdrawal of German troops from Russia began. For many Persians, this was not good news, as they had been waiting for the Germans and had great sympathy for them. The reason was simple: the German people had never harbored ill intentions toward Persia. On the contrary, in the early 20th century, they had contributed to the development of our country, aiding in the construction of the South-North 2,000 km railroad, as well as roads, factories, hospitals, colleges, an airport, and the training of pilots. Before World War II, Germans were everywhere in Iran, promoting the development of Persia. Apart from the economic benefits, ideological affinities were also studied. Persia, an ancient country with Indo-European, Aryan ancestry and an old written culture, had enjoyed good business and cultural relations with Germany for hundreds of years. Goethe, the great German poet, learned Persian to read and understand Hafiz, the great Persian poet. The philosopher Nietzsche studied ancient Persian religion to write about Zarathustra. On the other hand, as history suggests, the British and Russians brought only war and destruction to our country, an example of which I shall now relate.

The British remained in the Persian Gulf for an extended period of time. After World War I and the fall of the Ottoman Empire, they invaded Arabia with the help of British Intelligence Officer Thomas Lawrence—famously known as Lawrence of Arabia. They supported the Bedouins in their struggle against the Ottoman Empire and installed a desert Sheik of Saudi (a descendant of the King of Saudi), leading to the Arabian Peninsula being called Saudi Arabia ever since.

In this way, the British gained a foothold in the region. The discovery of the first oil fields in Chah Bahar, Persia, in 1908, caused interest in the area to spiral. They remained in this oil-rich area for a long time. In 1907, the British and Russians astonishingly divided our land among themselves through a treaty, which was later revoked by Lenin after the Russian Revolution.

WHEN THE LONG-AWAITED wheat was delivered, Mother was speechless with joy. We received a double quantity, allowing us to bake bread for a few weeks longer. During this baking time, long lines of people stood at our front door, evening after evening, waiting to receive some bread. Word spread quickly throughout the community, and people came on foot from great distances. As bread was scarce and local bakers' rations of flour were limited, our house became the main bakery—free of charge, of course. Despite this, many starved to death. Because of the war and persecution, Jews from Europe sought refuge in Persia, and naturally, they too had to be provided for.

My memories of post-WWII go back to when I was around four or five years old. I attended a local kindergarten where we were lovingly cared for by our teacher. One day, our dear teacher was absent, and we later learned she had committed suicide. This terrible event deeply affected me, especially at such a young age. It was devastating. The school director tried to console me, standing in a wet meadow and holding a red apple, but even today, I remember it with horror.

For the first six years of school, my siblings and I attended a nearby school. When I was about ten years old, my youngest brother was born, completing our family. Mother had given birth to and nursed ten children, raising them over a span of 30 years despite poor hygiene conditions and medical shortages, somehow managing to cope with all the problems that arose. My two older sisters were married and each had five children. Since they lived close by, they brought their children to our house almost every day —at Father's request. You can imagine how busy mealtimes were for us and the staff!

When World War II ended, Germany was divided and occupied. On March 1, 1946, the British troops finally withdrew from Persia. Then, on May 6th, the Soviets also withdrew their troops, but only after President Roosevelt seriously threatened them and forced them to leave. However, the Russians did not withdraw from countries such as East Germany or Moldavia, which became satellite states of the Soviet Union.

On January 22, 1946, the Republic of Mahabad in Iran was established. Later that year, in November, troops from the central government marched into Tabriz, overthrowing the provisional communist government. Some were arrested, while others fled across the border to Russia, where they met a cruel end. There were many good loyalists and patriots among the persecuted communists who saw socialism as a hope for our country, but they were bitterly disappointed.

However, on December 16, 1946, Iranian troops reconquered Tabriz, and the government established by the Russians was overthrown. A wave of arrests followed. My aunt's sons were fired from the factory, and those who were blond and fair-skinned were arrested, mistaken for Russians, and beaten. Father endured many complications trying to restore order. For example, one of my cousins, who with his blond hair, green eyes, and well-dressed appearance, went to the hamam (public bath) for his weekly bath, unaware of the dangers of being caught. Fortunately, an acquaintance found him in time and brought him safely home.

15

FATHER'S DREAMS

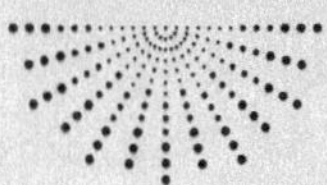

Father's desire was to send his children to Germany to study medicine, although our youngest sister studied in Switzerland. His dream was to build a hospital where his sons and daughters could work as doctors in different fields and help those in need. In Tabriz, there was an American hospital run by missionaries, one of the best in the area. While there were some government hospitals, they could not meet the needs of the locals. For the poor and needy, medical care was abysmal, but the wealthy had access to excellent physicians and specialists.

Reza Shah overthrew the Qajar dynasty and, with the approval of Parliament, took power in 1925, becoming King of Persia. He immediately began the difficult task of modernizing the country. Among other initiatives, he sent the first group of students to study in Europe, with the state financing their education. This started a competition among families who wanted their children to study abroad, although the cost of traveling, studying, and living abroad was very high. For example, a teacher's three-month salary was needed to cover the monthly expenses of a student abroad.

Within a decade, the country had many professionals in diverse fields who contributed to building modern Persia. Father wanted to do everything possible to provide his children with a good education, so he was pleased with the new developments improving the country, as he knew the old conditions all too well. Over the previous 125 years, the country had fallen into a deep sleep under the Qajar dynasty (1794 – 1925), which had done nothing for the country. There were many princes and princesses making claims, each of whom had received various villages as gifts from the ruling king, with town governors paying yearly dues to the royal house. State funds were collected as taxes, with about 1,000 large families owning 90% of the estates. After the abdication of Ahmad Shah and the change of dynasty to Pahlavi, the lower classes experienced a great awakening. They had great expectations from Reza Shah, who had somehow managed to rise from a simple citizen to become the king.

As I mentioned, the conditions of that time were well known to my father and his generation. He wanted to leave something more valuable than wealth to his children. He believed that studying and learning a profession would be useful not only to oneself but also to others. This became our mission, as he had made us financially secure through hard work and discipline, allowing us the freedom to study without worrying about money.

My eldest brother was the first to embark on the journey to Europe to study and endure the separation from family. When he graduated, I was about ten years old and had to change schools, moving to a well-known private school named after the Persian poet and mystic Saadi (1190-1283), whose verses are inscribed above the entrance of the UN building in New York. We had classes every day from 8 a.m. to noon and from 2 p.m. to 4 p.m. At noon, I had a Persian sandwich for lunch, which was just bread topped with feta cheese—not very satisfying. Mother pointed out that we should eat the same amount as other students. She was right; some children didn't even have a piece of cheese and ate dry bread in a hidden corner of the schoolyard. People knew us, even at school. Our father was a well-known figure, not because of his wealth, but because of his character.

He treated everyone with respect and understanding. Although he dressed in the European style (suit and tie), he was very attentive to the traditions and customs of our society. No loud music or big festivities came from our house because such behavior was not welcome in Tabriz. Even later, when we returned from Europe with our own cars and the narrow streets had been widened, we couldn't be noisy—Father was against it. He didn't want us to attract the attention of the neighbors, most of whom had small incomes or nothing at all. He was very considerate and regularly supported many families, financing some students as well. All of this was done in secrecy. He always greeted others first, even though according to Persian custom, the younger ones should greet first, and the older ones return the greeting. When someone entered a room, everyone stood up according to the guest's age, and once the guest was seated, everyone else could sit down. This polite and important gesture was customary in our country. Father, however, stood up when each guest entered his office and personally served tea to his visitors. This was unimaginable for the farmers and peasants. Many remarked that they had never witnessed such behavior, as many other wealthy merchants never even acknowledged the poor.

One late evening, we heard a knock on our front door, and an envelope was delivered for Father. He took it to his room to read privately. After a while, he returned and handed us the envelope, instructing us to return it without looking the bearer in the face. The letters were mostly cries for help from people in need. Our father didn't want us to know who they came from because he feared it might cause embarrassment if we met them later. This way of dealing with people benefited us, as we were accepted by our fellow citizens and not treated as sons of the rich. The gap between rich and poor was even bigger then. Many had a hard time making a living, especially when illness or natural disasters struck, causing financial ruin.

There was no health insurance available (except for civil servants and employees), and social services were inadequate, failing to cater to the sick, elderly, or orphans. The labor market was limited to the food and textile industries, and agriculture was still carried out using old methods, so manual labor, traditional workshops, and trade were the primary forms of employment. Unfortunately, no measures were taken to correct this imbalance, resulting in stagnation. In such a society, the wealthy were not well-regarded. Human nature, and perhaps envy, played a role. Many were curious about what happened behind the high walls of the wealthy. It was better not to hear cries of joy from our house, and at school, we suffered the envy of our classmates. However, due to our good reputation and thanks to Father's way of life, we had a certain advantage. With it came great responsibility, and we were forced to adapt, follow the strict rules he introduced, and behave accordingly. I can understand now how wisely he managed the family. He paid attention to Sadage and Zakat, which in Islam translate to personal generosity and obligatory self-taxation.

Depending on his income, he paid a portion of it to those in need, according to his own discretion. Whether it was a scholarship for study or financial support for certain families, relatives, or strangers, it was always done confidentially and under the strictest secrecy. If all the wealthy had fulfilled this religious duty, which in Islam holds high value and is even compared to daily prayer, there would be no poor in society.

16

GRANDMOTHER

Our grandmother, even after all these years, had not fully adapted to Persian conditions and continued to live in her accustomed way. She loved caring for us, washing us children one by one with warm water every evening—a task that required considerable effort since the water was heated over a wood fire. After drying us off, she would massage our hands with Vaseline, a cream made from oil that she had known from her earlier days in Baku and used as a body cream. Grandmother ensured that we went to the hairdresser regularly, wore clean white shirts, slept on white sheets, had clean hands, and kept our fingernails and toenails trimmed. We were taught to eat with a knife and fork and were not allowed to slurp while eating soup! We also had to be taken to the public bath every week, as we did not have a bath at home. Building a bath without running water had been too cumbersome and difficult. When we were small, Mother took us to the women's bath, Hammam, but as we grew older, the women began to grumble and protest that we were too grown-up to share the bath with them, so my brothers took me to the men's bath, separate from the women.

I loved sleeping over with my grandmother at night because she made me feel safe and secure. She was initially reluctant to have me stay, as she believed that the breath of the elderly was not good for small, sensitive children like me, but I stayed with her anyway. She loved all her grandchildren, some more than others, but she was especially fond of me. However, she had trouble with my oldest brother. As a little boy, he was clever and physically strong, often fooling the younger ones. For example, he once took chocolate from our younger brother by convincing him to plant a chocolate tree and sending him to fetch water for it. By the time he returned, the chocolate had been eaten—all under Grandma's watchful eye. She saw everything, including my brother Behruz watering the spot every day in hopes the chocolate tree would grow quickly!

As I grew older, I would carry my grandmother downstairs every morning so her bed could be freshly made, then carry her back again. She was very old, small, and light. One day, when I went to her room, she did not respond. She was asleep, sitting up in her pretty brass bedstead brought from Russia, which we called Krawat. I ran to my mother and told her that Grandma was not answering, so a servant was immediately sent to fetch Grandma's doctor.

The news spread quickly, and soon the house was full of relatives and neighbors before the doctor even arrived. He went straight to Grandma's room, and after examining her, he gave her an injection that revived her as if nothing had happened. Everyone reveled as sadness turned to joy, and the day ended with a celebration. The following day, I resumed my daily task of getting Grandma out of bed as usual.

However, one day, when I brought her back to bed, she held my hand tightly, looking at me with tired eyes. I will never forget the sight of her dainty little hand in mine as she said, "Please tell your father I want to talk to him." I left her without suspecting what was happening and went to my father to deliver Grandma's message. I also told Mother, who looked at me sadly and went to gaze out of the window. Whenever Mother was sorrowful, she stood in front of a particular window overlooking the courtyard and the blue sky of Tabriz. What she thought and said in her heart, or to whom she poured out her heart, I do not know.

A few days later, on a Friday in November, Father went to Grandma's room once again. We were curious but unsuspecting when we noticed Father coming out of Grandma's room with a bundle of papers in his hand, tears in his eyes. Whenever he had worries, he would retreat to his room for a few hours, and now he did so again. Grandma had handed over the land registers of the houses from Baku and all the securities and documents. Even after all these years, she had still hoped to return to her homeland, but now it was finally over. From Grandma's room, we heard the voice of my brother-in-law reciting verses from the Quran. What we didn't know was that she had suffered a severe heart attack weeks ago, and the doctor had only been able to prolong her life for a short while. Alas, not this time.

In our country, when someone dies, the deceased are laid in bed facing Mecca as part of the farewell process. My brother-in-law, who practiced his religion very conscientiously, continued to read verses from the Quran. Traditionally, funerals are held as soon as possible. The deceased are taken to a specific room at the cemetery, where the body is washed and then wrapped in a shroud called a "kafan." A spiritual Mullah is called to say prayers next to the grave before the actual burial takes place. All Islamic cemeteries are laid out in the direction of Mecca, Saudi Arabia. Grandma's lifeless body was taken away, and the whole house wept as she made her final journey.

As her life, filled with many trials and tribulations, came to an end, Grandma was finally reunited with her late husband. The room was vacated immediately after the maids performed their duties thoroughly. After an hour, there was no sign that our grandmother had lived there, and Mother never entered that room again. The first night without Grandma was expected to be filled with many mourners—family, relatives, and friends—so preparations had to be made. Rooms were prepared for hundreds of guests, and the large kitchen was opened, with the ovens heated as the cooks started their work. The ovens would burn for weeks.

A few days later, the official prayers were held in the nearby mosque. A huge crowd came to our house early in the morning, when the men took my father out of the house and accompanied him on foot to the mosque. The same happened with our mother and her siblings. The prayers lasted about two hours, and afterward, everyone returned, bringing our parents with them.

In the past, a funeral service was held for the deceased not only on the first night but also on the seventh day, the fortieth day, and the anniversary. Mother wished to hold a funeral service for our grandmother for forty days and to give Ihsan for forty days. Ihsan, which translates to donations to the poor, can be in the form of money, food, medicine, or assistance to the homeless. In Islam, Ihsan is extremely special. Everything had to be well organized to serve and distribute food for about a hundred people daily. So, Mother discussed what dishes should be cooked with her favored retailer, Agha Miri. After discerning what dishes were suitable for the season and could be easily distributed for forty days, Agha went into action.

How the cooks managed with all these people coming and going was incredible. A few hundred portions would be picked up, maybe more. After lengthy discussions, it was decided that a dish of lamb, carrots, and rice with saffron and spices would be prepared. Dozens of cooks and helpers worked day and night to meet the great demands!

Many guests were served inside the house, but distributing food outside was very difficult. People lined up in the alleys, pots in hand, to pick up the food. It became critical when the food ran out, and the cooks had nothing left to give. We often went to bed hungry because our mother would redistribute the food held back for us and everything edible in the house, ensuring that no one went home empty-handed.

After the food ran out, the front door was locked, and the cleaning crew went to work. The rooms had to be tidied and cleaned in preparation for the next day. Several dozen women were also busy washing dishes. Amidst all these activities, we children were almost forgotten and could do whatever we wanted. But we were all sad and very well-behaved. With the death of our dear grandmother, a chapter of our lives closed, and a new chapter began.

Memories of our grandfather, Haj Bekoff, and the city of Baku, as well as the old days in Russia, began to fade, although our mother, as always, listened to her daily radio program from Baku, with tears in her eyes as she listened to Caucasian music. I searched for my grandma every time I entered the room, unable to understand why God had taken her away from me.

At that time, there was no connection between the divided Azerbaijan. There was no mail, telephone, or transit communication to inform family and relatives on the other side of Mrs. Haj Bekoff's passing. There was also no other way to inform them. Mother continued to listen to Radio Baku, although the station was often jammed, and she could not hear it properly. Perhaps she silently hoped to hear something new from over there. But the Iron Curtain had fallen, and there was nothing new to hear.

MEANWHILE, things had changed in Persia, both in the country and within the family. The country seemed to have awakened from hibernation, and new construction was visible here and there. The family had stabilized, with Father's business doing well and our uncle's factory working at full speed. Mother's five sisters had also gotten their lives back on track. My mother's oldest sister, however, suffered a great loss when her only son died at seventeen from an illness. It was particularly sad as she was left with only one daughter. Two of my brothers were also seriously ill with the same intestinal disease at the same time, but they survived. My aunt's oldest brother in Germany was notified, where he had been for months studying medicine at the University of Mainz. My mother had a special relationship with him; having lost her father early and having no brothers, she called him "my son, brother, and father." The parting was very difficult for her.

However, Father's wishes seemed to be coming true, as he had accomplished everything he had planned so far. Now it was time to devote himself to religious duties, so he began preparing for the great journey to the Hajj, the pilgrimage to Mecca. It is a religious duty for every Muslim to fulfill this obligation, provided one is financially secure, has no debts, and is at peace with all fellow humans. Additionally, one must be ready to confess and seek forgiveness for all human offenses. Before leaving, one must secure the family financially, make a will, visit relatives and acquaintances to ask for forgiveness, arrange all earthly duties, and settle all accounts—as if it were one's last days on earth. All of this takes time, and it took about a year for my father to prepare himself for this pilgrimage.

17

PILGRIMAGE - HAJJ

*E*arly one morning, after bidding us farewell, Father was accompanied on foot by some family and friends to the bus terminal for his journey to Tehran. From there, he boarded a plane to Jeddah in Saudi Arabia. Although the journey to Mecca had become much easier compared to earlier times, it was still a gamble, and many did not return, mainly due to the torturous heat. The Hajj was made during the summertime, where temperatures on the Arabian Peninsula soared to over 50 degrees in the shade (122 Fahrenheit). I will try to describe the course of events in Mecca as best I can, though I have not yet managed to become a Hadji myself, so I must turn to books.

Upon arrival, the pilgrims, who are later called Hadji, must bathe and don the Ihram robes at the beginning of the ritual exercises. From this moment on, they are subject to many duties and requirements of the Hajj. For instance, within the purified district of the Hajj, it is forbidden to cut one's nails, remove even a single hair from the head or body, kill or remove any living creature that settles on the body, engage in sexual intercourse, quarrel, trade, or hunt. Additionally, within the prescribed time limit, there is an obligation to perform all the rites of Hajj. One such rite is the ritual of "sa'ee," which involves walking back and forth seven times between the small hills of Safa and Marwa. This ritual commemorates the desperate search of Prophet Abraham's wife, Hager, for water for her son Ismail, who later helped his father Abraham build the house for the One (God). It is said that she walked back and forth between these two hills searching for a watering hole without success, and when she finally gave up and sank to the ground, the Zamzam Well miraculously gushed out right in front of her. Drinking this water is also part of the Hajj exercises. One of the miracles of Hajj is that this insignificant desert spring flows abundantly every year during the pilgrimage, then recedes once the Hajj period is over.

Father's pilgrimage lasted about two months, and when he returned home, he had visibly lost weight. After arriving from Tehran, he was welcomed home with great celebration. Several sheep were sacrificed in his honor, as the family was happy and thankful to God for his safe return, unlike other pilgrims who had not yet returned or would never come back. He was repeatedly asked about the others, and he tried to reassure everyone by telling them that nothing unusual had happened and that all the pilgrims were healthy and expected to arrive soon. This important event was celebrated for an entire week, with guests served cool drinks, exquisite fruit, and delicious pastries. At noon and again in the evening, meals were served to family members and distinguished visitors who came to see my father.

Mother used all her cooking skills and experience, with the help of many cooks and maids who had learned from her over the years. At that time, Mecca pilgrims were considered honest and reliable confidants, highly respected in society. Father himself had never liked being called Hadji. For him, the Hajj was not only a religious duty but also an opportunity to express gratitude to God, who had always helped him through his problems and enabled him to help others in addition to his own family. He was now a Hadji, a well-recognized and well-earned religious title.

After the Hajj was completed, our normal life resumed. I was about 13 or 14 years old, and my second oldest brother had graduated from high school. His plan was to study in Germany, so he went to Tehran to sort out his passport and other necessary documents. Several weeks later, he was off to Germany.

Separations were always very difficult for Mother, who realized that studies would take years, and the future was uncertain. She wept as she took my brother in her arms, telling him many things we did not understand. Perhaps she was complaining to God or speaking to her late father about the hardships she had endured. Father, however, accepted my brother's departure and proudly gave him last instructions and advice, asking him to behave, study hard, and return home as a good doctor.

I had now moved up to second place on the list to leave—just one more brother to go before it would be my turn! I am the fourth of six brothers, two of whom were already in Europe.

UNCLE'S FACTORY WAS THRIVING, with full order books. He was now one of the first in town to own a limousine—an imported Cadillac—and we were often picked up in it. The driver would wait on the main street, as the lanes near our house were too narrow, and we would walk to the main road before driving to our uncle's estate with the curtains drawn.

The car moved slowly, often stopping to let passers-by or even animals pass. From afar, the odor of the leather factory smelled like rotten eggs. A sentry stood at the gate entrance, where the sounds of the big factory drums could be heard.

The path to the building led through a narrow lane, and behind a heavy wooden door, a beautiful large garden filled with plants and flowers appeared. Here, nothing of the factory was noticeable, as the air smelled of forest, rainwater, and fresh earth. Narrow, beautifully laid paths led us through the garden to our uncle's house. Native and exotic flowers lined the path, and I often watched the old gardener at work. Two farmers with sunburned faces could be seen lovingly caring for the animals.

From the kitchen, a wonderful aroma of delicious food wafted through the air—aromatic rice dishes prepared with saffron and spices, fresh bread, roasted poultry and lamb, strawberries, and melons. Our aunt prepared a mixture of Russian, Caucasian, European, and Persian dishes. The heavy wooden table from Baku was always laden with delicious food. The meal usually lasted a long time, as there was much to discuss and chat about. The latest news was exchanged, but above all, there was much laughter.

When I remember how heartily people laughed back then, it seems to me that we have forgotten how to laugh now.

Lunch began with soup and ended with various desserts, some of which were seldom known in Persia at the time. We also enjoyed different types of puddings, which I later sampled in Europe but had already tasted in Tabriz with my mother. Sometimes, when we returned home, we experienced stomach difficulties, but in those days, being overweight was considered a sign of health, and Aunt always wanted to see us healthy!

Father's passport photo

18

RAMADAN – THE MONTH OF FASTING

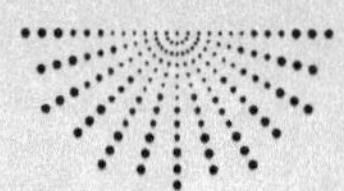

One of the most beautiful seasons for me as a child, apart from Nowruz, was the month of Ramadan. This month of fasting in the Islamic world follows the Arabic lunar calendar, which is about ten days shorter than the solar year, as measured by the Gregorian calendar. Because of this difference, Ramadan shifts forward by about ten days each year, aligning with the same season every thirty years. When I was a child, Ramadan fell during the hot summertime. From sunrise to sunset, almost twenty hours, people were required to fast.

Although I am not a theologian, I am writing about my life story. To provide some insight into the philosophy of Ramadan in Islam, I found a quote from Abd al-Qadir, a Sufi living and teaching in England.

"There is the obligatory annual fast of Ramadan, which is calculated according to the lunar calendar, so that it shifts according to the passage of the moon through the years. The opening of the fast depends on the visibility of the New Moon in the holy month. The fast lasts from dawn to sunset and is

broken immediately after the sun disappears. The fast is restriction-free and also includes any abstention from sexual intercourse. It goes without saying that fasting also includes the control of one's temper and tongue. The eye should fast at the same time as the other organs, and the ear should close itself to anything unhealthy. The overall impact of the one-month fast is profoundly shattering, and its effect on the constancy-fancy of the nafs (lust) is extremely lasting. It causes a shattering of the entire basis of the illusion of a detached self, breaking through the established dietary habits of adult humans, opening up memories of the childhood relationship to food. The reverberations of any imbalance and fear that were locked into that memory structure thought to be fundamental, are released and allowed to ring out like a gong whose vibrations were dampened, and which is now allowed to resonate out into absolute silence. Fasting, therefore, exposes the entire substructure of the nafs (desire)."

During the month of Ramadan, generally less work was done, although Father maintained his regular daily routine, fulfilling his religious duties with serene self-confidence. He did not want to show that he was fasting, and his demeanor remained as normal as before Ramadan, even while others appeared tired and sleep-deprived. Father's tea kitchen in his office was closed, and the atmosphere was quiet since few people stopped by. The farmers couldn't easily leave their villages, so Father missed their visits. Everyone aimed to conserve energy, avoiding sweating or becoming thirsty. At noon, in the peak heat, we heard the muezzin's call for midday prayers. Father rarely went to the mosque because he couldn't sit on the floor. Instead, he had a private room above his office where he would retire for prayer.

At home, the anticipation of evening meals, called "iftar"

(meaning to break the fast), made things more lively. The very best and most delicious dishes were prepared during Ramadan, and many new dish combinations were created as the need for anything edible heightened. I often thought that if everyone experienced this state of fasting, nothing would ever be thrown away! Even simple water, when thirst torments and one's tongue is dry, reminds one of plants wilting from thirst or a caravan in the desert craving water. I firmly believe that fasting is not only beneficial for the body but that eating and drinking in moderation also greatly benefits the soul and spirit, purifying the mind.

During Ramadan, we were awakened before sunrise, around three in the morning, to the smell of rice, saffron, and various deliciously spiced dishes. The meal prepared for this pre-dawn breakfast is called "suhoor." Great care was taken to set the table festively, with heavy tables covered in white embroidered tablecloths and adorned with a variety of flavorful dishes.

While we ate, the radio station repeatedly announced the time, helping everyone to adjust their food, drink, and medications, if necessary. Mother, a heavy smoker, found it challenging to refrain from smoking all day. Despite Father's endless efforts to help her quit, she continued to smoke, often replacing food with one or two cigarettes. We children intended to fast as well and ate with her. A few minutes before sunrise, the radio announcer recited a prayer from the Quran in a beautiful voice, signaling that it was time to prepare for the fast. We brushed our teeth, cleaned our mouths and noses, and took a final sip of water. Then, the muezzin delivered the Azan (the Islamic call to prayer), and the fasting began, lasting until sunset.

Salat, also called "namaz," is the first duty of every Muslim, and it is preceded by the ritual ablution known as "wudhu." This preparation is both physical and spiritual, as prayer is performed facing the qibla. Muslims observe the qibla not only in ritual prayer but also when sleeping and even during burial. While the qibla outwardly points toward the Kaaba in Mecca, inwardly, it directs one's focus toward God, as my father often said. The Sufi master, Abd al-Qadir, eloquently describes the qibla in his writings:

"In the act of Salat, daily prayer of the Muslim, a certain direction is to be followed whereby all human prayer is centered around a central point, the Kaaba in Mecca, so that an endless wheel of living praise of the reality (God) revolves endlessly around the four walls of the empty Old House built by Prophet Ibrahim (Abraham). This direction is called Qibla."

After we performed our morning prayer with Father, we children went back to bed. However, with so many siblings and cousins together, sleep was scarce. We always had so much to talk about—much of it was nonsense, but we would chat for hours! Around noon, we would finally get up, finding the house still quiet. There was also silence in the alleys and streets; nothing could be heard, and we usually made our way to the cellar, where it was cool and pleasant. A few hours later, hunger would strike again. In the kitchen wing, the staff were busy preparing and cooking for the much-anticipated dinner. We could hear the women talking and the chef giving out instructions. It was a hive of activity, with people coming and going, yet no one paid us any attention or questioned whether we were fasting.

One of my cousins, my best friend, convinced us that we didn't have to fast all day because we were only 12 or 13 years old and were only required to fast until noon. He was right, and many of us agreed. We voted on what to eat, deciding not to disappoint our parents by eating too much—just a little something. The cellar offered everything we needed: fruits, vegetables, pickles, some prepared dishes, and lavash (flatbread). We emerged from the cellar just before sunset, the end of the fasting day. The staff pitied us poor children who had supposedly endured the whole day without food or drink. We would rush into the dining room, always amazed by the beauty of the tables set for iftar (dinner).

It was a feast for the eyes, especially after fasting all day. The tables were covered with hand-embroidered white cloths, adorned with colorful carafes filled with cool drinks in bright colors—sherbets of roses, mint, or various herbs. There were also jams, baklava, halwa, huge bowls of seasonal fruit, soups, and various appetizers. The aromatic smell of the samovar boiling tea and singing like a bird added to the inviting atmosphere. It all looked so beautiful that we regretted breaking our fast with snacks, and the main course hadn't even been served yet—it wouldn't come until late in the evening!

Then our aunts arrived with their husbands and children, followed by other relatives. Everyone was welcome but had to arrive before our father, as it was customary not to keep the elders waiting. In our country, when an elderly man enters the room, everyone stands briefly to greet him; he returns the greeting and invites them to sit, then they all sit down together. If someone arrived after Father, he would have to stand again, which no one wanted to cause him. Slowly, the room filled with people. On the radio, happy music played, and there was always a solemn yet contented mood. Everyone was hungry, thirsty, and tired, but also proud. Mother had thought of everything, catering to every taste. Prayers of thanksgiving were read, then the Azan was announced, confirming sunset. First, hot water was served in small glasses. Father and Mother prayed, then took a sip in God's name, officially ending the fast.

After a long day of fasting, I learned that one gets full very quickly. You eat little but in several stages. Before the guests arrived, Mother had already sent trays of food and drink to neighbors, sick people, or pregnant women. My siblings and I also helped deliver food. The retailer, Aga Miri, whose small store was just around the corner, served warm meals as well. Since we helped him, we often received leftovers to eat!

Our temporary staff and servants were treated like family members. They learned a lot while working for Mother, and some later became well-known cooks and chefs. Mother's dishes were exceptionally good for Tabriz cuisine at the time. Besides Persian cuisine, she also prepared European and Caucasian dishes with dough and noodles. Her cooking was renowned throughout the city.

During Ramadan, the cinemas also showed the most wonderful movies. We usually went to the late-night show at 11 p.m. and enjoyed more cool drinks and sweets. The streets and restaurants were full of people. In the Armenian quarter, where my best friends lived, it was lively, and there were many good pastry shops. Armenians in Tabriz were very well-respected citizens, known for being hardworking and honest.

When we returned home, the lights were still burning, and preparations were already underway for the next day to begin again.

19

OUR BROTHERS ARRIVE FROM GERMANY

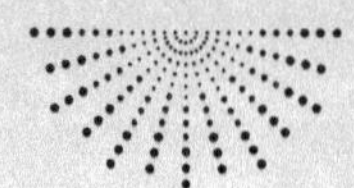

During this time of Ramadan, my eldest brother Farokh was in Germany. After passing his state examination and receiving his doctorate, he was now working as a doctor and completing his residency. My second oldest brother, Behruz, was busy with his exams. When Ramadan ended, Father shared the exciting news that both brothers would be coming home for a visit. As plane tickets were sent, Mom's joy was palpable—she was laughing again and sleeping better!

A trip from Europe was no small feat in those days. In Tabriz, the airport and railroad station were still under construction. Travelers had to take a propeller plane from Munich to Beirut, which had become the gateway to the Orient after the Soviet Union had destroyed the city of Baku. From Beirut, they traveled on to Tehran, and then by bus to Tabriz, since the railroad was still incomplete. None of us had flown before, though we occasionally saw planes flying high over the city—so high we couldn't even hear the noise of the aircraft. The journey was long and demanding, but both brothers finally arrived safely.

The time spent with our brothers was wonderful, bringing the house back to life. Two aunts from Tehran, along with their children—who had grown up and become parents themselves—also came to visit. The small refugee family from Baku had now become a large family with children and grandchildren. Mother and her sisters often sat together, reminiscing about the past, sometimes speaking in Russian so we children couldn't understand. Uncle hosted large parties at his beautiful house, where we sat on Persian carpets with comfortable cushions in the garden, listening to Mother play the accordion, which she played very well. My cousin Ali played the tar—a stringed instrument similar to a guitar—and my aunt played the gaval, a type of percussion instrument, creating quite an orchestra! They mostly played Caucasian and Russian songs, but it was always festive.

With many girls of marrying age, discussions and advice about marriage were common. However, our brothers visiting from Germany were naturally the center of attention, sharing stories about Europe. Father and Uncle were particularly interested in hearing what had happened to Hitler and the German Reich, and both were pleased to hear that Germany had recovered and that people were doing much better overall.

Our oldest sister, Firuze, was our confidante, and she discovered that Behruz was in love with a German girl who loved him back, and her family approved of their marriage. All Behruz needed now was our parents' blessing. The thought of telling Mother gave both my brother and Father a headache as they tried to figure out the best way to break the news.

Behruz had brought a tape recorder—a large, heavy device at the time—which we had never seen before. Hearing our own voices for the first time was a delight, and Mother had great fun with it. He had also brought tapes with music by Katharina Valente, Peter Kraus, and other well-known German artists of the time. Mother often spoke on the tape, enjoying hearing her own voice repeatedly. It was a novelty for all of us. We children received many gifts that were new to us, learning about things for the first time. Word of our brothers' arrival had spread around town, and Father received many congratulations and advice. Should they open a practice immediately, or perhaps start building a hospital as soon as possible? Father, ever agreeable, said the wise man gives in. As life goes, time flew by like the winds over the mountains, and soon enough, my brothers were preparing to return to Germany.

They had new suits, shoes, and shirts made to order, and they purchased gifts to take back with them. On their last day in Tabriz, Behruz finally revealed his secret. Mother was thrilled but also sad because she had longed to witness the weddings of her sons and to talk to her daughter-in-law about the prospect of future grandchildren. She was so used to sorrow and pain, feeling displaced from her own country, that she knew the weight of homesickness and being a stranger. She had experienced so much, even suffering from the grief of others, and she feared losing her sons. Yet, she agreed, as did Father. For him, the decision was ultimately up to my brothers, as he believed they would make the right choices on their own and did not want to interfere. After all, he himself had left home almost as a child and moved far away.

Behruz was relieved and happy, knowing he could now settle in Germany and start a family. He would no longer be alone; he would have someone who could perhaps replace a part of his mother, the family, and his homeland.

That evening, my parents hosted a big farewell party for them. There was much crying and sobbing, and gifts were given as suitcases were reopened and closed repeatedly until they could hold no more! The gifts ranged from a gold watch to pickled cucumbers, gold coins to handmade needlework. Both brothers must have had mixed feelings about leaving—torn between the love and warmth of family and the life awaiting them in modern Europe, with its foreign customs and traditions.

Early the following morning, after a tearful farewell, the staff helped carry their heavy suitcases through the quiet alleys of Tabriz. Occasionally, we heard a chicken or a passerby gracefully wishing them a good trip. The alley had been cleaned, and the ground was splashed with water, giving the fresh morning air a pleasant earthy smell. The motor coach departed promptly at 6:00 a.m. for Tehran. But as the route was under construction, the trip took more than 14 hours!

Mother was remarkably quiet and introspective after her two sons left. She stood by the famous window, gazing up at the sky. I wondered what she saw up there, as I was almost a grown boy now and wanted to understand everything. But as I approached her, I saw tears streaming down her delicate face. She stood very still, silently praying.

Shortly after my brothers left, great joy spread throughout our country as the imperial house was blessed with a crown prince. Mohammed Reza Pahlavi, Shah of Persia, and his wife, Farah Diba, had a baby boy.

Engagement picture of Margot and Behruz with friends, and my oldest brother Farokh, in Rheingau am Rhein in Germany.

MOHAMMAD REZA SHAH

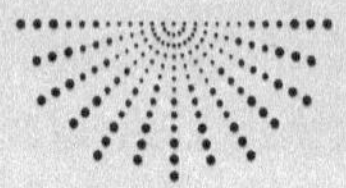

The Shah returned from Switzerland as a young prince in 1936 after completing his studies and, on the orders of his father Reza Shah, married Fawzia, the daughter of the Egyptian king, in 1937. It was a political marriage that ultimately failed, as expected, because she was a spoiled princess who had grown up in the luxury of Cairo and struggled to adapt to the foreign culture and language in Tehran. They divorced, and she returned to her homeland, leaving behind their daughter, Princess Shahnaz.

Sometime later, the Shah married the beautiful German-Iranian, Soraya. Her father was from the noble Bakhtyari tribe, and her mother was German. Their wedding was celebrated in both Persia and Germany, with the Germans claiming Soraya as their own and calling her their queen. The Shah was happy with her, and so were his people.

At the beginning of his reign, the young Shah gained great popularity by successfully pushing the Soviets back from the province of Azerbaijan. He relaxed the veil decree issued by his father, which was tolerated, made compromises with the clergy, and remained close to the people, gaining their favor. However, the one issue that stood between the two lovers was that Soraya had no children, a matter of great importance for the monarchy. The imperial couple traveled to Germany and were warmly received, but even after consulting doctors, they found no solution. After weeks of trying, they returned to their homeland, and Soraya, much to the Shah's sorrow, had to leave.

Years later, the Shah married for the third time, this time to a Persian architectural student from Paris named Farah Diba, who came from the well-known Diba family from Tabriz. After a grand wedding reminiscent of a thousand and one nights, their firstborn, Crown Prince Reza Pahlavi II, was born in a state hospital in the south of Tehran. The occasion was so joyful that we were given a day off from school, and people celebrated him warmly without the need for the usual state coercion.

IN MY FREE TIME, my friend Said and I often went to the cinema, which was the only real diversion we had back then. Movies from Hollywood, which were shown simultaneously in Europe and the USA, were also screened in Persia. Relations between the countries were excellent, and Persia was a good customer for Hollywood. Films were shown in various genres such as comedy, crime, drama, western, war, history, and romance. Our favorite was comedy, as it often reflected the living conditions we found ourselves in.

Said and I were soon to be among the lucky ones to travel to Europe to study, and we hoped to experience everything we had seen in the movies. At 15 and 16 years old, the stories in those films felt very real to us. We believed that everyone in Europe or the USA lived in elegant, beautiful apartments and modern houses, driving chic cars without a worry in the world. It was like a dream come true for us. We were often disappointed with our country and wondered why Persia seemed so sleepy and backward, missing out on so many developments in the 20th century. For Said, the movies were just a dream, but for me, I was determined to turn these dreams into reality—just like in the films.

In 1953, our country was deeply troubled, and Dr. Mohammed Mossadegh, the Prime Minister, was overthrown. The Communist Party, religious groups, those loyal to the king, and the king's opponents were all fighting each other. Mossadegh, who was still considered an idol by many Iranians, had nationalized the Anglo-Iranian Oil Company. Since the beginning of the 20th century, the Iranian oil industry had been in the hands of the British. Mossadegh was prime minister of Persia for only two years, from 1951 to 1953, but during that time, he kept the world in suspense.

Meanwhile, the Shah had gained a foothold and was building up an intelligence and secret service with the aid of America. He no longer respected the basic laws and constitution, which had been enshrined in our country by Parliament over 100 years earlier. The elections for the Majlis (Parliament) were manipulated, giving the king's loyalists the upper hand and leading to an undeclared war between rival parties. The newly established secret service uncovered communist associations within the army, leading to the arrest and execution of hundreds of officers.

A few years earlier, when free elections were still possible, Dr. Mossadegh had been elected Prime Minister. He came from a wealthy, feudal family, and his real name was Mohammed Hedayat. His father, Mirza Hedayat, had been the finance minister under the Qajar dynasty. It was said that the Shah was so impressed with his abilities that he gave him the name "Mossadegh." At the age of 18, Mossadegh was sent to France for training, where he later earned a doctorate in law. In 1916, he returned to Tehran and became Under State Secretary in the Ministry of Finance, and in 1922, he was appointed Minister of Finance. Mossadegh fell out with the new king, Reza Pahlavi, and was one of the few to vote against Reza Pahlavi's appointment as Shah. In 1928, he was forced out of all political posts.

As Minister of War and Supreme Commander, Reza Khan was a candidate for King of Persia. However, Dr. Mossadegh argued that "Reza Khan is a personality with special abilities, but he will not be able to do anything for the country as king, because according to the constitution, the king has only a symbolic place and is not allowed to rule. For this reason, his abilities will not be of any use to the country unless he bypasses the constitution and becomes a dictator."

In 1944, Mossadegh entered the newly elected parliament (Majlis) and became known for his activities with the National Front. On April 29, 1951, Mohammad Reza Shah, the second king of the Pahlavi dynasty, appointed Mossadegh as Prime Minister. On April 30, 1951, even before his confirmation, he initiated the law on nationalizing Persian oil fields, which was duly passed by Parliament. Mossadegh also tried to nationalize the Persian oil deposits, which had been pumped out and taken away since their discovery by the British. This was a dangerous decision and undertaking, as many of the top ten thousand families were half English and held English citizenship. Some sought protection in their embassies and were released from punishment only by pressure from their countries on the Persian government. Britain and Russia were particularly favored, and it was expected that the conflict of interest would pose challenges for Mossadegh, with various groups such as communists, anti-English, anti-Russian, religious, and nationalist factions opposing him.

The West stopped buying oil from Persia, leading to a boycott. England even set up a blockade in the Persian Gulf with warships, cutting off oil income and causing an economic crisis. People were under great pressure.

I remember that time well. Poverty was so severe that many were forced to live on bread alone. Nevertheless, Mossadegh was supported by the people. It was the first time in the Near East and in the Islamic world that a leader was willingly and sincerely followed by the people. They bought cloth from local producers, and women voluntarily donated their jewelry to support Mossadegh's government. Government bonds were issued, and the Persian people stood firmly behind their prime minister.

Dr. Mossadegh went to the UN with his followers and dozens of experienced lawyers, where they sued Great Britain. England was condemned, and Mossadegh got justice, winning the case. In 1951, Time magazine named Mossadegh "Person of the Year." However, under the pressure of great powers and international corporations, Mossadegh's government was finally overthrown on August 19, 1953. The conspiracy against him, called Operation Ajax, was carried out by the CIA on behalf of the US government under Eisenhower, with the help of Roosevelt Jr., who was in the country during the entire period. As a result, democratization in Persia was set back by a hundred years. The king became overconfident, leading history to take a different course, eventually culminating in the Iranian Islamic Revolution led by Ayatollah Ruhollah Khomeini.

At that time, I was in the ninth grade, and my brother Parwiz was preparing to graduate from high school, ready for his turn to go abroad. We had a good library at home, built up by my oldest brother and added to by the others over time. Parwiz was well-read and had contributed many books to the collection. I was now old enough to read them, and I eagerly made my way through the library!

As the years went by, many changes occurred. My eldest brother took over Father's responsibilities when he didn't want to participate. We had many great books, like *20,000 Leagues Under the Sea*, *Journey to the Center of the Earth*, *The Bees*, *The Ants*, and *Gone with the Wind*. Parwiz was a huge help, teaching me to read properly, which I enjoyed tremendously.

Over time, I developed good friendships at school, but Said continued to be my best friend. He was a quiet, romantic, and loyal person. We walked home together every day after school, first dropping me off at my house before he continued to his. Our route took us along the main street, Pahlavi, and then south to Shahnaz Avenue. At the beginning of the avenue was the Armenian quarter, where there were beautiful houses with natural stone facades and cozy little teahouses. At noon and in the evening, after school, the avenue was filled with boys hoping to catch a glimpse of the pretty girls from their school. A little further down the avenue was an elegant movie theater called Cinema Kristall, and next to it was a building with attractive stores that belonged to us. Across the street was a modern pastry shop, where we occasionally had a glass of iced coffee or a piece of delicious cake. I must confess, nowhere in the world have I eaten such delicious cakes as in Persia.

After a short walk, we reached the girls' school, Parvin, which was attended by the daughters of prominent families in Tabriz. It was the best private school for girls. On the left side of the avenue was a narrow alley paved with round natural stones, making it difficult to walk on due to the many holes! Halfway down the alley on the left was our mosque, and opposite it was the public bath, Hamam. Further along, toward our house, were two small stores, and right next to our house was the third small store, belonging to Aga-Miri (Mr. Miri), the retailer. His store didn't have much selection—just a few kinds of beans, rice, sugar, some overripe fruit, and children's candy.

His best offering was yogurt, which he got fresh from the dairy every day in large terracotta bowls. He hauled them to his little store and sold the yogurt with great pride. However, he couldn't possibly feed his family from the proceeds of his store alone. Later, I learned that Mother helped him by paying for his upkeep. He was also a good organizer when we had guests or for religious occasions in the mosque, like Ehsan (voluntary distribution for the needy). Whether in times of joy or sadness, he was always there to organize everything. In the fall, when the winter stock was to be stored, Aga-Miri was always present, taking over the supervision in place of Mother. During Muharram, the month of mourning, he was invaluable, rendering great services.

Me and my volleyball mates at the Ferdosi High School in
Tabriz.

MONTH OF MUHARRAM

Muharram is the first month in the Arab-Islamic lunar calendar. It is a month of mourning in Persia —the only country with the Shiite faith. Abd al-Qadir, the Sufi, writes in his book:

"After the death of the Prophet Muhammad, the caliphs succeeded him, namely the caliphs Abo Baker, Omar, Osman, and the fourth, Ali bin Abi Talib. There is no doubt that Ali was the most suitable for the task of the 'caliphate'. But the personal rivalry and tribal jealousy that set these men against each other, had to be acted out. As a result, as soon as the Prophet was no longer alive, the community began to tear itself apart in a previously suppressed frenzy. The house of 'Hazrate Ali' was set on fire. The door collapsed on Hazrate Fatima, his wife and the daughter of the Messenger (Muhammad). She suffered a miscarriage and died immediately after this incident, although her death was partly due to her burning desire to follow her father to the grave. The bitterness and distortions that arose from that

> *initial incident still reverberate in the Muslim community today, to the extent that it still exists as a living reality. Within just 29 years, the 'Gate of Wisdom', the 'Emir of the Trusting', Ali, was stabbed in the back by a Muslim as he was about to prostrate himself before God in the mosque."*

Soon after, the Prophet's two grandsons were assassinated. Imam Hassan was poisoned, and Imam Hussein, his younger brother, was killed on the battlefield of Karbala and beheaded in what is regarded as one of the most horrific massacres in the history of the Muslim community. The Prophet had known of their impending deaths during his lifetime, and the Hadith (Authenticated Tradition of the Prophet) recounts that he wept over them when they were still children. The division between Sunni and Shia did not arise at a single moment but developed over time. However, the brutal eradication and persecution of the Prophet's family remains a repulsive example of human greed and savagery, a blatant disregard for both Islam and the explicit warnings of the Prophet himself.

Imam Hussein, the younger son of Ali bin Abi Talib and Fatima, the Prophet's daughter, is a central figure in the Shiite faith. After the death of his brother Imam Hassan in 660, Imam Hussein led an uprising in Kufa (present-day Iraq) against the ruling Umayyad caliphs, but it was quickly crushed. On October 10, 680, he was defeated at the Battle of Karbala by the forces of Caliph Yazid I. He was captured and murdered. His tomb is located in the Iraqi city of Karbala. From his marriage with the Sassanid princess, Shahrabanu, came his son Ali Zain al-Abedin, the fourth Imam of the Shiites.

The mourning ceremony for the death of Imam Hussein is held on the ninth and tenth of the Arabic month of Muharram. Because the lunar calendar is ten days shorter than the solar calendar, Muharram shifts between winter and summer, alternating every fifteen years. In our country, from the first of Muharram to the fortieth anniversary of the Imam's death, nearly two months of mourning were observed.

Our mother dressed in black during this period. Laughter, joy, music, and the radio ceased, and our home became seriously quiet. During this time, Mother also provided for and cared for the poor, infirm, and needy. She often visited the cemetery to mourn her mother and unburden her sorrows.

The mosque in our alley was managed by our family throughout the mourning period. Every evening, six to eight clergymen preached, mostly about the life of Imam Hussein and the lessons derived from his martyrdom. They taught that every Muslim should be upright and steadfast, avoid killing, lying, and slander, help the sick and orphans, assist those in need, refrain from stealing, and observe many other good teachings.

During this time, sherbet, tea, and sandwiches were distributed. Father covered all the expenses, and Aga-Miri, the retailer, managed everything. He was busy with it for almost two months, occasionally opening his store to check on things, but otherwise keeping it closed. Despite his good organization, we children often had to walk home late at night through dark alleys to pick up sacks of sugar, tea, butter, and cheese. Most evenings, a hundred or so people attended the mosque, and on some nights, two to three hundred—it was unpredictable. The mosque was beautifully adorned with Persian carpets donated by various people, creating a soothing, heavenly atmosphere. The interior was simple yet elegant, with a large room supported by many columns and wide-span vaulted ceilings. The windows were exquisite stained glass, and each dome had a large crystal chandelier hanging from it. It was delightfully cool in the summer.

Father could not attend the meetings himself due to pain in his knee—his only ailment. Perhaps he also chose not to attend because, at the end of each meeting, the preacher would praise the donor and host and pray for him and his family. For this reason, the eldest son of the house always represented Father. As the host, one had to sit from the beginning to the end of the session, from about 6:00 p.m. until the middle of the night, right next to the entrance of the mosque. The host stood up at the entrance to greet each visitor, then took a seat again, as Persian tradition and manners dictated.

The tenth day of Muharram, called Ashura, is the culmination of the mourning ceremony for Imam Hussein. Our mother made special preparations for this day, as she did every year. Food and drink were prepared according to the season and served to a community of over a hundred people. The offerings were treated with special respect because they were donations in the name of Imam Hussein. You can imagine the zeal with which our mother worked as a hostess, serving her favorite Imam. The food was special, and people would even bring it from far away for their sick, expecting a quick cure. Many helpers assisted in the distribution, and the food was served to the guests on our best dishes, with portions delivered to the homes of relatives, neighbors, and the needy. In the early morning, mourners walked through the narrow streets and alleys of Tabriz, singing lamentations over the deaths of the Imam and his 72 followers.

There was a special, somber atmosphere. One could almost feel the events of 1,300 years ago. Every movement and word were precisely prescribed, following traditions that had been observed for centuries. Each funeral procession carried its own flag. The colors were black, symbolizing mourning; red, representing the bloodshed and massacre of the Prophet's family and descendants; and green, the Prophet's flag. The flags were large, heavy, and made of embroidered cloth with gold or silver threads. At the head of the procession, just behind the flag, walked the elders of the community, all dressed in black. As a sign of mourning, the men did not shave their beards during this period.

Aga-Miri had many tasks to manage but was given free rein on such days. Although he served only the men's section (women were served in separate rooms) and had a dozen helpers, he was sweating and, as always, nervous, smoking one cigarette after another. The women's department was the responsibility of the ladies who were almost always with us and who had helped raise us children. Some even stayed with us overnight if Mother wished.

As the day ended, several funeral processions came from other parts of town to express their personal condolences to our parents. Throngs of people, all dressed in black, sang sad dirges in unison, walking in the same rhythm and step through the courtyard. They left the house as they had come. During this ceremony, all the lights in our house were turned off. Our guests, mostly women, gathered in front of the large windows on different floors and mourned together. Mother took off her black mourning dress only after forty days, marking the end of the mourning period.

WHEN MY BROTHER successfully passed his high school exams with good grades, he flew to Tehran to obtain his passport and visa for Germany. By then, Tabriz had an airport and a railroad station, making travel easier. For our mother, it was the third son to leave home and move to a foreign country. The house became very quiet, with only four children still at home. As the eldest son, I had to represent my father whenever necessary, a responsibility that prepared me for an independent life abroad.

Summer had begun, bringing blue skies and bright sunshine over Tabriz, which both people and animals loved. The aroma of abundant juicy fruits, vegetables, and herbs filled the air—wonderful gifts from God!

Our mother provided large food rations to the servants every evening. During this time, she seemed satisfied and happy. However, her health was not good; she was often nervous, unbalanced, and exhausted, which worried us greatly. For our father, there was nothing worse than seeing someone sick at home.

He himself had never been ill and had never visited a doctor. His self-discipline, contentment, and positive attitude made him strong and self-confident, both physically and psychologically. Except for the occasional cold, I had never seen him sick, but we were deeply concerned about Mother's health.

Uncle and Aunt were preparing for the Hajj, the pilgrimage to Mecca, while we eagerly awaited news from our two brothers in Germany, hoping they would visit us that year. Our second oldest brother had become engaged and was working as a doctor in a hospital. Our cousin Nader, the son of my mother's younger sister, had also married. Many relatives had left the hot summer in Tehran to stay with us in Tabriz.

It was a summer like those of the past, but for me, it was different. I was now addressed by the staff as Aga (mister) and was taken seriously, confirming my role as the eldest son in the household. This transition happened without much fanfare, but I had to pay attention and behave accordingly. Mistakes that might have gone unnoticed before were now taken seriously.

In our house, certain rules were strictly followed. The word "I" was avoided as much as possible because it was considered a sign of arrogance. Instead of saying "my" house, "my" car, or "my" garden, we said "our" house or "our" car. In daily conversation, "we" was used instead of "I." When older people entered a room, those present stood up. The person thanked them and quickly took a seat so as not to keep others standing too long. Younger people always walked one step behind their elders, and we were careful not to sit with our backs to anyone or start eating before others had begun. It was considered impolite to blow one's nose in company or in public. When yawning, we kept our hands in front of our mouths. All these rules were ingrained in us as we grew into young adults.

One late summer's day, Father called from his office with the happy news that our brothers were on their way home for a visit. By then, we had telephone service, and our new phone was a large, black, heavy device with a rotary dial. It took several minutes of turning the dial to establish a connection with the central office and have the desired line switched on. We didn't know the exact arrival time of the brothers. My older brother had driven from Germany a few times and surprised us, but this time, they both came by plane, and Father was notified by phone from our store in Tehran.

When the news arrived, Mother was at the dentist, about a half-hour walk from our house. I ran there as fast as I could to share the good news. She was lying in the dentist's chair when I burst in with excitement. The dentist finished his treatment and wished us well. We quickly boarded a horse-drawn carriage to take us home, as it was much faster than walking.

After two long days of waiting, the brothers finally arrived with suitcases full of gifts. It was pure joy—chocolates in pretty packages, non-iron shirts, records, a slide projector with beautiful pictures, and more. After a long time apart, we were all together again, able to enjoy precious days as a family. Photos with all six brothers, three sisters, and our parents captured the beauty of those moments, which must have been around 1957.

During those days, the stove in the kitchen never went out, with cooking happening day and night. Mother usually asked our oldest brother what he wanted to eat, while the younger brother would complain, and I, of course, had nothing to say.

Father maintained his usual daily routine—going to the office at 7:30 a.m., returning home before dark, and going to bed at 9:00 p.m. While he was with us, we sat neatly, almost like soldiers—we didn't smoke, speak loudly, or laugh. He was always addressed as "sir," and we never used his first name. However, as soon as he said goodnight and went to his room, cigarettes were lit, and we made ourselves comfortable.

The good times passed quickly. Summer ended, and all three brothers flew back to Germany, taking brother Parwiz with them. Mother had to say goodbye to three of her sons this time, unsure of which son to hug first. It was heartbreaking to watch her standing there helplessly, trying to hide her grief. After they left, the house felt deserted and silent. Mother stood by her usual window, weeping uncontrollably, while the women in the house cared for her and wept alongside her.

Mother's helpers were more like friends than mere servants. They chatted with her while working and, before heading home in the evening, took their rations of prepared food, fruits, butter, and cheese, along with their wages. Besides these women, there were also gardeners, cooks, and a maid. They were always with us, but I never fully understood their specific roles.

Some of them had dreams, mostly about my dear, deceased grandma, Mrs. Haj Bekoff, which they usually shared with Mother during teatime. Kobra, a petite and humorous woman in her fifties, always remembered her dreams. One day, she dreamed about Grandma again and reassured Mother not to worry—that Grandma was in a good place, thanks to Mother's Ehsan (donations/kindness), and was being treated especially well. Mother listened intently, tears in her eyes. She often gave Nazri (a donation to the needy), which, unlike voluntary Ehsan, involves a promise to provide certain services if specific wishes come true. This could include supporting the needy, helping the sick and elderly, or engaging in charitable deeds like building schools or hospitals.

When letters from our brothers were delayed, Mother became worried and nervous, which was understandable, given that three of her sons were thousands of kilometers away in a foreign country. At that time, people knew very little about Europe.

As autumn approached, the winter stockpiling began, which was good timing as it kept Mother occupied and took her mind off her sons. Meanwhile, Behruz had gotten married, and Parwiz was studying at the University of Mainz. Father was very proud to have two sons as doctors. I, too, began thinking about my future, but I didn't want to be a doctor—I was afraid of blood! I told Mother I couldn't be a good doctor. She understood and said, "I know, my son. You have a very soft heart, and your father knows it too. What do you want to become?" I wanted to become a theologian, a real mullah. I didn't want to go to Europe; I wanted to study in Qom, Najaf in Iraq, or Beirut, where I could immerse myself in theology.

After my brother's departure, I was given his room on the upper floor of our house, complete with his books and furniture. It was nice to have my own space—no one disturbed me, and no one entered without knocking. Even my parents respected my privacy and ensured others did the same.

After school, Said and I would do homework in my room, where we were served tea and cake and treated like adults. We also painted, read the same books, shared interests, and complemented each other completely. Said was a good-natured, intelligent person, and it's a pity that fate separated us later in life.

In the afternoons after school, we often listened to German and American music on the tape recorder my brother had given me. Sometimes, our other school friends came over, and I proudly showed them our library and the tape recorder. Mother spoiled us with tasty snacks too.

We also went to the cinema, but I had to be home before Father returned from work. Our entire daily routine revolved around him. Whatever we did, he knew. When I smoked my first cigarette after a cinema visit, he already knew! Mother had taught us that smoking was one of the worst habits in our society. If Father could have, he would have done everything to get Mother to quit. Unfortunately, he didn't succeed, and I didn't follow his good advice either.

My brother wrote to me regularly, describing life in Germany. Having never seen anything beyond Tabriz, its surroundings, and a few nearby villages, seeing Tehran alone would have been a dream for me.

Mother's health wasn't improving. The doctors said her teeth were straining her nerves and suggested removing them all.

Looking back, I can't imagine that diagnosis was correct. However, the dentist proceeded, and within two weeks, all of Mother's teeth were extracted, making her look like an old woman at the age of 50. Those were sad times.

Then came a bigger problem for us. Mother's eldest sister, her husband, and their five children were planning to move to Tehran. Her husband, who was also Father's business partner, wanted to represent him and participate in decision-making in Tehran. Father didn't mind but didn't want to risk financial difficulties because he highly valued his reputation. In Tabriz, reputation was everything for merchants and businessmen. Father was so mindful of this that he ensured people didn't recognize his signature. He had his secretary withdraw money from the bank every morning and handled all payments in cash. When relatives or acquaintances needed money, they asked Father for a bill of exchange or a guarantee, but he never provided one. He believed that if the debtor couldn't pay, he would take on the debt himself.

Eventually, my aunt, uncle, and their five children moved to Tehran. Our house soon became quiet and lonely at times. It was a huge change for us all.

PILGRIMAGE TO MASHHAD

One day, Kobra arrived at our house earlier than usual. Father hadn't left yet, and we were still having breakfast. She seemed unusually excited, sitting in the corner with her veil pulled tight, revealing only her big red nose and one eye. After Father left the room, Mother, concerned, went straight to her. Kobra, still visibly agitated, told Mother that she had dreamed again about Mrs. Haj Bekoff, my late grandmother. In the dream, Grandmother had expressed a wish for Mother to visit Imam Reza —our eighth Imam and direct descendant of the Prophet. Overjoyed, Mother immediately agreed that we should make a pilgrimage to Mashhad, to the tomb of Imam Reza.

Mashhad, the capital of the Razavi Khorasan province and the second-largest city in the country, is located 850 kilometers east of Tehran, at about 985 meters above sea level along the Kashafrud River. The city was founded around 823 AD, and its name, Mashhad, means "place of martyrs," as it houses the tomb of Imam Ali ibn Musa al-Reza. Imam Reza, the eighth Imam of the Shiites, was poisoned by Caliph Mamun in 818 AD. Despite this, Mamun built a mausoleum for him, and since then, the site has become a major place of pilgrimage, earning the name "Mashhad al-Reza."

Over the years, rulers like the Mongols, Timurids, Safavids, and Nader Shah Afshar expanded the city and its pilgrimage site.

The Imam's Tomb is a vast sanctuary complex equipped to receive thousands of pilgrims daily. Pilgrims come from all over the Shiite world to visit this sacred site, which includes hotels, guesthouses, a hospital, a museum, and libraries. Throughout their stay, pilgrims are provided with free meals, thanks to the immense donations from the faithful. The Imam Reza Foundation, known as the Razavi Foundation, is one of the largest foundations in the world, owning numerous properties, including houses, stores, factories, entire business districts, hospitals, and many other facilities both within the country and abroad.

With construction at Tabriz Airport complete, we flew to Tehran first. It was an exciting adventure for me, as I had never been to Mashhad or Tehran before. Mashhad, formerly called Tus, was another thousand kilometers away, and we would travel there by train a week later. Mother, my youngest sister, and I flew for the first time in our lives on Iran Air, a new and well-organized airline. The experience was both thrilling and terrifying for my sister and me! However, Mother reassured us, saying that Imam Reza would protect his guests and ask God to keep us safe. After an hour-long flight, we arrived in Tehran safely. Mehrabad, the international airport in Tehran, had also recently been completed—it was a beautiful and well-planned structure. Many relatives and friends came to the airport to greet us. I was amazed to see how many people we knew there!

My sister's house, located in a new development area north of the city, was clean and modern, resembling homes found in some European cities. At that time, Tehran was one of the most beautiful cities I had ever seen.

Situated south of the Alborz Mountains and the Caspian Sea in the Iranian Highlands, Tehran lies at an average altitude of 1,200 meters above sea level. To the northeast is the 5,670-meter-high Mount Damavand, and to the north, the slopes of the 3,963-meter-high Mount Tochal, with its cableway bordering the city. Due to its hillside location, the capital has considerable altitude differences, with southern municipalities bordering the salt desert of Dasht-e Kavir.

In the northern part of the city, large gardens with old trees and flowing streams created a mild, dreamlike climate. The houses, built with magnificent facades along checkered, straight streets and surrounded by beautiful oriental gardens, offered a soothing sight. The area was filled with exotic trees, persimmons, fig trees, roses, and fragrant carnations—it was paradise for us.

Mother was happy again, especially since our family in Tehran had grown. Four of our aunts had become grandmothers, giving us numerous new cousins too! I also met many family members and companions of my father for the first time. In the evenings, well-dressed boys and girls would visit, speaking fluent Persian, but my accent gave away that I was Azari. We went to the movies together, rode double-decker red buses around the city, and visited the zoo and a circus. After a week's stay, our sister took us to the train station to continue our journey.

The main station of Tehran, built by the Germans before World War II during Reza Shah's reign, was massive yet functional, with a one-story building. The German construction and precision were immediately evident, although I didn't understand much about building at the time. But I already recognized the swastika symbol, which covered the entire ceiling of the large station hall. I was surprised that the Allies hadn't noticed them during all the years they occupied our country.

I boarded the train for the first time in my life. It was a German steam locomotive, offering first, second, and third-class carriages. We had a first-class compartment to ourselves. The departure wasn't sad; on the contrary, it was filled with excitement and joy— we were on our way to Mashhad to be Imam Reza's guests.

The disciplined train crew, trained and educated by the German Reichsbahn, caught my attention even as a young boy.

They were well-dressed, confident, and well-mannered, which surprised me since I had only seen such discipline in movies.

The 850-kilometer overnight trip to Mashhad took about 12 hours, stopping at roughly 35 stations. I spent much of the time gazing at the landscape, the huge mountain ranges, and the small sleepy villages, all draped in moonlight. The steady rhythm of the train was almost hypnotic, except for the occasional jolts that made the train shudder.

Before sunrise, the train stopped for morning prayers. Some passengers disembarked and went into a beautiful prayer house—not a mosque, but a facility for prayers. Toilets and washrooms were also available. After a while, we continued our journey.

As the sun rose, the landscape transformed, glowing in the sunlight—it was magical. The mountains were breathtaking, and the fields were abundant with vegetables and fruit, especially watermelon, stretching as far as the eye could see.

The excitement grew as we neared Mashhad. A fellow traveler told me that the first thing we would see were the minarets and the golden dome of the Haram. He also advised me that upon arrival, we should greet the Imam and make our requests, expressing wishes and petitions in our hearts. He told me that Imam Reza was popularly known as Ya Zamen-e Ahu, meaning "protector of the gazelles." Legend has it that a gazelle, pursued by a hunter, once sought protection from Imam Reza, who confronted the hunter and saved its life.

Time seemed to crawl, perhaps because I was so excited. All the while, Mother stood by the window, tears of joy in her eyes. Finally, I saw the minarets, the Mausoleum, and the Golden Dome, in all their splendor.

Our hotel was simple yet neat—pilgrims value peace of mind and hope over comfort. We were only there for four days. Visiting the tomb and touching it was difficult, as hundreds of thousands of pilgrims passed through daily, all attempting to touch it too! We went one evening during prayer time, with thousands of people standing for "Salat" (prayer). I pushed my way to the interior of the haram, with Mother and my sister close behind. We finally reached "Zarih," the outer protective cage of the holy shrine, and clung to the sturdy, solid silver woven tubes around the tomb, trying to feel a real connection with it.

Some pilgrims had brought their sick, blind, and even terminally ill children. After several days, with their last strength, they seized the Zarih, demanding a cure and recovery from the Imam, refusing to let go of the grate. They firmly believed in the power of the shrine. The guards had great difficulty trying to move them.

After a few days, we said goodbye to the Imam and flew back to Tehran. I had promised Imam Reza that if everything went as planned, I would fly to Europe to study, but before going, I would visit him again and give plenty of alms.

My most cherished memory, one I will never forget, was the splendor of the gate to the shrine of Imam Reza—resplendent with gold, silver, and beautiful green crystal discs—it was magnificent. Inside the shrine, heavy chandeliers hung from the ceiling, giving the room elegance and refinement. The entire space felt as though it couldn't be of earthly origin. Mother was visibly happy and had gained a lot of strength from this journey. As they say, faith moves mountains.

We flew back to Tabriz after a few days and saw that summer was slowly coming to an end. Life hadn't changed in this sleepy town, but I took great pride in the fact that I had flown in an airplane, traveled by train, seen the city of Mashhad, and visited the tomb of Imam Reza!

RETURN FROM MASHHAD

Our sister's move to Tehran had been a good decision—perhaps one day we would all follow. For our father, however, the idea seemed unlikely. Life continued as usual. As a young boy, I didn't mind the monotony; I knew I had my life ahead of me, with much to look forward to, especially the prospect of moving to Europe. But our mother, though only in her early 50s, looked worn and aged. Her ill-fitting dentures made her appear even older. She spoke to me more often now. After Father said goodnight and retired to his room, we would sit together, and she would look at me with sad eyes, sharing her dreams. She longed for everyone to be together again, but she knew it was no longer possible. I would soon leave home, followed by the next brother, and she was painfully aware of it. She would go to the window, light a cigarette, and gaze up at the sky for several minutes. In those moments, I saw not just my mother, but a saint—a woman who had borne ten children, breastfed for 20 years, lost her father, her homeland, and her first son at a young age, and yet managed to adapt to a new life while raising us and ten grandchildren.

I was excited but anxious about going to Europe, unsure of how I would cope with being separated from my dear parents and family. Mother reassured me as we sat at the massive dining table that came from Baku. She told me it was good that I had inherited many things from her but warned me not to place too much importance on money. She predicted that I would give away my shirt if I thought it was necessary, and she was right—I often did just that.

She reminded me of a time when I was around six years old. She had sent me to the corner store to buy some potatoes. There, I encountered an old woman who also wanted to buy potatoes but didn't have enough money. Using the money Mother had given me, I bought a whole sack of potatoes for her and carried it to her house. But then, I got lost on the way back and cried out for my mother. Fortunately, some strangers found me and helped me return home. When I arrived, I could see Mother had been distraught—she had been searching for me for hours. She calmed down when she saw me and told me how proud she was of my good deed. She also warned me that in foreign countries, people might not be as willing to help strangers, so I would have to take care of myself.

The summer of 1960 was one of the most beautiful in our house. Both my brothers arrived unexpectedly by car from Germany, bringing a friend along. My eldest brother was now a specialist surgeon, and my second brother arrived a few days later with his German wife, Margot. He had completed his internship and was an orthopedic surgeon. Parwiz, my favorite brother, was between studies and exams, so he came to visit as well. The house was full once more!

During that summer, Father had the house renovated to accommodate new refrigerators and gas stoves. As word spread, the front doorbell rang more frequently with neighbors asking for ice from our freezer. The maids constantly checked the water to see if it had frozen and packed the ice in plastic bags for distribution. Over the coming months, ice factories and storage units were built, and Pepsi Cola and Coca-Cola came to town. The streets were equipped with electric traffic lights, and advertising signs were installed.

We were thrilled to share these technological advancements with our brothers from Germany. However, Behruz's wife, Margot —a lovely, pretty woman from a respected German family— struggled at first with the climate in Tabriz. Our mother, who had grown up in Europe, understood and did her best to make Margot comfortable. Beyond the climate, Margot also had to adapt to different food, culture, and customs. Nevertheless, she settled in and was loved and respected by all. Father was very proud and pleased with his family. He had managed to send three of his six sons to Europe, though at great expense, he never spoke of it.

Our aunt and uncle, who owned the leather factory, often invited us to spend the day in their well-kept garden. A large area was covered with Persian rugs and plump cushions to sit and lean on. There, we were served fresh-smelling tea, homemade jams, and a variety of fruit in small bowls. We would take a spoonful of each jam and drink a sip of tea with it. The bowls were then cleared away and replaced with new ones, allowing us to sample two or three varieties of delicious jam with our tea.

At noon, they served delicious Persian soups and appetizers, followed by a main course of various rice dishes with grilled poultry and either a whole or half lamb. The meal lasted several hours, and afterward, we enjoyed cold drinks and fruit before most of us retired for a siesta. As the weather cooled down to around 25 degrees, everyone gradually gathered again, and more cold drinks and fruit were served.

Although Tabriz is only about 130 kilometers from the Caspian Sea, where all varieties of citrus fruits grow, I had not eaten oranges for most of my childhood. At our aunt's house, I experienced many types of fruit for the first time. Bananas were also new to me. Uncle had fruit brought especially for us from distant provinces and even from neighboring countries. The apples from Lebanon were famous at that time for their taste and wonderful aroma. Uncle was an epicurean and enjoyed his food tremendously. Sometimes, when I stayed there overnight, I would hear him calling for "kartoshka" (roasted potatoes), which had to be prepared for him at any hour of the night.

After dusk, we gathered again for dinner, which usually consisted of meat or poultry kebab marinated in saffron, olive oil, and lemon juice, then grilled on skewers and served with homemade pita bread and all kinds of side dishes on large silver platters. Margot, my sister-in-law, greatly enjoyed the meals and family gatherings, even though she didn't speak a word of Farsi. We couldn't communicate with her directly, but she had taken the family into her heart, and we hers.

A few days later, my brothers prepared to return to Germany. Suits and shoes were made, Persian carpets and gifts were bought. Behruz and Margot flew to Tehran earlier to visit our sister, while Farokh and Parwiz left a few days later. As autumn approached, the house once again sank into silence. Before leaving, my brother spoke to Father and promised to take me with them the next summer. I was relieved, knowing I wouldn't have to take this new path alone. And so began my last autumn and winter at home, in my homeland.

My sister-in-law Margot sitting with Mom during her first visit
with my family in Tabriz.

Behruz came with his wife Margot to visit us in Tabriz.

Gathering of us six brothers at my parent's home.

Mom, Margot, Dad, Ferangis, Firuze, and Manije.

24

TRAVEL PREPARATIONS TO EUROPE

In the evenings, I often went to my father's office after school, and from there, we would walk home together. Father would give me advice, trying to make the prospect of studying medicine more appealing. He would say, "Study hard and don't let European views of life influence you too much. Remember, God is everywhere, so hold on to your faith. Submit to your destiny, be patient, and don't make rash decisions. And most importantly, money can be lost, but what you learn will stay with you forever." He would have loved to study himself if he could have. Unfortunately, it hadn't been possible, and he considered himself very fortunate to have come this far. After being forced to leave Baku, my parents had promised that if God gave them children, they would do everything in their power to provide them with a good education.

My mother continued to spoil me as long as I was still at home. The autumn and winter months came and went, much like all the years before. But I began to feel restless—a strange mix of excitement and sadness. On one hand, I was thrilled at the idea of finally being free and grown-up, of seeing Europe like in the movies, driving sports cars, meeting girls, studying, and all the things a 17-year-old dreams about. On the other hand, I was sad to leave behind my family, my friend Said, the women who had helped my mother since my childhood, the retailer who always overcharged me, the Nowruz festival, the beautiful fasting period of Ramadan, and the solemn days of Muharram for Imam Hossain.

Despite my young age, I felt very close to God during this time and asked for guidance. At night, I would look up at the stars in the Tabriz sky and talk to my beloved Creator. There was a tremor in my soul, even in my sleep, and I would wake up drenched in sweat. My mother noticed my distress and tried to hide her own grief, sometimes even telling jokes to lift my spirits. People might have wondered, but I saw in her beautiful, innocent eyes the deep sadness that had taken hold of her—a sadness born from her longing for her children. I also noticed a certain perplexity in her demeanor, as if she were silently asking, "Why all this?" But she and Father were determined to keep their promise. We all loved our mother deeply. She was a kind soul, and I adored her. For me, there was, and still is, only one woman in the world: my mother.

I HAD to fly to Tehran to apply for my passport, visa, and other necessary documents for my trip to Europe. As Tabriz disappeared behind us and the high mountains of Sahand and Sabalan came into view, I felt a surge of excitement. I had just turned 17 but had never been independent. I wasn't allowed to grow my hair long, listen to loud music, stay out past sunset, smoke cigarettes in public, or neglect to greet everyone first.

The flight to Tehran took only an hour. I sat proudly in my seat, buckled in, and very excited. Drinks were served, the sun was shining—it was a pleasant flight. In those days, flying was something special, and the airport was a popular destination for family outings. People would watch the flights from a terrace in the terminal building, so it was always busy. Suddenly, I worried about whether they would find me at the airport—I had only been to Tehran once before. It was a scary feeling, and my hands were wet with sweat. Yet, it was also exhilarating, the feeling of being free.

When I arrived in the large arrivals hall, I saw many familiar and dear faces. My sister had come to meet me with her children, some aunts, cousins, and even some people I didn't recognize. I suddenly felt grown-up and full of confidence.

We drove through the beautiful, newly built streets of Tehran, heading north. During the ride, I imagined my mother standing at the window, a cigarette in her hand, while Father was likely still in his office, perhaps proudly telling his colleagues, "My fourth son is on his way to Europe to study. He doesn't want to be a doctor, but he wants to build houses, and that's not bad."

When we arrived at my sister's house, the differences between Tabriz and Tehran were immediately apparent. The house was in a quiet residential area and had three floors with a marble façade. In the front hall, a wide marble staircase led to the two upper floors, which were rented out. My sister and her family lived on the first floor. A large hallway served as a reception room, leading to various rooms, including modern bathrooms with European toilets, a kitchen with refrigerators, and a living room with a television! A short hallway led out to a beautiful garden filled with palm, lemon, and fig trees. In the middle of the garden was a water basin lined with blue tiles, full of goldfish swimming in clear water. The flower beds surrounding the basin were tastefully arranged with roses and other southern plants. The garden was large, but to me, it was idyllic.

In the evening, we dined on the large terrace under a star-filled sky. The aroma of fresh air and flowers made the evening feel magical. After dinner, we slept under the stars, with beds covered in pleasant natural fabrics and mosquito nets. As I lay in bed, my thoughts drifted to Tabriz and the high walls of our house—walls that were ten or twelve meters high. Our house had dark, sprawling cellars, no bathroom, and no hot water! Here, there were no high walls, just beautiful, low, and elegant partitions. You could see into all the neighbors' gardens, planted with flowers and shrubs, and enjoy the view. Apparently, there were no big secrets to hide here like in Tabriz, I thought. It was a pity that Mother couldn't live here. Father was very particular about his lifestyle in his old age and would not move to Tehran. I knew that and was very worried about my mother's future as she grew older.

Within about three months, I had gotten used to life in Tehran. I could speak Persian with almost no accent and had become very confident. I didn't blush when meeting women and could even dance!

Father's business partner was a dear, intelligent, and respected man. He was a member of the Tehran City Council and lived in the north of the city, in the posh Shemiran district, in a large house with all the comforts of the time. His son, Jamshid, was my age, and we got along famously. He drove a heavy American car, a Chevrolet. He was always elegantly dressed and had many friends. He often hosted parties in the big garden where we danced and listened to songs by Paul Anka. It was just like the movies—I will never forget those days.

Time passed in the blink of an eye. When I talked to Mother on the phone, I could sense a heavy, stifling silence around her on the other end. I tried to hide the lively and cheerful mood I was in. She again tried to hide her longing and told me everything was fine, urging me not to worry about her and to finish my preparations quickly.

Getting a passport wasn't easy because I was 17, and at 18, military service was mandatory. A lawyer from our office in Tehran was assigned to help with the application. Whether he was the right lawyer, I don't know, but he was well-paid for his efforts. We went from one office to the next until I finally got my passport. It was only valid for one year and had to be renewed every year while I was overseas. To renew it, however, I had to prove that I was studying, though at the time, I didn't fully understand what that meant.

My oldest brother Farokh married Jamshid's sister, Farideh.
Back row: Me and friends. Front row: Jamshid, Farideh, Farokh,
and Farideh's sister.

25

IT BECOMES SERIOUS

I returned to Tabriz at the beginning of summer. My brother Behruz had already arrived with his dear wife, Margot, and my other brothers were on their way by car, planning to take me with them by train through Turkey to Germany. Our sister from Tehran also came with her husband and children, so the house was full again, just like in the old days. Father was as cheerful as ever. I rarely saw him unhappy; he was a strong and grateful man who knew that nothing lasts forever, and everything eventually comes to an end.

Meals had to be served in two sittings. The oldest family members and guests dined first, then moved to another room for tea and cake. Afterward, the tables were cleared and set again for the rest of the family. We also used the garden, where guests were seated on large Persian rugs.

My mother, aunts, and sisters helped pack suitcases for the four of us brothers, filling them with gifts and goodies like chocolates, cookies, and canned goods. I packed clothes I had bought from boutiques in Tehran, with Jamshid's help, as he knew what would be appropriate in Europe. Luckily, money wasn't a problem—

Father had allowed me access to funds from the Tehran office and hadn't mentioned a limit!

In addition to packing, I began handing over my responsibilities as the eldest son to my younger brother. This included settling accounts for various purchases made with local merchants. Mother assisted in paying off my debts, some of which had grown quite large. She gently scolded me, advising me that I needed to learn to handle money more carefully in the future.

Once the accounts were settled, I started organizing my room, which my brother would move into after I left. I gave him clothes, books, photo albums, records, and other items I didn't plan to take with me. He was sad about it but also respected his new role.

Mother was deeply saddened by our impending departure, knowing the house would become very quiet with only three children left. Father would likely go to bed earlier to avoid thinking about it, and I imagined Mother would stand at the window more often, weeping as she thought of her sons and grandchildren so far away. I promised to write to her regularly and keep her informed. My best friend Said and I made the same promise to each other.

Despite my excitement for the new adventure, I felt a profound sadness at leaving my family. I knew I would desperately miss my sweet, kind mother, my father and his wise advice, and the noisy children always running around the house. My emotions were a confusing mix of anticipation and sorrow.

When everything was finally prepared and the suitcases were packed, the farewell celebrations began. Our uncle hosted a large party with many guests, and we attended several other gatherings to personally say goodbye to all our relatives, acquaintances, and friends. As always, Mother was very attentive, pampering me and cooking my favorite dishes. She gave me a lot of advice: to eat well, take care of myself, dress warmly, get enough sleep, not worry about her and the family, behave well, and honor Father's name. One of her favorite sayings was, "What you put in the soup, you get on the spoon."

Saying goodbye to my friend Said was also very difficult. We visited our regular coffee shop, had an iced coffee, and talked. I also said farewell to the kind Armenian, Mayak, the owner of the cozy pastry shop and café.

On my last evening, all the lights in our house were burning. I said goodbye to everything around me. After dinner, while saying goodnight to my mother, I wondered when I would see her again. I couldn't sleep for the longest time as I lay in bed, looking out the window at the sky, which was full of stars—the usual picture in the old city of my homeland.

The following morning, I got out of bed and was suddenly gripped by fear and homesickness. I was about to be thousands of kilometers away, in a place where people spoke a different language and practiced a different faith. I felt lost and paralyzed. At that moment, my mother came into the room and helped me get dressed. She was calm and serene, her beautiful eyes focused solely on me. She touched me lovingly, stroking my hair, and told me the story of her departure from Baku. She said, "Trust God and start the journey in His name. Everything will happen as it is destined. The destination is the same, but the paths are different. Find the shortest way, my son, and stay true to yourself, even if it is difficult in Europe."

The plan was for me and my two brothers to travel to Germany by train. At that time, the Orient Express passed through the city of Erzurum in Turkey. But first, we had to take a bus to Bazargan on the Turkish border, then continue to Erzurum. From there, we would board the train to Munich and finally reach our destination, Düsseldorf.

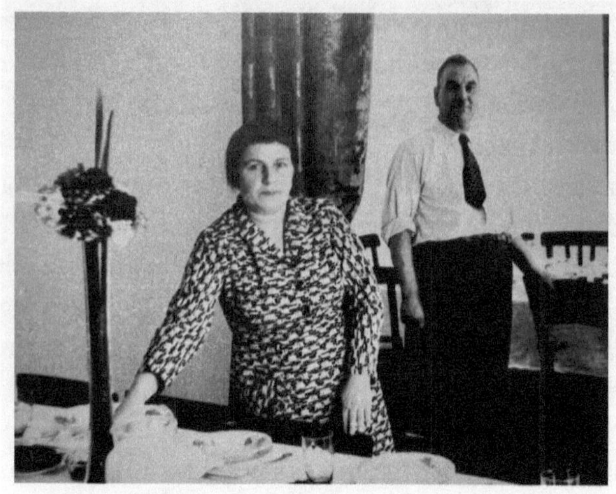

Mom setting the table for my last meal before my
departure to Germany. Dad in the background.

Dad with Darius in the garden. The door behind
them is the access to the water closet (toilet)
which was separated from the main house.

My niece, Jila, with her brother Darius, in our garden at home in Tabriz. They are standing in front of the lemon trees, and I can still smell their aroma!

26

MY STUDY TRIP TO GERMANY

My brothers and I were finally on the bus, heading toward our new adventure. How we had said our goodbyes, I could hardly remember. As the youngest, I was given the window seat, and I gazed out at the sleepy towns passing by in the dawn light. I silently bid farewell to everything I saw—houses, trees, villages, even the animals! The thought of returning home briefly crossed my mind, but soon we arrived at the border town of Bazargan. My mood shifted as we prepared for passport control. My brothers instructed me to answer the questions briefly and directly, nothing more. We agreed to meet again on Turkish soil. For the first time, I was on my own. I answered the questions correctly, was treated with respect, and passed through like a man.

We stopped for lunch at what seemed to be the only Turkish restaurant around. The food was similar to what we had in Tabriz, but it tasted different—like it had been cooked in old grease. Despite this, I was thrilled to be in a foreign country, surrounded by new sights, sounds, and languages. Experiencing a completely different culture was fascinating, and I realized I was just at the beginning of a long journey.

The waiter, a boy about my age, was clearing the table, wiping the old plastic tablecloth with a rag. Each movement sent half the rice and breadcrumbs onto my pants. He asked if I was going to Istanbul. To my surprise, I understood him! I told him no, that I was heading to Germany. He looked at me with wide eyes, full of amazement, and wished me all the best.

After lunch, we resumed our journey to Erzurum and from there, took a train to Istanbul. The city was enormous. It felt a bit like home, with many familiar sights reminiscent of Tabriz, yet some things were strikingly different from what I had seen in Hollywood movies. The grand bazaars bustled with people, much like those in Tehran, while the Bosphorus looked straight out of an Italian film with Vittorio De Sica and Sophia Loren—both popular actors in our country at the time. We explored the bazaar, visited the Hagia Sophia, and other significant sites. This great and historic city, about which I had read so much, was once called Byzantium until 330 A.D., when it was renamed Constantinople and became the Christian capital of the Western Roman Empire.

In 1453, after a long siege and with the help of locals and nobility, Sultan Mehmed II, known as Mehmed the Conqueror, breached the city walls and entered the magnificent Hagia Sophia church. Overwhelmed by its splendor, he ordered the notable and wealthy Greeks—who had betrayed their own people and faith to help him conquer the city—gathered there. "You have betrayed your people and your place of worship to save yourselves and your families. You will not be faithful to me either," he declared. That same day, he had all the men, along with their sons, killed. The church was then transformed into the famous Hagia Sophia Mosque.

We stayed in a simple, yet beautiful hotel owned by a Persian, and the atmosphere was warm and welcoming. In the evenings, we dined at local restaurants and marveled at the sights of the city. But as the sun set, my heart grew heavy, and I felt the urge to cry. My throat tightened with emotion. I wrote a telegram to my mother, reassuring her that I was doing well.

After spending two nights in Istanbul, we boarded the train for Munich. In just a few minutes, Istanbul faded from view. I never again experienced the city as beautiful as it was then. We traveled for three days by train, with rain falling the entire time. It was the first time I had seen rain last so long. When the sun finally appeared, it seemed different—weak, barely warming the earth. Back home, rain would stop after a few hours, and the sun would shine brightly again.

At night, I rested my head against the window, watching the train speed through foreign lands and dark forests. My thoughts returned to my homeland, to my family, and to my mother. She must have been standing at her usual spot by the window, thinking of me. Had she grown accustomed to the empty house? What were my brothers, sisters, and my friend Said doing? It was so hard to make friends, yet so easy to lose them. When someone leaves home, they also lose their friends. Mother always said that love withers without reunion.

We passed through Sofia, the capital of Bulgaria, in the night. Then through Bucharest in Romania, and Budapest in Hungary, with its beautiful bridges and old facades that delighted every traveler. By the time we reached Vienna, Austria, I was curious about this famous city, though I was dead tired. When the German customs officers in their green uniforms boarded our wagon, I knew we were close to our destination.

Finally, we arrived in Munich, the capital of Bavaria. The journey had been exhausting, with customs officers waking us at every border crossing to check our papers. At the Bulgarian border, they even opened our suitcases and inspected everything. Much of what we had packed became a source of confusion and trouble. The canned eggplants, in particular, caused a stir—my brothers had a hard time explaining what they were. Later, at the German customs checkpoint, I realized why: the pickled eggplants in the jar looked like grenades! After nearly ten sleepless nights and over 6,000 kilometers, we arrived safe and sound in Germany. We changed trains and continued to Düsseldorf, where my brother Parwiz lived. It was a rainy day in November 1961. Before disembarking and beginning this new chapter of my life, I asked God for help:

"In the name of God, the gracious and merciful!
Glory be to God, the Lord of the Worlds,
The Gracious, the Merciful,
Who reigns in the Day of Judgment.
To Thee alone do we serve, to Thee do we beseech for help!
Guide us along the right path,
The way of those whom Thou hast blessed,
And not those whom Thou art angry with
Or those who go astray."

This surah, Al-Fatiha, the opening chapter of the Quran, is similar to the Lord's Prayer in the Christian faith, which I had heard many times in Germany. It is with this surah that each new recitation of the Quran begins.

At that moment, my thoughts turned to my mother, who was now so far away from me, and to all the dear people I had left behind. My eyes filled with tears as I carried the two heavy suitcases off the train. We were standing in the main station of Düsseldorf. Our oldest brother bid us farewell, then headed to the post office to telegraph our arrival home. He took the next train directly to West Berlin, where he needed to return to his residency in surgery at the hospital.

My other brother and I stepped out of the station and stood in front of the old building, looking out at the city center of Düsseldorf. It was gloomy, with rain pouring down in torrents. Everything seemed gray and dark, much like the evenings back in Tabriz. We had no place to stay. Although my brother could have gone to stay with friends or at the university, he didn't want to leave me alone. We took a cab to a boarding house near the train station, where a friendly old lady showed us to a plain room with two beds and a small table with chairs. I stood there, paralyzed, staring out at the street through the old but clean windows. The scene bore no resemblance to what I had seen in movies or read about in books. I had imagined it quite differently.

After putting our suitcases down, we showered and changed before heading out to eat. Parwiz told me more about the city, describing how beautiful Düsseldorf actually was. I tried to listen, but my disappointment was overwhelming. I couldn't understand why everything seemed so different, so much less vibrant than what I had known at home. Homesickness gnawed at me.

We decided to visit a pub, or "Kneipe," as the Germans say. All eyes were on us as we entered, and it was almost frightening. We were watched at every turn, as though we were from another planet or there to beg for scraps. When we sat down, the waiter approached and, for the first time, I felt truly foreign and unwelcome. He tossed a small, dirty menu onto the table and gestured impatiently, asking if we wanted something to drink. Despite my brother's fluency in German, the waiter continued to speak in exaggerated gestures, unable to comprehend that a black-haired foreigner could speak his harsh, angular language so well. I never forgot that first encounter with a German.

Later that night, I struggled with a thick down comforter for the first time. The filling kept sliding down, leaving me with only a thin, empty sheet. I fought with it until early morning, my feet freezing cold.

The next day, Parwiz went to the university. I had to leave the room because it needed to be cleaned, and as I later learned, the room was meant only for sleeping. So, I wandered through the city, noting that everything I saw was drastically different from Father's stories about the greatness of Germany. The city was dark and gray, with houses that had crumbled from bombings. The ruins were overgrown with moss and ground cover. The buildings still standing were badly damaged, their facades pockmarked with bullet holes. The streets were eerily silent, populated only by the old and the very young.

Gisela in front of the building in Düsseldorf where she used to live with her mom, Mutti.

Gisela on a Sunday stroll. The buildings always looked grim and gray!

Strolling with my brother Parwiz in Düsseldorf, Germany.

27

OUR APARTMENT

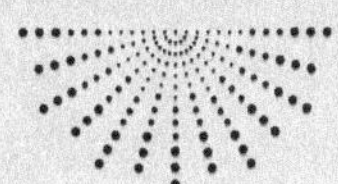

We hired a real estate agent to help us find a place to live, and four days later, he found us a modern apartment in the upscale Zooviertel district of Düsseldorf. The owner, an architect named Berger, lived in Spain and mentioned that he preferred it there. No wonder, I thought!

The apartment was beautifully furnished in the Art Nouveau style, consisting of three rooms and one bathroom. The master bedroom featured a classical French desk, a bookcase filled with valuable books, and a matching glass cabinet with elegant crystal glasses. The living room had a balcony and a pull-out couch for sleeping. The kitchen and bathroom were both modern and fully equipped. It was a perfectly furnished apartment, the kind few could afford in Germany at that time.

After we moved in, I spent the first few days locked inside. I didn't want to know anything about the outside world. I stood alone at the window in my room, gazing out at the endless horizon, just as Mother often did back home. Thoughts of her and our homeland filled my mind, and homesickness took hold of me. I longed for our house, my room, the familiar surroundings, and the comforting sound of my father's voice as he prayed in the morning.

Those were such good times. I mourned everything and cried silently. It was all in the past now, over and done with. Things would never be the same again. Even with Mother, it was all in the past.

My brother went to the university every day, diligently pursuing his studies, while I was often left alone. Gradually, I mustered the courage to leave the apartment and shop for essential food items. Unfortunately, I couldn't understand German yet, and the merchants seemed impatient and serious. I rarely saw people my own age; most were either very old or very young. My brother explained that millions of Germans had died in World War II, and the post-war generation was just beginning to grow up. Those who had survived the war were mostly pensioners with small incomes, many of whom still had to work. I saw many war-disabled and invalids, the traces of the war evident throughout the city— bombarded and collapsed houses, streets riddled with holes, and piles of rubble overgrown.

The city was always very quiet. No one spoke to each other on the bus or in the streetcar. As the stores closed promptly at 6 p.m., the streets became even darker and quieter. I marked my way home by the many advertising signs, especially one with two key symbols that caught my attention. I thought it was a sign for a key factory, but it turned out to be an advertisement for a well-known brewery. The local pubs were almost the only places where people seemed to enjoy themselves and converse. Mostly men gathered there after work, drinking beer, smoking cheap cigars, and playing cards in a cozy atmosphere.

My brother and I visited such a pub once, but it felt awkward. All eyes were on us until we left after our drinks. It was clear from their faces that we, as strangers, were unwanted and had no business being there.

The nights grew longer and the days shorter. November is a sad month for Germans, much like the month of Muharram for us Shiites back home. One Sunday is "Volkstrauertag," a day of mourning for soldiers who died in armed conflicts. The following Sunday is "Totensonntag," when people visit and care for the graves of the fallen. As I learned later, the mortality rate in this month is considerably higher.

Over time, I got to know some of my brother's fellow students. It was comforting to see compatriots after such a long time and to speak Persian with them. Amir, my brother's best friend, was a lively and likable young man from the north of Persia. He was an accomplished cook, and although Persian groceries were hard to come by, he managed to find suitable ingredients to prepare dishes similar to those of our homeland.

At that time, there weren't many foreigners in Germany. Most of the students at the universities were Persian, with only a few from other countries. After all, studying wasn't cheap, and the cost of accommodation, food, and everything else was high in the post-war period. Italians were the first guest workers and pioneers of the German economy. Ludwig Erhard, the Minister of Economics under Chancellor Dr. Konrad Adenauer, had revived the economy, leading to what was known as the "economic miracle." Germany was rebuilding quickly and successfully, laying the foundation for a modern and democratic nation after the war. Meanwhile, East Germany remained occupied by the Soviet Union, becoming one of its satellite states and referred to as the "Eastern Zone" where people were forced to follow the Communist system. Just before our arrival, even Berlin, the former capital of Germany, had been divided by an ugly wall.

During the war, many Germans had perished on the frontlines or been taken prisoner. Hundreds of thousands of civilians, including women and children, were killed in the bombing of cities. The human toll of WWII was immense and cruel for all involved. Beyond the personal tragedies, there was now a severe labor shortage in all sectors—not only in factories but also among doctors, engineers, lawyers, professors, civil servants, and even judges.

Studying at our apartment during my university days in
Germany.

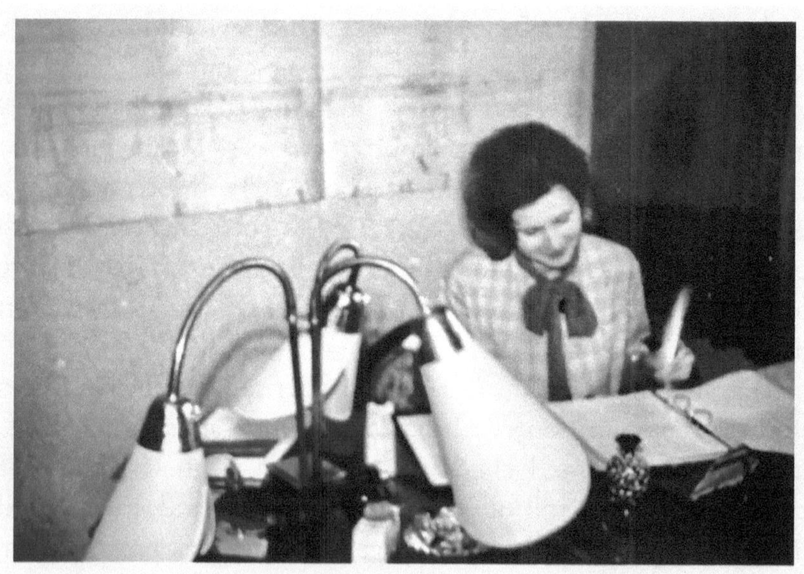

Gisela checking out my work with her curious spirit.

The three brothers at a university party in Mainz, Germany. Left to right: Behruz, Farokh, and Parwiz.

28

NATIONAL SOCIALISM

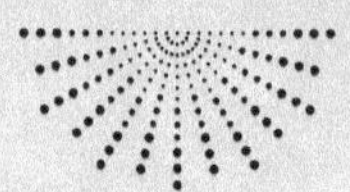

On January 30, 1933, Adolf Hitler was appointed Chancellor of the Reich. He and his party quickly moved to suspend the Weimar Constitution, banning all political parties except their own or forcing them to dissolve. They brought trade unions, the press, state governments, and all aspects of public life under the control of national socialist ideas. Resistance was minimal. Even the churches, though they maintained a certain distance, did not actively fight against the regime's totalizing grip on society. The political left, divided and weak, tried to organize underground, but they could not mount any serious resistance.

How did this happen? How could Hitler, after being appointed chancellor, so effortlessly secure dictatorial power over Germany? This uncomfortable question remained largely unasked in Germany for a long time because to answer it would mean acknowledging how much of the regime was accepted, or even desired, by large parts of society. What did this society look like? What was everyday life like in Germany? Finding answers to these questions became crucial when one realized that German daily life unfolded against a backdrop of monstrous, state-initiated crimes. Persecution and extermination did not occur in secret; they were blatant. The Third Reich lasted long enough to infect generations with its ideology. The same professors, civil servants, and judges who had supported the regime were now tasked with rebuilding the new democratic Germany, which naturally caused great headaches for the upright democrats.

Italy, Germany's ally in World War II, did not experience the same "economic miracle" that transformed Germany. The demand for labor was not as strong in Italy, so Italians became the first foreign workers to arrive in Germany. They were welcomed with open arms and found employment in factories and the catering industry across the country. Over time, Italian cuisine became a staple in Germany.

Persian students made up the largest group of foreign students in Germany. Most lived with German families as subtenants because household incomes were insufficient due to low wages, so the rental income helped families make ends meet. Almost every family had one or more rooms rented out. We were fortunate to have our noble apartment, which we deeply appreciated. This was possible because our father sent us funds every month. The three of us brothers shared the rent, although our oldest brother, who lived in Berlin and worked as a doctor, paid his share and helped support us. I began learning how to cook, starting with fried eggs, hoping that one day I would be able to prepare more elaborate dishes for us.

I eagerly awaited letters from home, checking the mailbox several times a day, almost every hour. Our janitor, a kind middle-aged woman, tried to explain to me when the letter carrier would arrive, but I couldn't understand her. I tried to convey that I was waiting for letters from my homeland. She often visited me in our fourth-floor apartment, bringing me fruit or a piece of cake. Later, when my German improved, she told me that her son, who was about my age, had been killed in the war. She had watched me and cried when she saw me walking down the stairs to the mailbox with a sad face and teary eyes. I still remember her sweet face.

When I received the first letter from home, I was overjoyed. It was the first time I had seen my parents' beautiful handwriting—my mothers in Russian and my fathers in Persian. My younger brother wrote that Mother had almost fallen ill after our departure and that most evenings she retired to bed early. There was little more to say; it was all very sad. Now, I was the fourth one missing from the house.

I started attending German language classes full-time at the world-renowned Berlitz School. The school was in a very beautiful, old building on Düsseldorf's most famous street, Königsallee, known for its elegant boutiques and cafes. Here was the Europe I had seen in movies and read about in books!

In the middle of the wide avenue flowed a river, surrounded by magnificent trees. Snow-white swans swam alongside ducks, undisturbed. Elegant old lanterns lined the beautiful avenue, lighting the way for pedestrians in the evening. The old buildings, with their stone facades, housed big banks and financial giants. Life-like stone figures adorned these massive structures, and I was fascinated by them. My German teacher, who was originally from France, was a very kind, patient man. Within four months, he taught me and my classmates enough German that I could speak and write it almost flawlessly.

One day, about four weeks after our arrival in Germany, Parwiz told me he had a date with a girl on the weekend. She was bringing a friend, and he suggested that I join them. They were going to help me familiarize myself with German society, customs, and traditions.

29

FATE'S ENCOUNTER

I was going on a date with a girl for the first time in my life—and conversing in German, no less. The excitement was overwhelming, and I bombarded my brother with questions: Where were we going? What should I say? What would we eat? What should I wear? He reassured me, explaining that we would go to a restaurant, chat, and maybe even dance if I felt like it. I admitted that I didn't know how to dance, so he gave me a quick lesson in waltzing, teaching me that dancing usually involved pairs. I also prepared myself linguistically, memorizing key phrases like where I came from and what I wanted to study.

Saturday evening, we took the streetcar to our meeting place. Two young blonde girls were waiting for us, their faces full of smiles and their eyes sparkling with mischief. One had a fashionable high hairdo and wore a knee-length skirt; the other had simple, straight hair and a longer, less trendy skirt. Parwiz introduced me to Gisela and Marlene. Marlene, with the high hair, paired off with him, while Gisela took my hand, and we headed to a pub.

I was excited yet confused by this first encounter with a girl. However, Gisela's simple, kind, and friendly demeanor put me at ease. I didn't know much about dating etiquette—like which side to walk on or what to say—but as the evening progressed, and despite some language barriers, we grew comfortable with each other. It felt as if we had known each other for a long time, thanks to my brother helping with translations now and then. By 10 p.m., Gisela had to head home, despite our pleas for her to stay longer. She insisted, worried about getting into trouble with her mother. We escorted her home, then saw Marlene off on the streetcar. It was an evening I will never forget.

My German was improving day by day. With no internet, and television being too expensive for most, the radio became my primary tool for learning the language. We often tuned into Radio Luxembourg, which played wonderful music around the clock. It was a great way to immerse myself in the language. This station had many listeners and later became the well-known television station, RTL.

I met with Gisela several times after our first encounter. She even visited our apartment, helping me with various tasks. As Christmas approached, the streets and stores were beautifully decorated, and I was introduced to Christian traditions for the first time. In Tabriz, I had often gazed at the Armenian quarter's shop windows, dreaming about Santa Claus and reindeer. Here, it was a reality. Gisela explained the customs to me as best she could, given my language skills.

In Germany, Advent is celebrated on the four Sundays before Christmas Eve. The word "Advent" comes from the Latin *adventus*, meaning "coming" or "arrival." The four weeks symbolize the 4,000 years that mankind waited for the arrival of the Savior, according to the Church. A wreath with four candles is placed in the home, and one candle is lit each Sunday until all four are burning on the fourth Advent.

Shortly before Christmas Eve, a fir tree is brought into the home and decorated with candles and glass ornaments. The size of the tree corresponds to the size of the house or apartment. Gisela and her mother lived in a modest two-room apartment, yet it was tastefully and comfortably furnished. Cleanliness and order were immediately evident, and her mother reminded me of my grandmother in Tabriz, though she was much younger.

World War II had destroyed or burned many houses. Under Chancellor Konrad Adenauer, Germany began a housing program with great zeal. The first recipients were displaced persons and refugees. Due to time constraints and high costs, some quality measures, like soundproofing and thermal insulation, were skipped, creating what became known as social housing. Gisela's mother, a single war widow who had lost everything to the Russians, was grateful for such an apartment on the fourth floor of a multi-family building—despite the lack of an elevator. After years of hardship, she was happy to finally have her own space again. With her pension and Gisela's income from working at a pension insurance company, they had a secure and quiet life.

As I got to know more about the German people, I began to appreciate their characteristics—cleanliness, efficiency, order, and determination. These were traits my father had always admired. He used to say, "I want to give you something that no one can take away from you, something you will never lose." By this, he meant a good upbringing and a successful education.

I received regular letters from home, and each one brought me immense joy. Seeing the letter carrier approach the mailbox was a moment of anticipation. Friends and family who had received our address wrote loving letters, eager to know everything about Germany. Some of the boys back home asked about the girls, curious about what was happening in the movies. The older ones gave advice, inquired about our studies, and asked about my progress in learning German. Before opening the letters, I would make myself comfortable—fixing a cup of tea, just like at home with my uncle—and then savor every word.

Some letters made me laugh out loud, and I was glad to hear my own voice in the silence of our apartment. I laughed at how wrong my thoughts had been about Europe and Germany. This was a country where people worked hard from dawn until dusk, often with only a few slices of bread to sustain them, then returned home in the evening content with sandwiches or a glass of beer at the pub. Maybe on Sundays, they might have a roast on the table—yet they were happy and satisfied.

I often thought about home, comparing our two cultures. There were good and bad qualities in both. In our country, every event, whether success or failure, sickness or health, is seen as God's will—it is called "kismet," or fate. In Germany, on the other hand, people seemed to have little to do with God.

Later, when we had a television, we often watched a program called "The Word for Sunday" every Saturday evening. A priest or pastor would speak for a few minutes about religion, faith, God, and Jesus. But I don't think many people watched or listened to it. Religion was not at the forefront of German society as it was at home. The aftermath of World War II had torn apart many families. Many children lost their parents and became orphans, and many women became widows. Social shortages meant that many children lacked proper education or a normal family life. Displacement due to the war was a common experience.

Whenever I heard Gisela's sad family story, I couldn't help but think of my own family's fate. It was astonishing—both her family and mine had been affected by the same tragic forces, displaced by the same power, despite being thousands of miles apart. Now, displaced children and grandchildren, Ramsauer and Haj Bekoff, had met in this new and diminished Germany.

GISELA'S MOTHER was a petite but strong and kind woman. Her face bore the marks of a life filled with hardship. From the moment we met, she welcomed me warmly, and I instantly liked her, treating her like my own mother. She came from a well-known family from East Prussia, the Ramsauer family, who had been expelled from Austria about 300 years ago during the religious wars between Catholics and Protestants. They had settled in East Prussia, where over centuries, through the work and diligence of generations, they had built up and cultivated a large estate with extensive lands.

I often sat with Gisela and her mother in their cozy two-room apartment, at a round table covered with a beautifully embroidered cloth. A small lamp stood on the table, casting a warm glow as I listened to the stories she had to tell. Gisela was her only child. Her husband, Gisela's father, had been sent to the Russian front shortly after his daughter was born, like many other unfortunate men. He was killed in the war, though the exact circumstances were unknown. Initially, he was reported missing in action, and his burial site remained a mystery. It must have been terrible to lose a loved one and not even know where they were laid to rest.

Shortly after her husband was reported missing, Hitler's army collapsed on the Eastern Front, and the Russians swiftly occupied East Prussia—the breadbasket of Germany. As the story goes, the invasion of the Red Army in 1944-1945 is said to be one of the cruelest campaigns in history. On the night of January 30, 1945, the cruise ship *Wilhelm Gustloff*, loaded with 10,000 East Prussian refugees, was sunk by Soviet submarines. More than 9,300 people, including 4,000 children, were killed. After East Prussia was taken, the Russians began their revenge. In total, 387,000 people were murdered, a post-war loss that went down in history.

As the Red Army advanced, Germans fled in terror. People were raped, murdered, or abducted, and hundreds of thousands perished in Soviet prison camps. Gisela's mother had to flee, much like my family, with her young daughter and three sisters, taking only what little they could carry. They left everything behind for the Russians. With only a horse and carriage, they embarked on a perilous journey that claimed the lives of thousands. Her fate was strikingly similar to that of my parents—losing home, fortune, and a husband, which at first remained unclear. When the Red Cross finally confirmed her husband's death, she refused to believe it. She lived with the hope that he had been taken prisoner by the Russians and would one day return to her and their daughter. She never remarried.

Gisela's parents, Mutti and Edwald, on their wedding day in 1939.

It was a double wedding as Mutti's sister Elli, got married on the same day!

Gisela at age two with Mutti behind the barn.

Last picture of Gisela and her parents before her
father was killed in 1944.

The entire four generations of the Ramsauer family in their estate in Jodschinn, East Prussia.

Gisela's grandmother's estate in East Prussia on a winter's day.

Mutti visits her husband Edwald while serving in the military.

30

RESIDENCE PERMIT IN GERMANY

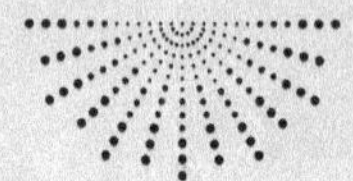

My residence permit in Germany was extended for six months at a time. The first time I stood in front of the official at the Foreign Office, he asked in a low voice where I was working. I tried to explain that I intended to study, but he was in a hurry, moving slowly and carefully yet without letting me get a word in edgewise. I left the office without any results. My compatriots, who had already been through this experience, showed me the way forward. They suggested that I leave Germany via a border and then re-enter. At that time, Persians did not require a visa for most countries except Israel and Switzerland. So, my brothers and I went to Holland for an overnight stay, and when we returned to Germany the following day, I was granted another six months of residency.

As my language skills improved, I became proficient enough to consider studying. However, I didn't pass the entrance exam at the art school in Düsseldorf. The University of Wuppertal, then known as the Engineering School, required a two-year internship in various subjects before I could begin my studies. On top of that, my Persian passport was only extended for one year at a time, and only if I could provide proof of my studies. If not, it wouldn't be renewed, as I was 18 years old and expected to do military service in my home country. It was a vicious cycle, as the Germans say, and I felt stuck.

My brother, who worked as an assistant doctor in a hospital in the Rheingau along the Rhine, lived with his wife and her parents in Winkel—a cozy town surrounded by vineyards, far from the noise of the big city. Margot's parents had a well-respected family business, a plastering and stuccoing company that always had work in the small town where everyone knew each other. My brother, aware of my predicament, suggested that I start my internship in plastering and stucco work there. Behruz promised to speak with his father-in-law about securing the position for me.

One day, my brother called to tell me to come immediately, signaling that my internship was about to begin. His father-in-law had to finalize some formalities and obtain permission for me to work there. In Germany, there are many regulations, and if not, a clever official can always find a reason to impose one! I packed my bags and said goodbye to Gisela and her mother, who, aside from my brothers, were the only people I knew. Along with my brother and dear sister-in-law, we drove towards the Rheingau. Parwiz stayed behind to prepare for his state examination.

We drove along the Rhine, passing through Bonn, Koblenz, and Mainz, marveling at the beautiful, quaint villages along the way. Everywhere, people were busy—older men carrying firewood, repairing garden fences, or tending to their small vegetable gardens, and women cleaning windows or scrubbing the entrance halls of their homes. It was fascinating to see so many active people. The large vineyards, meticulously planted in rows on the slopes of the mountains, were a sight to behold. If I hadn't seen it with my own eyes, I wouldn't have believed it. We also passed many bombed bridges from the war and old, abandoned fortresses stretching as far as the eye could see. The roads, however, were well-built, and the villages and towns blended seamlessly into one another, with no patches of unused land in between. Germany was clearly an industrial country, but agriculture was also practiced with modern, effective, and orderly methods. I saw many well-fed cows grazing in the pastures and thought they must produce much better cheese here than my father's cheese from the village of Liqvan.

I had resigned myself to the gray and unfriendly atmosphere of Germany and was ready to take the first steps toward my studies. My brother knew what lay ahead for me. He understood that I would have to work hard from morning until night, like other workers, and even more so as an apprentice. Nobody would know me, and they probably wouldn't even remember my name. As a trainee in Germany, I knew I had to obey and learn.

31

INTERNSHIP ON THE RHINE

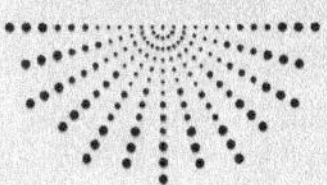

rriving at the Merscheid family home, my brother's parents-in-law, I was warmly greeted and welcomed. I quickly bonded with their oldest son, Werner, who was about my age. And so, the seriousness of my life began.

Our days started early, waking up at 5 a.m., with my work clothes and a white cap ready for me. Every day, except Sundays, we began work at 6 a.m. At 9 a.m., we had a half-hour breakfast break, then worked until noon. We would return home for a hearty lunch, then head back to work at 2 p.m., continuing until 5 p.m. After my first day on the job, I was so exhausted that I fell into bed without even washing or eating dinner and slept straight through until morning.

The work was tough, both physically and mentally. I wasn't used to such hard labor. Even if I had wanted to, I wouldn't have been allowed to do such work back home—it would have been beneath my station. The employees drank several beers throughout the day, and I think this helped dull the harshness of the work. Every morning, they sent me to fetch beer, but there was a large German Shepherd guarding the pub, who didn't seem to like me. Often, I had to wait outside until someone came to help. When the coast was clear, I grabbed the beer and ran back as fast as I could. The dog's behavior remains a mystery to me to this day—sometimes he was calm and let me pass without a fuss, other times he seemed ready to pounce.

Over the next six months, I learned a lot—bricklaying, cleaning, wallpapering, painting, and more. I also learned to endure long hours of hard labor, often accompanied by insults. The first few months were the hardest. My muscles ached constantly, and I was frequently injured, yet I still had to put up scaffolding, move ladders, haul cement buckets, and tackle countless other strenuous tasks as an apprentice. I often wondered what my mother would think if she saw me like this. After a long day, I would look at myself in the mirror and laugh at the sight—but often, I cried. Gisela regularly called and sent me letters full of encouragement and hope, which was a great comfort. At least one person was thinking of me. My brothers had their own problems and worries with their studies or work in the hospital. At the worksite, I was just another foreigner, an apprentice. No one cared who I was or where I came from.

We mostly worked in a nearby village where everyone knew each other. The Merscheid family was well-known as entrepreneurs, especially since their son-in-law was the Persian doctor. We always went home for lunch, where Mrs. Merscheid prepared traditional German dishes. I was always hungry due to the physical work, but I often didn't eat my fill—not because there wasn't enough food, but because I was too embarrassed to eat too much. I also missed the bread from home. In Germany, bread was only eaten at breakfast, unlike at home, where it was a staple at every meal.

Sometimes we were lucky and had breakfast at the farm where we worked. The farmer's wife would serve us fresh rolls with sausage and fragrant coffee, which lifted our spirits. Werner, the junior boss and the youngest among us, always got the best pieces. As I worked, I often thought of home, and tears would come to my eyes. The other workers laughed at me and made fun of my sadness. No one ever asked what was wrong, or why I was feeling so down.

However, I was very happy to hear that my brother Behruz and his wife Margot had become parents to a little girl named Jila, making me an uncle. Although they were happily living with the in-laws, they planned to find their own place soon. You could see how much in love they were and how excited they were about their future.

The six-month apprenticeship eventually came to an end. With hands full of calluses and a body bruised and scratched, I returned to Düsseldorf with a certificate in hand. When the train arrived, it felt like coming home. Düsseldorf had become my second home. I had my own apartment with beautiful rooms and a well-equipped kitchen. My brother and friends visited regularly, always bringing ingredients to prepare Persian meals, making my return even more welcoming.

Gisela was thrilled about my return. Having grown up without siblings or fatherly love, our family and friends became a substitute family for her. She took great pleasure in being with us. In the evenings, I would pick Gisela up from her office, and we would take the streetcar home for dinner. Later, I would walk her home, where her mother would be waiting impatiently for her return. Her mother was very strict and old-fashioned. Gisela wasn't allowed to wear short skirts or makeup, and she had to come straight home after work. Due to her strict upbringing, Gisela didn't have a large circle of friends and had no boyfriend, but she enjoyed my company as long as she was home at a decent hour—just like it was back in Tabriz.

Now that I had completed my apprenticeship, I began searching for a university to continue my studies. One day, a friend of my brother called from Kassel. He told me he was studying architecture there and that I might be able to enroll right away. Kassel was a city on the border of East Germany at the time. After the war, Germany was divided between the victorious powers, with the eastern part of the country and Berlin falling under Soviet control, while West Germany was divided among the Americans, French, and British. Berlin was later divided by a wall, separating East and West.

I took a slow train to Kassel, as express trains didn't run as frequently. The train stopped at nearly every village along the way, and I was on the road all night. Tired and battered, I arrived in Kassel and searched for my compatriots, but it wasn't easy as many lived in dormitories, and I had no access. After finally finding my friends the next day, it turned out that there were no available apartments or even rooms in Kassel. It was a university town with many students, and due to its proximity to East Germany, nobody had invested in housing construction. I didn't know where else to go, so I returned to the train station. Friends didn't even ask where I was sleeping or what I was planning to do, and I couldn't afford a hotel.

I spent the next three days wandering the university by day and sleeping at the train station by night. A young Italian waiter sympathized with my situation and lent me his razor, showing me where I could freshen up. He helped me as much as he could, but after three days, I realized it was all pointless. I returned to Düsseldorf by slow train, empty-handed.

Soon after my return, I began an internship as a technical draftsman at the well-known construction company, Beton und Monierbau AG. It was a requirement of the University of Wuppertal and necessary for the entrance examination. After completing this internship, I could now study civil engineering. My life slowly took shape, and my goals became clearer. If everything went according to plan and with God's help, I would start my studies in the winter semester and take my exams in the summer of 1967.

At the construction company, I was given tasks such as copying, folding, and labeling the meter-long plans. Sometimes I was allowed to change and draw reinforcement plans. Every day, I had to be in the office punctually at 7:45 a.m. Engineers and technicians wore white coats like doctors, and every employee stood at his drawing board. I will never forget my first day because I had no place to work and just stood in the corner of a room. After two days, an engineer finally asked me what I was doing there. When I explained that I was there for my internship, everyone laughed heartily and then gave me a work desk.

Time passed slowly as I learned technical terms and how to use a copying machine, which at that time was very complicated and harmful to my health. The smell of ammonia was everywhere, and my hands and clothes always reeked of it.

During this time, my brother Parwiz passed his state examination with good grades and began working in the emergency room at a hospital in Duisburg. My oldest brother married the daughter of my father's business partner in Tehran and now lived in Bochum, working as a senior physician at a hospital. Behruz became a father for the second time, welcoming a son named Darius, and had moved to Stadt Karlsruhe with his wife and their two children, where he worked as a surgeon in the local hospital. All of Father's wishes had come true; now it was my turn to fulfill my duties.

BEGINNING MY STUDIES IN GERMANY

I commenced my studies at the University of Wuppertal. The city of Wuppertal, named after the river Wupper that flows through it, is vast and unique, with a suspension railway called the Wuppertal Schwebebahn. Built over a century ago, this railway runs above the river, with train cars suspended from an iron framework, giving the appearance of floating in the air.

Every day, I walked from my home to the nearest streetcar stop, which took me to the train station. From there, I caught a slow train to Wuppertal-Barmen, where I disembarked and walked to the engineering school. The entire journey took four hours each day. Over time, my fellow students and I formed a carpool, which made the long commute more bearable. We passed the time playing chess, listening to music, telling jokes, or discussing politics and art. I vividly remember one morning in February 1964, when world champion Muhammad Ali (formerly Cassius Clay) knocked out Sonny Liston. We spent the entire train ride animatedly debating the fight.

After school, life was fairly regular and quiet. Friends came and went, and we often cooked and ate together. In the afternoons, after tea, I would study in the fading light of the evening, though often with a sense of unease. I was frequently overwhelmed with sadness and homesickness. In these moments, I would leave the apartment to get some fresh air or visit Gisela. We would sit comfortably with her mother, talking about our families and shared experiences. Sometimes, I met friends to go to the cinema or listen to music. Our newly acquired television set also attracted many friends. German television at that time had only two black-and-white channels. The news and weather were broadcast at 8 p.m., followed by German crime series and a few foreign films.

Despite the limited programming, the mere presence of a television was a sensation.

On the evening of November 22, 1963, our regular television program was suddenly interrupted by a special announcement. After a brief pause, the news broke that U.S. President John F. Kennedy had been shot. We were shocked and deeply saddened. Kennedy was an idol for many around the world, especially in Germany, where his famous words, "Ich bin ein Berliner," spoken at the Berlin Wall alongside then-mayor Willy Brandt, had resonated deeply. Hours later, with great sorrow, his death was confirmed.

Despite the advantages we had, my student years were not carefree or particularly pleasant. I was often insulted by both fellow students and professors. What might have seemed like jokes were, in reality, far from it. I was sometimes called derogatory names like "carpet seller" or "camel driver." The lecturers were not particularly welcoming either, with only a few exceptions. They often questioned what I hoped to achieve and why I had chosen Germany for my studies. I frequently felt that we Persians were not welcomed there. No one seemed to care that studying in Germany was expensive for us, despite the fact that we brought significant amounts of foreign currency into the country.

Moreover, they didn't understand how popular Germans and their reputation were in our homeland. Most didn't even know where Persia was and often confused it with Iraq, a country that had only come into existence after World War I. The average German knew of Persian carpets, Princess Soraya, Empress Farah, the Shah of Persia, and perhaps their family doctors, who were often Persian. What they didn't know was that after the war, there was a great demand for doctors in Germany. Thanks to the initiative of some Persian families who had sent their sons to Germany after the war, many Persian doctors graduated from German universities and went on to serve the German people.

There were maybe six or seven foreigners in total at the university, and only two of us were Persian. One of my lecturers told me from the start that he didn't expect me to succeed and would ensure that I returned home without a degree. I was determined to prove him wrong. Despite the daily challenges, from morning to night, in the university, restaurants, cinemas, or on trains, the times were somehow beautiful. I was young, and youth is one of the most precious gifts of God. The heart blossoms like a rose in spring, and even the smallest and simplest occasions can bring immense joy. I was curious and full of energy, despite the serious problems and difficulties I faced. I never doubted that I would succeed.

I had great faith in God, in our Creator, and I was sure that my parents' prayers would be answered. In my religion, loving and honoring one's parents is equal to daily prayers. My siblings and I loved and honored our parents, and this gave me a strong sense of self-confidence. I always kept my pride, and I wasn't overly bothered by how the Germans treated foreigners. I even understood their behavior to some extent.

In 1918, the German Empire was abolished by a revolution, and from 1918 to 1933, the Weimar Republic came to power. It did not bring significant improvements for the Germans. After that, the Third Reich rose to power in 1933, lasting until the end of World War II in 1945 and the subsequent demise of Adolf Hitler. He had aimed to create a master race and turn the Third Reich into a superpower, but instead, he left the country and its people vanquished and divided. Apart from the millions of Jews who were exterminated, millions more fled, leaving their homes, farms, and businesses behind. Now, twenty years on, the populace had to work hard and pay reparations to the Jews and those affected for many years to come. The history of this hardworking and capable people is both strange and sad.

I had meanwhile obtained my residence permit and Persian passport for one year. I planned to visit my homeland and family, so I wrote to my father requesting an airline ticket. Just the thought of going home made me incredibly happy. I could now better understand and appreciate Persia and its beautiful customs and traditions. I thought of my mother and family, the hot terracotta floor of the courtyard, the blue sky, and bright sun of Tabriz, and all the delicacies that the good Lord had given us.

Getting ready for a costume party at Mutti's place. Left to right: Parwiz, girlfriend, Gisela and me.

Karneval Party, March 1962, Rheinterassen in Düsseldorf,
Germany

FIRST VISIT HOME

We frequently received guests from home, often people we didn't know personally. They usually came for medical care or business, often distant relatives or acquaintances who had sought my father's help. All four of us brothers took on the responsibility of hosting them, which involved a lot of work and inconvenience. As the one responsible for hosting guests in our apartment, I was grateful for Gisela's help. She assisted with everything from cooking and shopping to washing and ironing. Some of our guests appreciated our hospitality so much that they thanked us for years afterward. Others simply disappeared from our lives without a word of thanks, never to be seen again.

One day, as usual, we were to pick up an acquaintance of my father from Düsseldorf Airport. He suffered from severe asthma. My brother Parwiz, who had just obtained his driver's license and bought a big Citroen, offered to drive. About half an hour into our journey, at the first major intersection, someone rammed into us on the driver's side. We landed in a ditch by the side of the road. Thankfully, neither of us was hurt, but the car was a total loss.

After the police handled the formalities, we took a cab to the airport.

Since we didn't know the arriving passenger personally, we held up a sign with his name on it. When we met him, we explained the reason we had to take a cab. He was a kind, well-mannered man of about 50. Hearing our story, he turned red with embarrassment and apologized profusely, insisting on covering the damages. We assured him it wasn't his fault, explaining that it could have happened to anyone.

Upon arriving at our apartment, he was impressed by the clever layout and efficient use of space in our 90 square meter living area. When he learned that I was studying architecture, his admiration grew. He was a considerate guest, moving quietly and trying not to disturb us. Gisela, who had learned a few Persian words, chatted with him, impressing him with her ability to juggle her office job, our household chores, and caring for her mother. He asked me if all German girls were like that.

With the help of my brothers, our guest received thorough treatment for his asthma during his hospital stay. Although he couldn't be completely cured, he left Germany grateful and with good memories.

In February 1965, the winter semester ended, marking a difficult period in my life. The technical aspects of my studies weren't challenging, as I had already mastered mathematics and geometry in school back home. The real difficulty lay in the human relationships. I was frequently insulted by both lecturers and students, even by those who considered themselves friends. In society, it was no different. Everywhere I went, people asked where I was from. Despite always being neatly dressed, I was often offered old clothes or shoes, as if I were in need. It was disheartening to realize how inattentive and ignorant some people were. On the other hand, when I compared Gisela and her mother or some of our friends, I realized that not all Germans were alike. However, I didn't dwell on it, focusing instead on preparing for my trip back to Persia, like buying gifts and packing.

~

DURING THE TWO years I had been away, many changes had occurred in Persia. Land reform was implemented by the Shah as part of his "White Revolution," under pressure from U.S. President John F. Kennedy. The imperial family's landholdings were distributed among peasants, followed by the property of other large and middle-class landowners. The Bank of Agriculture purchased the villages, then allowing peasants to purchase land from them with long-term repayment plans. However, this well-intentioned reform did not go as smoothly as hoped. The Shah had not sufficiently consulted or coordinated with Islamic dignitaries and Ayatollahs. According to Islamic law, property is particularly protected, and the reform faced significant resistance.

While the program did create a broad middle class, it failed to balance the extremes of wealth and poverty. The Shah and his advisors also overlooked the fact that peasants traditionally had a special relationship with the village owner. He, as Arhab (landlord), had the duty to always help and support his subjects in times of drought, illness, mourning, or for even weddings and celebrations. Now, as independent landowners, the peasants were left without guidance or support, relying solely on the banks. Other reforms, such as the suffrage for women, schooling, health services, military, etc., were not accepted and supported by the society.

~

I FLEW from Frankfurt to Tehran on a brand-new Lufthansa aircraft. At that time, passengers were treated with exceptional service—there were no security checks, smoking was allowed onboard, and meals were served with many extras. We first flew to Beirut, Lebanon, one of the most beautiful cities in the world. Known for its gorgeous beaches, elegant streets, and magnificent homes, Beirut was a popular vacation destination for wealthy Arabs, oil sheiks, and Europeans. The famous casino of Beirut was a global hotspot for the rich and famous. After a brief layover, we continued our journey to Tehran.

I was filled with excitement. After such a long time and so many experiences, I was finally returning home to see my family again. Memories of my early days in Germany flooded my mind: arriving with my brothers at Düsseldorf's train station, spending nights in the station restaurant, enduring the loneliness of the boarding house, my internships in the Rheingau and at Beton und Monierbau in Düsseldorf, and the beginning of my studies in Wuppertal, with all the insults and verbal abuse I had endured. In a way, I was proud of my resilience. Father always said that a wise man knows when to give in, and I believed he would be pleased that I had followed his advice.

As we approached Tehran, the city below sparkled with lights, contrasting sharply with the gray and rainy Germany I had left behind. The sight of Tehran's lights and the starry sky above filled me with joy. A restlessness overtook me, and I could hear my heart pounding. An elderly lady sitting next to me, returning home after visiting her son in Cologne, noticed my anxiety and tried to calm me down. She asked if my mother would be at the airport, and when I heard the word "mother," I couldn't control my emotions and cried tears of joy. The lady reassured me that my tears would flow properly only when I was in my mother's arms, and her words brought me a sense of peace.

After disembarking, I immediately felt the pleasantly warm, dry air of Tehran. I savored every step as I walked toward the airport terminal, taking deep breaths that eased the pressure on my chest. Passport control was smooth, and I was greeted by the sight of my entire family and relatives gathered in a corner of the arrivals hall.

The moment they saw me, shouts of joy erupted, and there was laughter, crying, and many hugs.

We drove home through bustling streets filled with the scents of jasmine and roses, scents that can only be fully appreciated in the dry, warm air of the 2000-meter-high Iranian plateau. Few places in the world have a similar climate.

My eldest sister now had five children. Her eldest daughter was studying English and French at Tehran University, and her eldest son had graduated from high school and planned to study chemistry at a university in Texas. The three younger siblings were still in school. Father's decision to send his children abroad for their education had inspired many families who could afford it to follow suit.

My flight to Tabriz was scheduled for the next day, so I stayed with my sister overnight. Mother had not come to Tehran with the rest of the family, as she expected many guests and did not want to leave Father alone. That night, I hardly slept, eager to tell my parents everything. Germany felt distant, as if the past few years had been a dream.

The next day, we drove in a long motorcade to Tehran International Airport. The sun was shining, and the weather was pleasantly warm—a stark contrast to the dull, cold climate of Germany. My sister and some cousins accompanied me on the flight to Tabriz. I was even more excited than when I had arrived in Tehran. My sister tried to distract me, but my thoughts were with my mother. I longed to hold her in my arms and feel her warmth after years of separation.

When we landed in Tabriz, my father was waiting at the bottom of the stairs, a surprise I hadn't expected. He pulled me into a strong embrace, and after our greeting, we walked together into the arrivals hall. There, surrounded by family, stood my mother, upright in her elegant black veil, her faithful eyes fixed on me. It was one of the most beautiful moments of my life. To experience such a heavenly moment, one must endure years of separation and learn to live in solitude within a foreign culture. Finally, I was back in my mother's arms, hearing her kind heart beating. We cried tears of joy as she held me tightly under her veil, asking repeatedly about my brothers and how we had managed living so far away for so long.

When she calmed down a bit, I turned to greet the other friends and relatives who had come to welcome me. Among them was our guest from Germany, the one who had suffered from asthma. He embraced me like his own son, inquiring about my brothers and Gisela.

As we drove home through the city, I noticed that not much had changed. People seemed more comfortable, and there was a sense of calm. The factories, refineries, and many other buildings were either under construction or being refurbished. The industrial area and highways were still incomplete, but traffic had increased significantly. The roads were now bustling with cars, making it impossible to cross intersections as we had in the past. I had always enjoyed my walks through the old alleyways, but I wondered if they would soon disappear completely.

When we arrived at our house, I was relieved to see that nothing had really changed. The lemon trees were in the same place, the large pond was still full of goldfish swimming in the clear water, and the garden was nicely pruned. The terracotta plates seemed to shine under the warm late afternoon sun. I stood there, taking in every corner and niche of the house. Everything that once seemed old-fashioned now appeared beautiful and precious—like an old friend.

Said, my dearest friend, was overjoyed to see me again. However, I spent the first few days visiting the oldest relatives and friends, as is customary in our country. These visits were usually brief, just long enough for a glass of tea or a refreshing drink, before moving on to the next relative. The order of visits was strictly observed, as it held great importance. It took me over a week to complete my visits, each filled with joy and sometimes sorrow if someone had passed away.

In the mornings, I eagerly awaited breakfast in the garden under the blue sky and warm sun. The garden was filled with the fragrance of flowers and plants, and the only sounds were the chirping of birds. During breakfast, my family left me alone to spend time with friends. No one complained that after three years away, I wanted to spend my time reconnecting with old friends.

After breakfast, my friends and cousins took me into town. I was now interested in the urban development of my hometown and visited the bazaar with renewed curiosity. The bazaar, a kilometer-long, covered complex built of brick and mud, was like a large department store. Each section, called a Raste, sold different goods—shoes, leather, fabrics, carpets, silver, gold, jewels, spices, fruits, and more. The Tabriz bazaar, one of the most beautiful and largest covered shopping areas in the world, was a city unto itself, protected from the sun and wind, and well-ventilated. To see the entire bazaar, my vacation wouldn't have been long enough.

The fire watch tower of Tabriz was another site we visited. Built over a century ago, it towered above all the houses in the city. People kept watch day and night from the top, alert for any signs of fire to help extinguish them quickly.

I DISCUSSED Gisela with my oldest sister, sharing her family's story and my intention to marry her. I sought her opinion and advice. She was positively impressed but uncertain about how and when to tell Mother. We decided to wait and let fate guide us. It would have been a great shock for Mother if we surprised her with a second German daughter-in-law. I had already decided to marry Gisela after my studies. She was an honest and good person, good-natured and trusting. However, I worried whether Gisela could adapt to living in Persia, a country unknown to most Europeans.

Sometimes, during tea with my mother's friends, they would mention this or that pretty girl from their circle of friends and wealthy families, suggesting potential matches for me. I laughed and jokingly redirected the conversation to my brother Parwiz, the older brother who would be first in line for marriage, since I still had a few more years of study ahead.

Two months passed quickly, and soon preparations were underway for my return to Germany. Suits, shirts, and shoes were ordered, and Persian handicrafts were bought as gifts. My uncle even gave me a gold wristwatch. Mother packed all kinds of goodies for me to take back. Before embarking on a long journey, it's customary to distribute gifts or money to the needy and children, so that the traveler reaches their destination safely.

As I made my farewell visits, the tears began to flow again. Mother became restless, standing more often at the familiar window. I held her in my arms, condemning the separation. She had experienced pain and separation as a young girl and responded with tears in her eyes, saying, "Because of your future, my son! If the same happens to you as it happened to us in Baku, no one can take your knowledge and skills away from you. This is parental love, my son—you are better protected there, and you will have a better future. Don't let my tears affect you. It's motherly love that I can't control. Don't worry, I will get used to being alone again."

I stopped by Father's office to bid farewell. In our final moments together, we were alone for the first time since I arrived. He asked the usual questions: How were my brothers doing? Were they satisfied with their work as doctors in Germany? Were they good doctors? He wanted to know everything about my studies and whether I needed anything. When I told him that his oldest son was a senior physician in a large hospital in Bochum, performing surgeries; that my second brother was a specialist in orthopedics with a great reputation; and that my dearest brother was an emergency department surgeon in Duisburg, Father's eyes filled with tears of emotion.

He looked up and said from his heart, "Glory to God, Lord of the Worlds," and prayed with deep gratitude. His face shone with joy and pride. He thanked me and said he hadn't known that his sons had become such good doctors in a foreign and highly respected country like Germany. He was proud of us and pleased with himself. He told me he wanted to enable his two youngest children to study as well, and then he would have achieved his goals. At that moment, I saw not just my father, but an upright, steadfast, and proud 65-year-old man who had worked all his life and remained true to his principles. He wanted to leave his children not just money and fortune but also secure their futures through education and help his fellow men. Perhaps the fate of my grandfather, Haj Aga Bekoff, from Baku, the great baron, also influenced him in his decisions.

Father offered me a cup of hot, aromatic tea, which he had prepared himself, as he always did for visitors. He also gave me a bundle of banknotes to distribute as farewell gifts. Before I left, he asked how I traveled to the university. I told him I took public transportation because I didn't have a car. He praised me for my frugality but said that time was precious and that I should buy a car.

I flew to Tehran accompanied by my mother and siblings, with plans to continue to Germany from there. Father stayed behind, continuing his daily routine. After a few days in Tehran, my beautiful time in my homeland came to an end. I was sad to leave all these dear people behind. I was also sad to return to a foreign country, because in my heart, I belonged here, in my homeland. Here I had my pride, and I was someone. Here I had peace, I thought. I hated goodbyes—they were always so unpleasant.

Saying goodbye to my mother was the hardest. She knew it too and tried to make it as short and painless as possible. As we drove through the streets of Tehran to the airport, passing much construction, I said my silent goodbyes with my eyes.

As the Lufthansa plane circled over Tehran, I saw the stately

Mount Damavand (elevation 5671 meters) towering in the sky one last time and prayed silently. After a stopover in Beirut, we arrived in Düsseldorf late in the afternoon. It was raining and cold, as usual. Gisela and Parwiz were at the airport, and it was a great joy to see them both again. Once home, I talked for hours about my experiences and unwrapped gifts—sweets, treats, and real Persian tea for my brothers and Gisela.

Serious student life resumed. I also took driving lessons and got my driver's license. When I bought a used but well-maintained Opel Rekord, I felt more independent, and life seemed brighter. I no longer needed to use the streetcar or train and face the constant insults from strangers along the way. My contact with people outside was now limited to the university or shopping.

When the winter semester began, I was fit and ready to learn. The German economy was booming like never before. The "Gastarbeiter," or foreign workers, from Italy and Spain were no longer sufficient to meet the demand. German industry sought cheap labor from non-European countries. The Persian government refused, so millions of workers from Turkey, economically weak and politically unstable at the time, arrived in Germany over the years. They were mostly from eastern Turkey, Anatolia. Arriving by train, they were immediately distributed among factories. This migration had long-term effects on German society. With the Italians came pizza, pasta, ice cream, and many other dishes and specialties unfamiliar to Germans. Spaniards brought their own cuisine, red wines, and Spanish music. The Turks, however, brought entire grocery stores. Soon, Turkish specialty stores were everywhere, significantly changing German food culture.

～

GISELA and I had our first vacation together in Mallorca, a Spanish island in the Mediterranean Sea. At that time, it wasn't as popular as it is today. When we returned to Germany, we brought watermelons in our luggage. In Persia, watermelons are often served as dessert or as a refreshment on warm summer days. Many Germans were unfamiliar with this fruit, and everyone asked what it was, as only local fruits like apples, pears, plums, cherries, and berries were commonly available—the only exotic fruit being bananas. The beloved banana was imported from South America with government subsidies, thanks to Chancellor Adenauer's efforts after the war. Citrus fruits were imported from Spain. Now, we could buy almost everything we knew from home in Turkish and other foreign stores.

I started cooking in my spare time, as eating in restaurants was too expensive for us students. My brother Parwiz and his friends had to work long hours at the hospital, but I had enough time to manage the household despite my studies becoming more challenging. By then, I had a good command of the German language, so in some subjects, like mathematics, I was even better than some of my fellow students. I also had no trouble understanding lectures. In subjects like economics, history, or construction chemistry, we sometimes had to recite historical facts, and I often found myself unintentionally drawn into discussions. With most Germans, these discussions often centered around the Third Reich and Hitler—a topic that was always uncomfortable.

So happy to be back home from Germany during my semester
break. Here with Mom (Sara Mama)

My first visit back home in Tabriz - it was good to see my
friends once again. A feast, ready on table in front of us, is one
of the iconic gestures of great hospitality in the Persian culture.

THE TERM "THIRD REICH"

The term "Third Reich" was coined by Joachim of Fiore, a realist historical theologian from around 1135-1202. He envisioned three empires following one another:

1. The Old Testament Kingdom of the Father.
2. The Present Kingdom of the Son.
3. An eternally lasting age of salvation, or the "Freethinking of the Holy Spirit."

Fiore believed that temporal salvation, according to the concept of the "Heavenly Jerusalem," should be established on Earth for eternity, similar to the Shiite expectation of the twelfth Imam. This understanding of "Heavenly Jerusalem" was why the term was used by the Nazi regime until January 30, 1933. From that date, at Hitler's request, the term was no longer used. The idea was that "Heavenly Jerusalem" could only be realized after solving what the Nazis referred to as the "problem of the Jews, Roma, and Gypsies."

At 16, I had read about nationalism and Hitler's book, *Mein Kampf* (which was banned in Germany), so I was already familiar with his ideology and intentions. I tried to avoid discussions on the topic but was sometimes deliberately drawn in by others. Our lecturers had different views, shaped by their own experiences, both good and bad. One professor, who insisted I sit in the front row, would greet us with a military bearing and during his lecture, he would stand next to me, rhythmically tapping my head, jesting that our "foreign guest" would now explain how construction was done in his homeland. The students found this amusing and laughed loudly, assuming I came from a desert, with a father who owned camels.

Sometimes, I shared interesting facts about the history and culture of my homeland, like stories of Cyrus, the king of the Persians; the great physician Avicenna and his book *Canon*, which was taught in European universities until recently; or the chemist Razi, who discovered alcohol (from the Arabic *al-kuhl*), and the origins of words like alchemy (from the Persian *kimia*) and algebra (from Arabic *al-jabr*). Persia produced many great scientists who contributed to solving humanity's problems and advancing science. However, after the Arab conquest and the arrival of Islam in our country, the Persian language was condemned and forbidden, so many books were written in Arabic. Unfortunately, a reasonable academic discussion about these topics was rare, and there was little interest in learning about them. I often felt disappointed, remembering how we treated visitors in Persia where no one was insulted without good reason, and the weak were protected at all times. I didn't understand why foreign students like me were mistreated in Germany. Despite following all the societal rules—dressing well, being polite and punctual, and communicating in the language—I was still treated as an outsider.

But as far as Gisela was concerned, I played the role of her friend, brother, and father all at once, and often confided in her. Her mother, who had become like a substitute mother to me, was also very fond of me. Despite her small pension, she always had the best food on the table, served on fine dishes in a beautifully decorated, typical German-style apartment. The two small rooms were always clean and comfortable, with pictures of earlier, happier times adorning the walls showing her parents and grandparents, and men with long braided mustaches who sat proudly in rows. Gisela's mother, though only in her early fifties, dressed like an old grandmother and insisted that Gisela also dress decently, avoiding short skirts and flamboyant hairstyles.

After dinner, we often sat around the small dining table, where Gisela's mother, with her East Prussian accent, would tell stories of her past—of her deceased father, her mother and three sisters who lived in the country, and her only brother who had recently returned from Russian captivity. She spoke of her childhood home and large farm in East Prussia, where dozens of people were employed to help care for the many cattle that provided good and sufficient food. She recounted her double wedding with her sister, the great celebration, and even remembered the names of the individual musicians who had played. But these happy days were short-lived. When their only child was born, her husband saw his daughter only a few times before he was killed in the war in 1944 at the age of 35. Shortly after that, the Russian invasion began.

Happy days were like autumn leaves blowing in the wind. I enjoyed listening to their stories, often thinking of my own family's history and the strange coincidence that, despite being thousands of miles apart, both families experienced the same tragic fate. It reminded me of my mother and her life, and I would often excuse myself to hide in the bathroom and wipe away my tears.

At the university, after passing the exams, we were called "the old ones," and newcomers respected us. Many were even surprised that two foreigners had made it this far. Despite everything, I had made some friends. One day, they wanted to visit me, so we went to my apartment to work on our schoolwork together. When my fellow students saw my apartment, they were shocked that I could afford such a place, even with its frugal furnishings. The apartment, owned by Mr.

Berger, was tastefully decorated, with a library full of classic books like Goethe, Nietzsche, Tolstoy, and Victor Hugo. They asked if I was familiar with any of the books, and I informed them that I had already read most of them at home by the time I was seventeen. They were astonished and finally began to take me seriously.

Meanwhile, the German economy was flourishing as never before. Industry was rebuilding on the strength of German goods, which were once again being exported. Unions were formed, wages increased, and people's incomes improved, leading to greater purchasing power. The desire for a better life after the long years of war and displacement grew stronger, increasing demand for better housing and apartments. Construction and renovation of highways, public buildings, and facilities resumed, and the demand for civil engineers soared. Senior-level employees from construction and architectural firms were invited to attend exams as observers and to negotiate employment contracts directly with the graduates. For us in the final semester, the future looked very hopeful. However, I had no intention of staying in Germany. Although I was grateful for my education and degree, I felt uncomfortable with how I had been treated as a foreigner. Some professors couldn't bear the thought of an Asian holding a diploma from their university. That was reason enough for me to return to my homeland immediately after graduation. Especially since the National Democratic Party of Germany (NPD) had recently been founded from various radical right-wing and xenophobic groups. It was astonishing how quickly people could forget the hatred and consequences of war. My decision was firm: I would turn my back on Germany.

November arrived once again—a particularly sad month in Germany. In the evenings, I often visited Gisela's mother, whom I affectionately called Mutti. She had bought a television, so after she cooked for us, we would watch the evening news together. L.B. Johnson was the U.S. President, and the Vietnam War was in full swing, with U.S. forces deploying over 500,000 soldiers and using napalm bombs as a weapon of choice. The news was grim.

So, 1965 became a year of decision-making for me. After graduating, I had to think about Gisela's and my future together. She left the decision up to me, agreeing with whatever I decided without forcing me into anything. Gisela was always selfless in that regard. Ours was a real and great love. She advised me not to do anything that would hurt my mother or my family. I could discuss everything with her and often talked about my homeland, our habits, and how we lived. I deliberately made it sound much worse than it was and asked if she could live in such a country. Her answer was always without hesitation: yes. I also discussed the idea with Mutti, not wanting to take her only daughter away from her, yet not wanting to live in Germany. Mutti's only wish was for Gisela to be happy and to have a better life than she herself had. Fate had not been kind to her and her family, but maybe it would be different for her daughter. She often asked what my mother would say, and I assured her that my mother would love Gisela like a daughter. Mutti was visibly relieved and gave me her blessing.

I also discussed the idea with my brothers, wanting their blessing as well. In our culture, the elder brother represents the father. However, all three of them believed we should make this important decision ourselves. About Gisela, they all agreed—she would be a faithful companion in my life.

We celebrated our official engagement with a small party at Mutti's, together with my brother. I now had greater responsibility and stood by my word—to complete my studies, graduate, and get married. Learning of our engagement, Gisela's employer promised us an apartment in Mettmann, near Düsseldorf. When construction began, we often drove there to inspect the progress. It was located on the edge of a forest, offering a magnificent view over beautiful fields. The German economy continued to improve day by day. There were parliamentary elections, and the CDU party won with an absolute majority. Ludwig Erhard became chancellor, and as a minister of economics in the Adenauer cabinet, he had realized the economic miracle happening in Germany and could now pursue his programs further.

At the university, I no longer had any inhibitions and defended my theses with determination. I didn't take everything said too seriously and even made fun of some lecturers and their attitudes. Mr. M. could no longer use my head as a drum kit!

35

OUR WEDDING

"The garden of love is green without limit and yields many fruits other than sorrow and joy."

— RUMI

Our future apartment was ready in late summer, so we gave up our shared apartment in Düsseldorf. Parwiz had been living in the hospital for weeks now, and my oldest brother had been given a villa in Bochum by the hospital, where he lived with his Persian wife. At the registry office, we had requested December 17th for our wedding, coinciding with Gisela's birthday. However, the registrar married us on September 17th, 1965, instead.

As the wedding day approached, I found myself juggling multiple responsibilities—studies, the wedding, furnishing the new apartment, and the move—all without informing my family in Persia or seeking the consent of my dear parents. Financially, I was also stretched thin. Although I received an allowance from my father every three months, by the end of the second month, my funds were nearly depleted.

Gisela and I went to the city together to search for furniture for our apartment. I couldn't help but think that if we were in Persia, my mother would have been there to help us in every way. A grand wedding feast would have been organized with many guests. Gisela would have experienced a wedding like something out of "One Thousand and One Nights." I would have given anything to celebrate our wedding with both families in my home country, but unfortunately, it wasn't possible.

On our wedding day, after breakfast, we went to the registry office for the official ceremony. Weddings were scheduled every half hour, so everything moved along quickly. When it was our turn, we were ushered into a room with a large desk where an officer stood behind it. He first confirmed our names, then asked Gisela if she would like to marry me. She immediately said yes. He then asked if she had considered everything because Persia was a "poor developing country" and reminded her that, as a Muslim, I could marry four women. He repeated the question, asking if she still wanted to marry me and what surname she would take. Gisela, without hesitation, responded that she would marry me and take my last name—of course! The official finally finished, and we signed the marriage documents. Happily, and hurriedly, we left the room.

This encounter highlighted the prejudice some people harbored. The official had no real understanding of Persia or Islam. Our issue was not about my homeland or faith but rather about people like him who held such misconceptions. Despite this, we proudly and happily drove in our old car to join our small wedding party, where we were welcomed with much love.

I had reserved a table for eight people for lunch at a posh restaurant on Königsallee. Our guests included Gisela's mother, grandmother, her only uncle, my brother Parwiz, and two friends. To make it festive, a wedding menu was specially printed, and the table was tastefully decorated with candles and flowers. This was the start of our wedding celebration.

We enjoyed a five-course meal, served in a very festive manner. Gisela wore a black suit, and I wore a black suit with a bow tie. I hadn't considered the cost of the meal, but thankfully, Parwiz treated us all. After lunch, we drove to Mutti's apartment and continued the celebrations. She had prepared everything with a lot of love and attention—just like my mother would have. Late in the evening, we said goodbye to the family and drove home to our newly furnished apartment in Mettmann.

As Gisela's mother faced the prospect of sleeping alone in her apartment for the first time, I fully understood her tears, having experienced similar emotions in my own life. I had promised her that I would always honor and love her daughter. I told her that my mother had said goodbye to two daughters and four sons and that if she were here, she would be proud of Gisela. Perhaps one day they would meet—who knows?

My life now had new meaning and had changed completely. I was married, and Gisela bore my name. Before our official marriage, I had performed the wedding ceremony myself according to Islamic law. In our religion, if no clergyman is available, the couple can perform the ceremony themselves if both agree to begin their life together in God's name. Gisela had already given her consent of her own free will, so we were married religiously. We still had to go to Bonn, the German capital after the war, to register our marriage at the Iranian consulate, where Gisela would receive her papers and Iranian citizenship.

We quickly settled into a daily routine: waking up at six o'clock every morning, having breakfast together in our small kitchen, then I would drop Gisela off at the bus stop in Düsseldorf before continuing to the university. The winter semester had begun, and I had a lot to do. My brother Parwiz often visited us. I would pick him up in the evening after work at the hospital in Duisburg, and we would drive together to our place. Gisela tried her best to cook and serve us like her mother used to. Though her cooking skills were still developing, the meals were edible, and we enjoyed our time together.

On Sundays, I brought Mutti and Oma, Gisela's grandmother, to our place for lunch. Mutti always brought delicious home-cooked dishes, with enough leftovers for us to have meals for the week. After lunch, we would take long walks in the forest, holding hands and chatting about the beautiful times in East Prussia. Upon returning home, we would enjoy some of Mutti's delicious cake.

My other brothers from Bochum and Karlsruhe also visited us when they had time, and we sometimes spent weekends at their homes. All the while, Gisela listened attentively, trying to learn family names and a few Persian words and phrases.

Gisela and I were married on September 17th, 1965, in Düsseldorf, Germany.

36

IMPERIAL IRANIAN EMBASSY

One day, we traveled to the Imperial Iranian Embassy in Bonn to register our marriage. Gisela also received her Persian identity card and passport. When they asked her religion—a customary question at that time, even in Germany—she stated Islam. I had not discussed religion with Gisela, and it was entirely her decision. In Islam, there is no compulsion; Muslims are expected to know their own religion and accept it out of conviction.

My oldest sister already knew about our marriage, as I had written to her, but she was the only one informed back home. My plan was to wait until I completed my exams in the summer and then fly home to announce the news. However, the Iranian ambassador, in a well-meaning gesture, wrote to my father to congratulate him on the marriage of his son in Germany, completely disrupting our plans. I had wanted to personally introduce my wife to my parents, to show them that I had followed my mother's advice and chosen a life partner wisely. Gisela was sweet, good-natured, and pure in spirit, and I couldn't have simply walked away from her, despite the challenges we might face.

My younger brother later told me that when Father first read the letter from the ambassador, he was initially shocked, thinking it might be a special message or invitation. After reading it, he handed it to my brother, who then opened the envelope and read the contents aloud: "The marriage of your son with Miss .... has been registered here. Both are officially husband and wife." The ambassador had congratulated my father and wished him continued success in raising his children.

Father was silent for a few moments, then finally said, "God bless them both, they have my blessing." He then asked my brothers how they should go about telling Mother that I had gotten married in a foreign country and without asking them. After much discussion, they decided to wait for the right moment to inform her.

My family managed to keep the news a secret for a few months, but in the spring of 1966, we received a telegram telling us to pack up immediately and fly home. The Lufthansa office also called to confirm two round-trip tickets to Tehran. Luckily, Gisela had been learning Persian at the local language school. I helped her as much as I could, teaching her the customs and habits of our homeland. We practiced how to wear a veil correctly using a bedsheet and how to sit and eat according to Persian customs. There were still many things for her to learn, like standing up briefly when older people take a seat, waiting for others to start eating before you do, and accepting offerings politely.

Gisela applied for leave from work and went shopping for gifts for my family and relatives, while I stayed busy preparing for my exams in the summer. However, sometime later, I received a telegram from my father's secretary advising us to delay our return home and that they would inform us of the exact time and date later. We were devastated by the delay, and my brothers tried to comfort us. Gisela returned to work, and I continued attending the last remaining lectures.

Our mathematics professor, Mr. W., was an older gentleman with long white hair, one of the kindest people I had met in

Germany. He was calm, businesslike, and above all, good-natured. He could solve quick and complicated calculations in seconds without using a slide rule or pencil, doing it all in his head. He had noticed my sorrow. One day after a lecture, as I was leaving with my head down, he called me into his room. He asked me privately what was wrong. In the short time we had, I told him the story of my life and explained that I was desperate.

He looked at me for a while and said, "Your decision is quite right; it all takes time. When people from different cultures come together, they contribute to international understanding. Of course, there are special challenges to overcome. If this fact had been considered earlier, many misunderstandings, and perhaps even wars, could have been avoided."

I also told him that some lecturers didn't care for foreign students and might even cause trouble during the final exams next summer. He laughed softly and said he would check my grades in other subjects first. If everything was alright, he assured me of his help. He said goodbye to me affectionately, leaving me full of hope and energy. He was a good man, and his kindness gave me the strength I needed to carry on.

37

HONEYMOON IN PERSIA

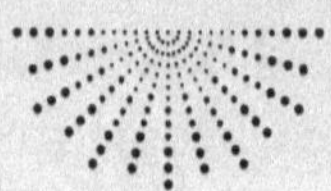

When I got home, there was a note from the post office in the mailbox. A telegram had arrived, and I could pick it up at the post office by 6 p.m. I felt a strange anticipation—who could it be from? I immediately drove to the post office. It was from Tehran. The secretary wrote that everyone was eagerly awaiting us and that I should fly home together with my bride. I called Gisela to tell her the news. She was so happy; I could hear her telling her colleagues that she was flying to the Orient. Our vacation plans were back on track. I called the airline to reserve our seats and sent a telegram indicating our arrival.

A few days later, on a beautiful morning, we said goodbye to Mutti, Grandma, my brothers, and friends, and flew off to Persia. Gisela was excited, yet calm. I could see the happiness on her face. Despite the long journey to an unknown country, she wasn't anxious. On the contrary, she embraced it with a special calmness, looking forward to meeting my family. During the flight, with a short stopover in Beirut, we rehearsed everything again. She repeated many Persian words and practiced the names of my brothers, sisters, and close relatives.

As we flew over Tehran, the city lights flickered below us, and

Gisela realized that I had understated my stories about my homeland. She became restless, eager to disembark the plane. Soon, we were off the plane, walking in the pleasantly warm air towards the airport building. She looked around, holding my hand tightly.

I had forgotten about myself, as all my thoughts were with her. She was now my wife, a guest in my country, and I felt a great responsibility for her—but she was doing well so far. After passing through immigration and customs, we went to the arrivals hall. My sister, her children, aunts, cousins, and many others were there, laughing, and happy, with flowers to welcome us. They embraced Gisela first, then me—it was a warm and touching welcome. Gisela had tears in her eyes. We drove together to my sister's house, and it all felt like a dream. Later, Gisela told me that it was as if she had embraced her own sister and family, although she had never had a sister.

Gisela was captivated by the brightly lit, bustling streets of Tehran. Everywhere she turned, she heard beautiful music, vendors hawking their wares, and saw a mix of ancient and modern architecture. It was a special and beautiful experience for both of us. When we arrived home, she was full of enthusiasm. I had exaggerated everything in my stories to her. It was all very comfortable and welcoming. Gisela was overwhelmed by the loving interactions, especially with the children, the respect shown to parents, and the attention from my family. She felt at home from the first minute after our arrival. It was love at first sight with my, and now our, home. Although my home was actually in Tabriz, and we would be flying there the following day.

My sister was delighted with Gisela after only a few hours. She had already become a member of the family. With her broken Persian, she tried to answer many questions. Her accent was pleasant, and everyone enjoyed listening to her. She paid close attention to the local customs, which I had taught her and which she had learned eagerly.

My sister was reassured and couldn't stop hugging Gisela. She was confident that our parents would be proud of her and praise my decision. It was a beautiful evening with the family. We dined outside under a clear sky, the air fragrant with jasmine. We ate and talked for hours, losing all sense of time.

Finally, it was time to sleep. Our beds were set up outside, covered with white nets. We lay side by side, staring up at the starry sky. Gisela could hardly believe that we were finally in my homeland. I had told her so much about it, trying to describe such nights under the open sky, and now she was experiencing it firsthand. I told her about Tabriz, my city, where I grew up. For the hundredth time, I spoke about my parents and siblings, telling her that the old Persia still existed there and that we would experience it the next day. In the meantime, she slept like an angel until the warm rays of the sun woke us early in the morning.

After breakfast, when we were about to leave the house, my sister fetched the Quran. It is customary in Persia, when travelers take their leave, for the Quran to be held over their heads as they exit the door. While the book itself may not have any power, the belief in it reassures the traveler and strengthens self-confidence. The Quran is more than a book to us because it is God's word. One does not touch it if one is dirty or impure; it is treated with great respect. My sister wanted to explain this to Gisela, but before she could, Gisela took the book, kissed it gently, returned it to my sister, and walked with her innocent face under the book to the door.

When we landed in Tabriz a short time later, I saw my father waiting impatiently to greet us. He hadn't changed a bit—still looking tall and strong. I introduced Gisela, and she embraced Father without hesitation, as if he were her own father. I was so moved by this that I had tears in my eyes, and so did Father, which was rare. He was so impressed by Gisela that he spoke to her in his own language, Azeri, without realizing that she didn't understand.

He said, "I know that my sons do not decide anything against our will. I agree with everything and am satisfied. You are our daughter, and now you are home."

I inquired about Mother, and he told me she was waiting in the car. I was anxious, but Father assured me that everything would be fine.

We got into the car, and Gisela immediately hugged Mother and called her Mama. She took her in her arms without hesitation, then hugged me and cried. We arrived home to find my younger siblings waiting to greet us, with the maids running back and forth. They hugged Gisela and tried to talk to her, though the atmosphere was a bit awkward since I didn't know what to say. Gisela finally sat down and glanced around the room.

My mother took out a cigarette, and Gisela immediately jumped up, took the lighter, and lovingly held it out to my mother to light her cigarette. Mother was surprised by this gesture and thanked her. Gisela then sat on the floor next to her—Mother always liked to sit on specially-made cushions on the floor—and slowly began to chat with her in Persian. Mother was amazed that she could communicate with her daughter-in-law, even if only a little. Her eyes shone with joy, and I could see that Mother had already taken Gisela into her heart.

That same afternoon, one of my cousins was getting married in the house across the street. My mother asked Gisela if she would like to come with us, if she wasn't too tired, because she wanted to take this opportunity to introduce her new daughter-in-law to the relatives. Before I could answer, Gisela eagerly said yes and jumped up to change her clothes. She asked Mother what she should wear and offered to wear a veil if there was one. Mother was thrilled to hear this but told her it wasn't necessary, as she was dressed more decently than most young Persian women. She suggested that Gisela just put on her prettiest dress, which she had brought with her. Gisela had taken my parents to heart from the first meeting. Father and Mother were now like her own parents, as she hadn't known fatherly love before. I left her with him and went to my mother, hugging her and apologizing for any hurt I may have caused.

A while later, they had changed into simple but beautiful dresses, and we set off for the wedding celebration. I sat with my father and told him about my studies and life in Germany with my brothers and their families.

He responded, "Inshallah," (if God wills it). But he added that after that, I should return home immediately.

My Mother's arrival in Germany with Gisela.

I was so excited to show Mom around.

38

ETERNAL FRIENDSHIP

Upon returning home after the wedding, Gisela was exhausted and went straight to bed. So much had happened in the last 48 hours! My father, true to his routine, had gone to sleep around 9 p.m., which gave me some time to chat with Mother. Naturally, she wanted to hear all about Gisela. I shared how we met, about her mother Mutti, and how Gisela had lost her father during the war when she was very young. We also discussed the fact that I hadn't asked for their permission to marry Gisela. I reminded Mother that she hadn't known Gisela at all, so it would have been a difficult decision for her and Father. Now that they had met, Mother assured me I had made the right choice. She told me Gisela was a very special person who would remain faithful to me always. After only 10 hours in Tabriz, Mother shared these beautiful thoughts and gave me her blessing for a happy life with Gisela.

I hugged Mother tenderly, tears welling up in my eyes. She gently told me to go to bed but reminded me not to leave Gisela alone as she was a stranger here and far away from her own mother. I went upstairs feeling content and slept like a baby.

The following morning, we were awakened by the brilliant

198

sunshine. We went down for breakfast to find the table beautifully laid, with my mother and siblings waiting for us. Gisela, with her usual gusto, enjoyed the meal, clearly comfortable after just one night. It had taken me many months to adjust to life in Germany, but she managed it from the very first day. When our tea was served, Gisela skillfully poured a glass from the samovar and brought it to my mother. Everyone watched attentively. My mother was delighted with her, appreciating the natural, unforced way she did everything with love and attention.

Word of Gisela's arrival spread quickly through the community, and soon we were inundated with invitations for tea. My uncle even hosted a large party in her honor. Gisela was now experiencing everything I had told her about—the beautiful nature, the hospitality, and the warmth of the people. She received gifts and was fully accepted as my mother's daughter-in-law.

After a few days, Gisela expressed a desire to visit the city and the bazaar. Mother readily agreed and asked my youngest sister to accompany her. Gisela surprised everyone by asking for a suitable veil, as younger women rarely conformed to this tradition. Mother brought her a silk veil and skillfully draped it over her head. Gisela looked angelic as she walked with my sister to the bazaar. They had a fun time, and when Father came home from work, he proudly told us that businessmen from the bazaar had called to congratulate him on his beautiful daughter-in-law from Europe. They even noted that Gisela wore her veil better than most women in the country.

Gisela quickly grew to love Persian cuisine, tolerating everything and developing a good appetite. Persian food is very healthy, and my family was pleased that she enjoyed it, hoping she wouldn't fall ill. However, one day she did feel unwell and mentioned it to my mother. Mother, with her sharp instincts, immediately recognized the symptoms and gave me the happy news: Gisela was pregnant. The family doctor soon confirmed it.

From that moment on, Gisela was treated like a young child, everyone looking after her while I was more or less ignored!

I spent much of my time with Said and other school friends, visiting our former teachers or going to the cinema. I also started preparing for our return to Germany, getting suits and shoes made and buying gifts for my brothers and their families.

One evening, Father brought home a package containing various diamonds. He told Gisela to choose some so our jeweler could make her a beautiful ring. She was thrilled, not just with the ring but with the fact that she had a father figure in her life again. This gesture confirmed that she had been fully accepted by my parents. I was grateful to God that, after months of worrying about my parents' acceptance, everything had settled perfectly. I had trusted in God and married with good intentions. Gisela's happiness was my greatest wish, and with the blessings of both her mother and my parents, we knew we would be happy. My parents were more than satisfied with their new daughter-in-law. Her charm and good nature had won over the entire family. She was no longer a stranger and had found a second home in our country.

A few days later, Mother asked Gisela about her job and what she planned to do now that she was pregnant. I explained that Gisela still had to work, and while her mother could help, she suffered from asthma. This greatly concerned Mother. The next day, she surprised us by announcing her decision to accompany us back to Germany! She simply couldn't let Gisela go without knowing how she would manage, especially since I was clueless about dealing with a pregnant woman! Father was fully supportive and agreed immediately.

The news traveled fast throughout the family, causing both astonishment and trepidation. Mother was a firm believer who had never removed her veil in public. We all wondered how she would adapt to life in Europe. After much discussion, her decision was final, and our joy knew no bounds.

Her preparations began much like mine had—organizing her

passport and travel documents, shopping for new clothes, and buying gifts for our family in Germany. She even selected the most beautiful Persian rug for Mutti.

The day before our departure, Father had a father-son chat with me. He praised me for my marriage and thanked God for giving me such a noble person as a life partner. He advised me to always take great care of Gisela. I looked at him fondly, seeing the peace and wisdom that radiated from him.

After attending several festive events hosted by relatives, the day arrived for our departure. My father stayed behind to care for my younger siblings, happy to be left alone in the big house with them. He never complained in his life—always a grateful person.

We arrived in Tehran in the early evening, with Gisela walking hand in hand with my mother through the airport terminal. It still amazed me how quickly such a deep affection had developed between them. They had formed a true mother-daughter relationship, despite the language barrier. Many relatives and friends came to the airport to greet us, particularly because of Mother's arrival as the head of the family. Over the years, she had helped and advised so many, and many were curious to meet my new wife and hear about Mother's journey to Europe. We were received with joy and enthusiasm, and all went together to my eldest sister's home. Everything was new and wonderful for Gisela, and we were both spoiled. Mother was transformed, her eyes shining once again with laughter and joy, but her focus remained on Gisela, watching over her like a protective guardian.

We stayed in Tehran for several weeks, allowing us plenty of time to visit relatives. My cousin, Ali Aga, who worked as a customer consultant at the Russian Bank, often had his driver pick us up in his American car to show us the city. We also visited my father's business, Magaseh - Iran, a delicatessen store in the city center. There, we met customers who remembered Gisela from when they had been guests in our home in Düsseldorf. They had not forgotten her warm hospitality and welcomed her with open arms.

Our stay in Tehran was a memorable experience, but eventually, it was time to return to Germany. The farewell was especially difficult for Gisela, who had developed a deep connection with my family. As she sat on the plane with tears in her eyes, my mother comforted her, assuring her that as soon as I finished my studies, we would return to Persia. It was Mother's first time flying to a foreign country, and she was nervous, but Gisela calmed her by sharing stories about East Prussia and her family's fate. By the time we landed, Mother had forgotten her fears.

When we arrived in Düsseldorf, my mother donned her elegant brown coat and matching silk headscarf. As we walked through the arrivals hall, I couldn't help but feel immense pride for these two remarkable women—one, my dearly beloved mother, and the other, my dear new wife. Gisela's mother, my brother Parwiz, and some friends were there to greet us. Both mothers hugged each other like old acquaintances.

We drove directly to our apartment in Mettmann. During the drive, Gisela enthusiastically recounted our trip, translating for my mother as she spoke to Mutti. Despite the language difficulties, a bond quickly developed between the two women—a bond that would last for many years.

Gisela's mother had taken care of everything at the house. The beds were made with fresh linens, the table beautifully set, and the refrigerator stocked with fresh fruit and vegetables. Mother noted the care and attention to detail, seeing much of herself in Mutti's preparations. Fate had brought together two families from different lands, both with similar life experiences—dispossessed, robbed, and expelled by the same perpetrators.

I noticed that both women, though from different cultures, shared the same qualities. They were kind-hearted and always ready to give everything they had. Whether it was a hot meal for a homeless person, a warm coat for someone in need, or even a cup of water for a thirsty dog, it was the deed and the mercy that mattered.

When we were young, Mother often told us stories. One I'll never forget is the story of Moses and the Shepherd.

A shepherd, moving with his flock through fragrant meadows, was talking to God, saying, "O my beloved, where are you? Show yourself. I will sew for you the most beautiful dress. I will crochet stockings from my sheep's wool, so your feet do not freeze. I will massage your shoulders, so you do not feel pain. I will cook for you, care for you, and provide for you with all my strength."

When Moses heard this, he scolded the shepherd. "How can you say such things? God is not a man. You know nothing." But then Moses heard a voice: "The shepherd is a true believer. Why do you insult and disown him?"

Mother meant that beyond our religious duties—daily prayers, fasting, even pilgrimage to Mecca—we should never forget our responsibilities to our fellow human beings. We should be at peace with ourselves and with our Creator.

WITH THE WINTER SEMESTER UNDERWAY, our daily routine resumed. Gisela went to work in Düsseldorf, and I traveled to Wuppertal to study. Mother often stood at the window, admiring the diligence and order of the people below riding their bicycles early in the morning to work, returning late in the evening to provide for their families. In the afternoon, I would pick up Mother, and we'd drive together to collect Gisela from work. Mother often surprised her with a sandwich, figuring she'd be tired and hungry after a long day.

On weekends, we visited my brother and his family in the Black Forest, where we were pampered by my sister-in-law. We also toured monuments and beautiful old castles along the Rhine. Mother was particularly enchanted by the lovely spa town of

Baden-Baden, with its old houses adorned with beautiful stone facades. The town rekindled memories of Baku and Russia for her. Fortunately, my old, used car served us well and never let us down.

We often gathered with my three brothers and their families—it was like being back home in Tabriz. Though Mother was content, she began to miss Father and my siblings, as it was the first time she had been so far from home and for so long. However, she was grateful for my brothers, who gave her a thorough medical examination and referred her to a renowned dentist. Due to an incorrect diagnosis in her early 40s, all her teeth had been extracted, and she received a full set of dentures that never fit properly. Now, with a brand-new set, she was satisfied and happy.

The time was approaching for Mother to return home, so we began shopping for gifts once again. However, Mother's supply of traveler's checks was running low. Unaccustomed to financial limitations, she told me to go to the bank and withdraw more cash! Unfortunately, by the end of the month, our account was always in the red. With my money transferred from Tehran and Gisela's salary, we were only just making ends meet. I felt helpless. Through my friends, I learned about a pawnshop where I could borrow money. The young lady at the shop scrutinized me closely as I placed my gold watch—a gift from my uncle in Tabriz—on the counter. After examining it, she handed me a few hundred German Marks. Having never experienced such financial need, I felt a strange mix of shame and relief. But I would have done anything for my dear mother, even if it meant pawning a cherished possession.

A few days later, Mother noticed I wasn't wearing my gold watch and asked where it was. I made up a lame excuse, but she wasn't fooled. She looked at me with her kind eyes, already knowing the truth.

So, the wonderful time with Mother in Germany came to an end. She had spent much of her time with Mutti, and despite the language barrier, they had communicated in their own way.

Watching them, I had the feeling that they could read each other's life experiences in their eyes.

When we took Mother to the airport, everyone was there to bid her farewell. We all had tears in our eyes as we hugged and kissed her goodbye. She, on the other hand, remained composed, speaking calmly to everyone. She reminded me of the great responsibility I had to my wife and our baby and urged me to take good care of both of them. I gave her my word and promised that we would return home together with Gisela's mother in the summer after I finished my studies. It was also Gisela's wish. After her departure, our apartment felt empty—not just for me, but for Gisela and Mutti too.

WE ENJOYED our last Christmas in Germany, and for Gisela's sake —being seven months pregnant—I prepared everything in our apartment. With her mother, grandmother, uncles, and my dear brother Parwiz, we celebrated the holiday with great joy.

Gisela could no longer work, and she was well looked after by a renowned Persian gynecologist. We received numerous letters from home inquiring about Gisela, how she was coping, and when the baby was due. From Mother's stories, I heard that everyone was thrilled, believing that Gisela had worked miracles. We were very happy and grateful to our mighty and merciful God.

Hanging with old school friends in Tabriz.

39

BIRTH OF OUR DAUGHTER, MINOU

"Let yourself be silently drawn by the strange pull of what you really love. It will not lead you astray."

— *RUMI*

The Persian New Year, March 21, was approaching. Despite Gisela being heavily pregnant, we decorated the house together in preparation for the festivities. My experiences at home with Mother guided us in bringing everything to fruition—new clothes, spring-cleaning the house, and preparing a festive table with wheat sprouts, new banknotes, and more. Mutti visited almost every day, bringing food and filling up the refrigerator for the entire week. It was uncanny how similar she was to Mother, a true blessing from God. Why weren't more people like that?

Spring arrived, and with it, our beloved child—a daughter. The Persian New Year was just 8 days old when she came into our world. When Gisela went into labor, I rushed her to the hospital. We were unprepared, unsure of what to bring or what papers were required. I parked the car on a quiet, deserted street outside the hospital, and we went in together. After handling the formalities, a nurse led Gisela to her assigned room.

When I returned to the car, a policeman with a large German shepherd dog was waiting for me. He asked why I had parked the wrong way. Excitedly, I told him I was going to be a father, expecting a "Congratulations!" Instead, he took me to the nearby precinct.

He ordered me to take a seat, and I complied immediately, with the German shepherd sitting at attention between us. The officer asked me numerous questions, jotting down my answers while deliberately insulting me. Each time I spoke, the dog growled and inched closer, making me fear it would bite. After about ten tense minutes, the phone rang, and the officer announced he had to leave for a call. He told me I was lucky and allowed me to leave without paying a fine. I will never forget how cold and insensitive he was at a time when I was rejoicing in the birth of our child.

A few days later, I brought Gisela and our new baby home. We had become a family. We had wished for a girl, and our wish had come true. We named our sweet daughter Minou, which means paradise in Persian. She was paradise for us—a true gift from God. We always have faith in our dear God, knowing that each of us is a tiny part of Him. Sleepless nights followed, filled with feeding, burping, and changing and washing diapers (since disposable diapers were yet to be invented). Mutti was a tremendous help during this time, teaching us how to care for our baby.

I was so proud of our daughter, often thinking that when I reached my 40s, I would be in my prime, and she would be 17 years young! "Inshallah, isn't it beautiful," I kept saying to Gisela.

~

IT WAS the middle of exam time, and I was busy writing my thesis and preparing for the oral exams. I had already passed the written exam, as had my friend and compatriot. However, our "dear lecturers" could be troublesome during the oral exams, and they were. My friend didn't fare well in his oral, and his dream was over. Five years of study and expenses were gone. It was a mean-spirited act, deliberately carried out by the so-called professors—inhumanely and deceitfully.

When it came time for my oral exam, I was extremely nervous, especially after what had happened to my friend. Dressed in a smart black suit and tie, I entered the examination hall, which felt more like a Roman arena. The room was filled with directors, architects, lecturers, entrepreneurs, and professors from the examination board. I was to be tested on surveying, a subject I had prepared for (or so I thought). However, the questions were framed in a way that even a lecturer might struggle to answer within the 30-minute time limit under the gaze of so many observers. The professor drew some fixed points on the board and asked a difficult question that couldn't be answered in such a short time. Standing there with no chance to sit down or put the question on paper to solve it, my heart cried out to God for help. "God, please do not leave me alone; injustice is happening here."

Suddenly, I heard the voice of Mr. W., my mathematics lecturer. "You are from Persia, aren't you?"

"Yes, Mr. W.," I answered.

"How can we help your country, and what will you do when you return to your homeland?"

The audience became attentive, their eyes narrowing as they looked at me. "Please do not give money to the Persian government," I said. "Instead, build more technical schools like the one you built over 30 years ago in my hometown, Tabriz."

The interest of the audience was piqued. I continued, "In the past 30 years, thousands of qualified technicians have been trained there. These specialists are now employed in various industries, such as electricians, plumbers, carpenters, and locksmiths. The

German order and accuracy have become well-known in the local labor market thanks to these technicians."

I spoke the truth, as my best friend Said had studied there and told me about the great service this school had done for our country. All Persian teachers were trained in Germany, and the school was under German management, just like the German official at that time. Naturally, I compared such people to my wife, her mother, and other decent people I knew. When someone experiences such vicious attacks in a situation like mine, they do not forget it quickly. Many atrocities by the Third Reich are also not forgotten, and blame cannot undo them. Education is the only cure—if there were any real educators.

Thirty minutes passed quickly. A specialist lecturer tried to challenge me, but Mr. W. intervened. "Colleague, we don't have until eternity. The other examinees want to get it over with too. Besides, he is one of our best students from abroad. You are dismissed," he said to me. And so, I made a quick exit! Mr. W. certainly helped me pass my oral exam.

Gisela with our baby daughter, Minou.

Summer time in Tehran, Minou surrounded by
flowers.

Sitting with Minou on the staircase in Firuzeh's garden during my lunch break.

40

AFTER GRADUATION

few weeks earlier, on June 5, 1967, the Israeli Air Force launched a surprise attack on Egyptian bases in the Sinai Peninsula. In just six days, Israel captured not only the Sinai and Gaza Strip but also the Golan Heights from Syria—a major water reservoir for the region—and from Jordan, the West Bank, and the eastern part of Jerusalem, which is a holy site for Muslims on par with Mecca. We students watched these events unfold with great interest. The war was over almost as quickly as it began, with Israel defeating the combined armies of its neighbors. It was a humiliating defeat for the Arabs and their leader, Abdul Nasser.

My classmates laughed about it, treating it as some kind of dark humor, but to me, it was a tragedy. In many Islamic countries, the leaders themselves were often the biggest enemies of their own people. Despite the laughter, we had great pity for the Arabs, as I believe many others around the world did as well. I thought of the sad story of Lawrence of Arabia, where the young Faisal, who would later become the King of Saudi Arabia, charged into battle with a sword in hand, trying to fight against planes and machine guns with the Turks.

The Six-Day War might have been a great military achievement for Israel, but the political consequences were profound, leading to ongoing instability and violence in the Middle East—an issue that would persist until the conflict was resolved.

~

ON THE MORNING of my last day at the university, I encountered trouble with my car for the first time. My good old Opel grew louder and louder as I drove, but it held on just long enough to get me to the university parking lot before giving up and falling silent forever. For me, this wasn't a mere coincidence; it felt like it was meant to be. I left the car and went into the city with some friends, including my compatriot Hasan, to celebrate our graduation. I promised Hasan that we would work together when we returned to our homeland.

Everything else happened in a whirlwind. We went to the Persian Consulate and had my certificates and diplomas notarized. Gisela and Minou, our little princess, received their Persian identity cards and passports. We were informed that we could take our household belongings and a car back to Persia without paying customs, so we decided to pack up and move as soon as possible. Even Mutti agreed to the plan.

Gisela had her pension paid out, and with the money, we bought a new Opel Rekord. Her willingness to give up everything —even her pension in Germany—to accompany me to an unknown country and future, was the greatest proof of her love and affection.

We planned that I would go home first by car to prepare everything, and then she would join me with our daughter and her mother. However, shortly before I was set to leave, I received a telegram from my father. He informed me that his good old partner was on his deathbed and wanted to see his son, Jamshid, one last time before he passed away. The doctors had given him only one to two weeks to live, so my father asked me to bring

Jamshid with me. Jamshid, who was studying in Graz, Austria, was unaware of his father's condition as he hadn't been granted a residence permit in Germany.

With a heavy heart, I said goodbye to everyone—my brothers, friends, my dear wife and daughter, Mutti, and to Germany itself. I was grateful for my education, but I was also eager to return to my homeland.

Around this time, the German Federal Railroad was bringing trains full of Turkish "guest workers" to work in German farms and factories. The millionth guest worker even received a new bicycle as a gift! I felt sorry for them because I knew from my own experience what was in store for them, their children, and grandchildren.

After packing the new TV and my personal belongings in our new car, I set off for Austria. I arrived in Graz around midnight, where Jamshid was studying and living. The city's dark, rough-looking streets appeared even more foreboding than those in Germany. When I arrived at the house, some lights were still on, and a young man was standing at an open window. I asked after Jamshid, and a few minutes later, he came out to greet me. We talked for a while—he was very pleased to see me. I told him I had completed my studies and was heading home, and if he wanted to accompany me, we could be in Tabriz within four to five days. Although he didn't know about his father's illness, he declined my offer because he planned to visit the Persian Consulate first and then fly home. There was nothing more I could do.

Jamshid offered me a place to sleep overnight, but I declined as I was eager to get back on the road. We hugged and said our goodbyes. I declined his request to stay until the next morning, as my longing for my family and home was far too strong to lose another hour. As I reached the car, he suddenly called out from his apartment window, "Wait, I'm coming with you!"

Left: Final graduation exam at Universität Gesamthochschule Wuppertal. Right: Dancing with Gisela at my graduation party.

Having coffee with Gisela at a cafe in Düsseldorf.

41

OUR ROAD TRIP HOME

Our great adventure had begun. Two young men—I had just turned 24, and Jamshid was about six months older—headed home like thirsty horses that smelled water. I kept a secret from Jamshid. His father was on his deathbed, and I thought it best not to tell him, as we had a long journey ahead and uncertainty about when we would arrive.

We drove overnight through Romania, the land of the Ceausescu clan, and didn't see much of the capital, Bucharest. Passing through Bulgaria, we were supposed to visit one of my father's suppliers in Sofia, but we pressed on without stopping. At every border crossing, the television we were carrying caused much trouble. I had to lug the heavy set through customs alone and then back to the car. In Budapest, we allowed ourselves a brief rest and bought a Khleb, a delicious dark round bread.

By the time we reached the Turkish border, we were both exhausted. For three days, we had subsisted on dry bread and cough syrup. But we felt more relaxed now, having driven through only Eastern Bloc countries so far. It also helped that I could understand Turkish, as it was similar to my mother's native language, Azeri.

Unfortunately, we didn't know the route, and there were no good road maps available. Turkey at that time was a poor developing country, suffering from inflation and governed by the military. The roads were poorly lit with virtually no signage, leaving us to rely on chance. We asked passers-by for directions and kept driving until we found a gas station to refuel and inquire about the way.

Soon, the road became narrower and almost impassable. We crossed a rickety bridge made of irregular wooden planks that led over a deep gorge, where we could see the glistening water between the boards! As we continued along the mountainside, the path became so narrow that no other car could pass, barely wide enough for us. We honked continuously to warn oncoming traffic, though later we discovered there was none—not a car or a soul in sight.

As daylight broke, I looked down and realized the severity of our situation. It was an extremely dangerous stretch of road, made even more treacherous by the humid air that left the ground wet and slippery. There was no protective wall or guardrail, so the slightest mistake could have been fatal. I started to pray, recalling everything I had learned from my mother. I promised the good Lord that if we made it out alive and Jamshid saw his father before he passed away, I would donate my first paycheck to a needy family whose daughter, Nazr, was getting married.

After a much-needed break, Jamshid took over the driving, and we set off once again. Although we weren't fully aware of the danger, we had a subconscious sense that we were lost. I thought of my wife, our baby Minou, and my mother, who was likely standing at her usual window, wondering where we were.

There was no turning back, so we drove carefully at a snail's pace. Jamshid, a good driver, skillfully maneuvered through the tight curves while chatting with me. After about two hours of navigating this perilous route, we spotted a building in the valley below.

We breathed sighs of relief as we approached a small teahouse, where an elderly man was washing out front. My joy knew no bounds. Thank God, I said to myself. When we got out of the car, looking disheveled, unshaven with long beards and dirty clothes, the man gazed at us, horrified, as if we were ghosts. He cautiously approached and asked where we had come from.

When I replied in Turkish and pointed up to the mountains, "From up there," he couldn't believe it and burst into laughter, making fun of us.

"You came by CAR? From up there?" he inquired.

"Yes," I replied.

"Since the Ataturk era, no car has passed by here! That road is impassable! I don't know how you managed it!" he exclaimed.

Within half an hour of resting and eating eggs and bread for breakfast, all the villagers had gathered around us, listening to our tale as if we had fought Samson while driving the old, deserted road. It was our fate and God's will that we had escaped unharmed. It was time to move on, so we said goodbye to these simple folk, who refused to accept money for the breakfast.

After five days of driving, we arrived at the border. As we drove through the small town of Bazargan on the Persian side, Jamshid asked, "Why are we in such a hurry?"

I couldn't tell him the real reason, so I answered, "Soon you will see your family. Isn't that nice?" He laughed and gave me a big hug.

After about two hours, we arrived in Tabriz and drove straight to my father's office, parking the car with its German number plates right in front. We entered the office to find Father tallying the cash from the cash register, as he did daily after the close of business. The safe was open, his glasses perched on his nose, and he was busy counting. He glanced up briefly, without really seeing us, and said, "My friends, please come back tomorrow as we are closed now."

Then suddenly, someone rushed into the office, exclaiming, "A car from Germany has arrived!"

At that moment, my father looked up, recognized me, and rushed over to embrace me. "Who is this gentleman?" he asked.

I introduced Jamshid, and Father quickly advised him, "Your parents must be worried, so you must leave without further delay."

Jamshid flew to Tehran and was just in time to say goodbye.

Beautiful mosaic structures on a mosque in
Isfahan.

42

ARRIVAL IN TABRIZ

"Your heart and my heart are very, very old friends."

— HAFEZ

I left my car in the garage at the office, and a small van drove us home, carrying all my luggage and the TV. As we entered the house, Father called out, "Guess who's here? Yunes, our son!"

I then heard my mother's voice, filled with relief, saying, "Thank God. I was so worried; I've had such bad dreams."

The reunion was special because I was the first son to return home after graduating. I had left in 1961, and now, six years later, I returned as an engineer. Everyone was eager to hear about Gisela, Minou, and my brothers and their families. It was a beautiful summer's day, and though my home was always cozy and welcoming, with Mother's delicious cooking, it all felt surreal. My time in Germany seemed like a distant memory, and if I hadn't left my two loved ones there, I might have thought the past six years were just a dream.

My old and faithful friend, Said, who was studying mechanical engineering at the German Technical School in Tabriz, along with other friends, came to welcome me home. Everyone was content.

In the days that followed, relatives and friends hosted homecoming parties for me, including those whom I had cared for in Germany. I visited Mr. Jawadi in his office, and he proudly told me his asthma had improved. He was now the head of "Loewe and Sun," the Red Cross of Persia in Azerbaijan. At that time, alongside the Red Cross and the Crescent, we also had our "Lion and Sun," which was allowed to exist in parallel.

Not long after my return, I found myself struggling with indecision. Every thought and observation felt like a conflict—should I think in German or Persian? I saw no future in Tabriz. As an engineer, I needed to be close to construction, but I also wanted to be near Father and Mother as they grew older. Now that I had returned, I wondered—was it for good?

One evening, after Father had gone to bed, I sat with Mother. We smoked a cigarette and drank tea. I knew she could sense my turmoil because she gently advised me to leave Tabriz, wanting to free me from my indecision.

"Maybe we will move to Tehran too," she said, but we both knew Father would never leave the life he knew in Tabriz. She held me close and said lovingly, "You are a father now, so you understand parental love. Our only wish is for your happiness. In Germany, you are safe, but here you must be cautious. Beware of false friends, and above all, don't trust everyone. My dear son, I know you—you would give away your shirt if someone asked. Don't be reckless; you must consider your wife and daughter now."

Her words were a relief, freeing me from the burden of my decision. Mother knew that Tabriz was a quiet, sleepy town with little to offer. While my brothers, being doctors, could work anywhere, I was limited to construction.

Sadly, Jamshid's father passed away, but not before he had the chance to see and embrace his son one last time.

I went to see Father at his office. He was sitting alone and was pleased that I had stopped by. As usual, he poured a glass of tea, which he did for every visitor. He knew I had something on my mind, though I hadn't said anything yet. He inquired about his sons and grandchildren in Germany and, of course, about Minou, asking when he would finally meet her.

I told him, "As soon as I have a place to stay and our household items arrive from Germany, Gisela and Minou will join us."

He responded, "Why are you waiting? You should start preparations immediately. Your mother and I want you to live where you work, and we want what is best for you and your family. Don't worry about us."

When the subject of work came up, I remembered that the Persian Consulate had offered me a job as a technical manager in Isfahan. I had studied urban planning and traffic management, which was a new and highly demanded field at the time. When I shared this with my father, he was thrilled and immediately called Mother to tell her the news with pride. He then asked if I would prefer to drive to Tehran in my own car or fly, offering to send the car with a driver. The decision was made, I wanted to drive my own car.

That evening, I asked Mother if she would like to drive with me to Tehran. Father had already agreed, and he would never say no.

The following day, Mother and I drove to Tehran, leaving my younger sister and brother with Father. The journey to Tehran was a vast improvement compared to our trip through Turkey three weeks earlier. The landscape was captivating, ranging from barren deserts and rocky mountains to lush orchards and plantations. We arrived at a large oasis, and as I opened the car window, I breathed in the cool air, a refreshing mix of the oasis's coolness and the desert's warmth.

Upon our arrival in Tehran, I asked for directions several times before we finally found my sister's street. She had already rented a spacious apartment in a two-family house in her neighborhood, so Gisela, Mutti, and Minou could soon join us.

When I left Tabriz, Father reassured me not to worry about money, reminding me that I could get anything I needed from his store. He had always thought of everything and was always prepared. Within a few days, our household items arrived from Germany. Fortunately, there were no issues with customs, so everything was cleared quickly. Gisela, with the help of our good friends in Germany, had packed everything—except diapers for Minou. Those were beautiful, joyful times, and I was happier than ever!

Said meets the Shah while he was on a tour of the campus at the German Technical School in Tabriz.

Mutti came to visit, and we took her to the famous landmark in Tehran, called Shahyad Tower (Freedom Tower). This marble structure stands 148 ft tall and was built in 1971.

43
LIFE IN PERSIA

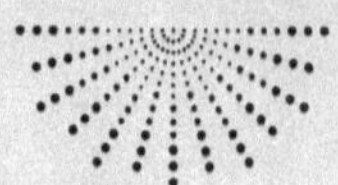

My younger brother Jacob was about to begin his military service and proudly wore his Persian Army uniform. When he wasn't on duty, he eagerly helped us prepare our new apartment, ensuring it was ready within the week.

When Gisela, Minou, and Mutti arrived at the airport in Tehran, the entire family gathered to welcome them. We could hear Mutti's joyful shouts as she entered the arrivals hall. Mama (as we called our mother) embraced Gisela's mother first, then Gisela, who was holding Minou. Finally, I was able to greet my loved ones. We drove home through the beautiful streets of Tehran, with me sitting between both mothers, acting as an interpreter. When we arrived at our apartment, both women were delighted with all our preparations and happy to be in Tehran.

1967 WAS a significant year for us. I had completed my studies and graduated with an engineering degree. The big move to Persia was successful, everyone was healthy, including our beautiful baby Minou, and we were together in our own apartment.

Our oldest sister assisted Gisela by showing her around the city, introducing her to the best shopping areas, and teaching her how to negotiate with merchants.

One day, I received a call from my college friend Hassan, whose father was a contractor with extensive experience and a large amount of heavy construction equipment. Hassan thought his father could be of assistance to us. Knowing that Hassan didn't have a diploma, I believed I could help him, so I suggested he join me on a trip to Isfahan. He accepted my invitation with enthusiasm.

We embarked on the five-hour drive to Isfahan together. Since my position had already been confirmed by the Ministry of the Interior, I was able to register Hassan as my assistant at the mayor's office at City Hall, located on the famous Chahar Bagh Avenue.

Isfahan, once the capital of Persia, has a rich history. In 640, it was conquered by the Arabs, marking the beginning of its Islamic era. During the 7th to 9th centuries, under the rule of the Umayyads and Abbasids, Isfahan became renowned for its silk and cotton. In 1051, it was taken by the great Sultan Tughril Beg, founder of the Seljuk Empire.

By 1388, the city, then home to 70,000 people, fell to the destructive forces of the Turkish-Mongol conqueror Timur Lenk. However, in 1453, with the construction of the Darb-e Imam Shrine, a new cultural era began under the Qara Qoyunlu, a Turkmen tribal federation. The Safavid conquest in 1502 marked the start of the city's greatest transformation, and by 1590, Isfahan had become the capital of Persia.

By the 17th century, the city's population had grown to roughly 600,000. Under the rule of Shah Abbas I, Isfahan flourished, attracting artists and craftsmen from across the country.

The Allahverdi Khan Bridge, also known as the famous Si-o-se-pol (bridge of 33 spans), in Isfahan.

44

ISFAHAN

Isfahan is the provincial capital of the province that shares its name, located in central Persia about 430 kilometers south of Tehran at an elevation of approximately 1,500 meters. The city sits in the fertile valley of the Zayandeh Rud River, on the edge of the Zagros Mountains.

Upon our arrival in Isfahan, we were taken to a magnificent old building and directly to the mayor's office. After a brief greeting, we were led into a large room, beautifully decorated with old, heavy wooden desks and chairs. A map of Isfahan adorned the wall, and various files were scattered across the tables. After a short discussion, the mayor scheduled an appointment for us to meet with the Governor.

We began preparing for our new life in Isfahan by renting a house, which I later discovered belonged to the Attorney General of Isfahan. We were unexpectedly provided with a cook and several servants, though neither Hassan nor I knew who had hired them. A few days later, the Attorney General's official car arrived to take us to the Governor's palace. Upon our arrival, we were led into a grand room with an enormous Persian rug, elegant seating, and a large oil portrait of the emperor. After a brief wait, the Governor emerged, and a well-dressed gentleman introduced us as the two engineers sent by the Ministry of the Interior to work for the Technical Department in Isfahan. I was introduced as the Technical Director. The Governor handed our certificates to the mayor and promptly returned to his room, leaving me with a cold impression of the exchange. Although we were young engineers, a handshake would not have gone amiss!

That evening, I asked the young man serving tea some questions about himself, where he was from, and who had hired him. He only asked how best he could serve. I turned to Hassan, puzzled about how we were going to pay all these people since our salary, while adequate, was not enough to cover such extravagant expenses. We soon discovered that several contractors and interested parties had provided everything for us—from the cook to the furnishings. It became clear that these people had encountered difficulties and now sought our help. This was their way of expressing gratitude.

We started work promptly at 8 o'clock every morning. An old man would bring us various files and serve tea daily. One day, he brought a particularly thick file, weighing about four kilos, with a note from the senior department requesting we process it. The file contained a complaint about a piece of land near the river running through Isfahan. This prime piece of property was where distinctive houses and villas had been built, and the plaintiff claimed a large portion of it belonged to him.

The old man warned me to be cautious, explaining that wealthy residents of Isfahan, with special connections in Tehran, would take whatever they wanted, regardless of the law. This file had been unresolved for countless years, with much dubious information, and several officials had lost their postings over it. Realizing the sensitivity of the matter, my friend and I decided to survey the land ourselves. The next day, Hassan took the surveying equipment and headed to the piece of land in question. It was a peculiar sight since most engineers had assistants to carry the instruments.

After completing the survey, it was clear the plaintiff's claim was unfounded—he was trying to unjustly enrich himself at the city's expense. Later that evening, we discussed how to proceed but found it difficult to talk openly with so many people in the house, possibly even spies. We spoke mostly in German and decided to hold off on any action for the time being.

Every city has a development plan naturally, which is called B-Plan, but this one was very exaggerated and for a city like Isfahan, not at all suitable. The green areas and the necessary biotopes and hydroponic landscapes were designed in such a way that thousands of properties were affected. However, some of them only by a few meters, so a building permit could not be obtained, which in turn meant their properties could not be sold. The planners wanted to create green areas and biotopes in oriental shapes, with flowers and leaf ornaments in a large format, without respecting the old structure of the city. In the Islamic countries, most houses are built in the direction of Mecca, therefore creating a checkerboard cityscape with straight streets. I made a report about this and tried to explain that it would not be important, from the urbanists point of view, if the green areas were to be changed in shape, but only in intended size—meaning that hundreds or maybe thousands of families could get a roof over their heads—which to me seemed a sensible solution.

Just as I was sending the report to be typed, the mayor called, asking if I questioned the B-Plan. I hadn't realized he was already aware of my report's contents before it was even finalized. I requested a technical conference to present my ideas and arguments.

The Shah's 48th birthday and his coronation both took place on October 26, 1967. This occasion sparked intense competition among the provinces and cities, each striving to outdo the others by erecting monuments across the country. I had personal reservations about whether the Shah genuinely desired such displays, as they seemed largely to serve the purpose of self-aggrandizement. Our governor in Isfahan was no different. Despite the fact that it provided no real benefit and was essentially pointless, he felt the need to create a large and conspicuous tribute. His proposal was to erect nine steel pillars in front of the public utilities as a symbol of the "White Revolution" (the nine new reforms). Unfortunately, this meant that Isfahan, the former capital of the Safavids, with its stunning mosques and blue domes featuring oriental designs, would now be marred by the addition of nine unsightly steel columns—an utterly inappropriate choice for such a historic city. Although we were tasked with designing the plans, I was reluctant because the maintenance alone—de-rusting and painting—would be costly. Moreover, the pillars did not complement the cityscape, nor did they provide any tangible benefits. I believed a more fitting tribute for the coronation would have been to build kindergarten schools or facilities for the disabled, but our suggestions were dismissed as pompous.

Every weekend, I drove home to Tehran with Hassan. We often drove through the night to maximize our time with our families. I had sold my German car and bought a more affordable Peykan, a locally made car from the burgeoning Iranian auto industry. The Khayami brothers built a modern car factory called Iran National which eventually became a model for South Korea at that time. Gisela and Mutti enjoyed living in Persia, especially the climate, so my family was happy. Minou, our beautiful daughter, was healthy, and everything seemed to be going well. I suggested moving to Isfahan, and they agreed wholeheartedly. Upon my return to Isfahan, I rented a house for us all.

Back at the office, things weren't going as smoothly as I had hoped. Despite doing everything correctly, I sensed trouble. The next day, I was summoned to see the governor, experiencing his enormous office for the first time, and being permitted to take a seat at his desk. I introduced myself, explaining I was from Tabriz

—something he had already guessed based on my name and accent —and that I had studied in Germany and was excited to bring my knowledge to bear on behalf of my country.

He asked me why I was opposed to erecting the proposed monuments for His Majesty's coronation, as he was receiving complaints. I noticed that none of my files were on his desk and wondered if perhaps he had been misinformed about me. He might also have assumed since I had only recently returned from overseas, I had no idea about the political situation in our country. This was my first encounter with a politician, but I told him succinctly that I was unaware of any errors and explained my point of view about the plan. He became impatient, so I suggested that we share my proposals with the Shah and ask for his approval.

Pressure from leftist newspapers and other opponents began to mount. Hassan completed and signed off his report regarding the riverfront properties and placed it on my desk. Despite warnings, I decided to move forward with the report. Shortly after, I received a phone call from someone with a strong Azari dialect, threatening me with death if I did not process Mr. K.'s file fairly. He added that he would gladly serve the jail time for his crime in order to get justice for his people. I calmly responded in Azari, that he had been misled with inaccurate information and that the claim was not valid, based on the survey work we had just completed. I showed no fear because the prayers of my parents have always protected me, and I have great faith in our Creator.

As I left the office that day, I was confronted by a tall, strong figure. To my surprise, he bent down and asked to kiss my hand, apologizing for his earlier threat after learning more about me. He admitted that he had been misled. At that time, the "Lutis" were akin to vigilantes who took the law into their own hands. Lutis were very religious and fanatical people who kept peace and order in their districts. There was no stealing, and no one was cheated. If a newcomer wanted to assert himself as a Luti, he had to deal with the senior one first! Sometimes there were bloody outcomes, so he gave me his name saying that if I had any problems, I should send him a picture and the address of the person and he would "send them back to me in a coffin!" As he walked away, I glanced back and saw all my co-workers prepared to assist me. It was a nice acknowledgement from those I had only known for a few weeks, and it encouraged me to persist with my beliefs and values.

Returning from Tehran, I was accompanied by Gisela. We drove through a barren but warm landscape, filled with hope and confidence. Looking back, we were young, healthy, and full of adventure, with no real problems. I kept my work worries to myself, trusting that everything would work out. Gisela's faith in me and our future was strong, giving me strength. Her trust in our common destiny was so strong and natural that it sometimes scared me. Things always panned out in the end, and I believe her pure heart and soul were the source of our strength. God was always gracious to me, perhaps because of that. When we arrived at our new home in Isfahan, it felt cold and empty, needing the warmth of our family. It was a large house with typical Persian architecture, and a sizeable garden with numerous old trees. Many rooms had stained glass windows, adding to the eerie atmosphere. The final straw was the kitchen which was overrun by cockroaches. Having left Minou and Mutti in our beautiful apartment in Tehran, with so much family nearby, we were quick to reevaluate this move to Isfahan. Gisela took my hand, and we hurried out the door to go dine in a local restaurant instead!

Gisela was excited to explore Isfahan for the first time. As we walked through the streets, I noticed many curious eyes on us, making me feel like a stranger in my own homeland. In Tabriz and Germany, we had lived somewhat isolated lives, but here in Isfahan, we were viewed as outsiders. This confusion among my own people would later cause significant difficulties.

Returning to the office, I found chaos awaiting me. A crowd had gathered, and it was clear that my helpful attitude had attracted attention. The old file carrier cautioned me saying that my opponents were growing in number. Illegal requests and recommendations from officials began piling up on my desk, conflicting with my principles. Realizing that our stay in Isfahan might not end well, I sought advice from the mayor. He offered little guidance and warned me to be careful with my decisions.

Driving through the countryside near Isfahan.

Greeting the Governor in Isfahan.

45

GOOD TIMING

Gisela and I had been in Isfahan for only a week, and despite the difficult connection with Tehran, we phoned home every evening. She couldn't bear the separation from our little daughter. So, on a sunny autumn afternoon, we decided to return to Tehran. The road was clear and almost empty, snaking through bright, barren mountains and valleys like a gliding serpent. Gisela asked me to stop for a moment to enjoy the fresh, clean scent of the desert.

As we resumed our journey, we suddenly noticed a fully loaded truck driving recklessly in the oncoming lane. Without warning, the front left wheel of the truck came off and rolled in an arc directly towards us. The truck tipped to the left on its front axle, slid across the warm asphalt right in front of our car, and crashed into an embankment. I swerved left into the oncoming lane, narrowly avoiding the rolling tire, which then landed harmlessly on the embankment. I applied the brakes, and thankfully, we came to a stop completely unharmed. The truck driver, appearing uninjured, got out and asked if we were all right. After ensuring everyone was fine, he dashed off to retrieve his lost tire, and we continued on our way. It was pure luck that

Gisela had asked to stop—those few minutes likely saved our lives.

As we approached Tehran from the south, passing through the holy city of Qom, the road wound through a pass, and suddenly, the capital city came into view. Emerging from the dry desert, we entered a lush, green oasis. The city was ablaze with lights, specially illuminated for the upcoming coronation celebration of the imperial couple. Streets were decorated with luminous wreaths in various colors and shapes, resembling Christmas in Germany. Thousands of fairy lights hung from street lamps and consoles, each street glowing in a different hue. We drove home through these freshly decorated streets, feeling a sense of joy and relief.

When we arrived home, the apartment was full of guests, including my mother, who had come from Tabriz, and my younger brother, who was doing his military service. Gisela had arranged a special room for him as a gesture of appreciation for taking such good care of the family during my absence. Minou was being spoiled by everyone, and Gisela's mother felt at home, especially since the dry climate in Tehran had improved her asthma. Life was good, and for the time being, I could forget about Isfahan and its problems.

Tehran's nights were long, and it seemed as though the city never slept. The streets buzzed with life, filled with new attractions —American fast-food chains, drive-in cinemas, large department stores, and luxurious hotels (for those days) like the Hilton and Sheraton. The city had transformed with new highways and a modernized appearance.

I often ventured to the south of the city, near the bazaar, to observe the common folk. Many seemed dissatisfied, exposed to foreign influences via radio and television that clashed with our culture. Almost every house had a television antenna on its roof, and as I wandered through the bazaar, stopping at traditional teahouses or shops, I overheard loud and clear discussions. I couldn't understand why those in power didn't recognize the significant culture shock and its consequences. Every country has its customs and traditions, which form its cultural identity. Persia was no exception; its traditions had been respected for millennia, and I had grown up with them. The flashy, foreign-influenced exterior of the capital did not reflect the true depth and beauty of the city and the country, which concerned me deeply.

WHEN I RETURNED TO ISFAHAN, a notable visit was scheduled from Khrushchev, the party leader, and President of the Soviet Union. He was to be received at Chehel Sotoun (Forty Columns) a beautiful pavilion built by Shah Abbas II of the Safavid dynasty. I had received an invitation to the event, and protocol required me to attend. I also had orders from the mayor's office to visit the plant and report back. At the event, I was greeted by the sight of a self-service buffet, where food and drinks were brought in for the guests but also discreetly taken away by others. Puzzled, I asked my driver what was happening, but he just laughed, thinking I was joking. He explained that the food was naturally taken home by directors, office heads, and big bosses, as was customary. When state dignitaries visited, they were served on the upper floor of the offices.

I was speechless at the spectacle—wine, beer, whiskey, caviar, southern fruits, and many other delicacies were on display, with tables set for about a hundred guests. When I returned to the mayor, I jokingly reassured him that everything was fine, just like in our office.

My thoughts drifted back to Tabriz. When farmers came to pay, they often brought large baskets of fresh fruit from their villages, but Father never took any of it home, leaving it for the needy. Instead, after a long day at work, he would buy fruit from the local vendor and carry the bags home himself.

Mother used to teach us about "Halal" and "Haram" in

Islam. Halal means everything permissible and good for humans and the environment—healthy food and consideration for others. Haram encompasses what people should avoid in order to achieve the goals of Halal. She believed that if people had adhered to the concept of Haram, such as refraining from consuming certain foods like fish without scales or pork, the world would be in a better state. Father's donation of the farmers' gifts was rooted in these beliefs; he worried that accepting such gifts might be Haram, as it could be seen as taking advantage of the farmers.

These principles of Halal and Haram guided me throughout my life, and as I grew older certain principles learned as a young man remained as great companions in my journey. As a result, I found it difficult to accept generous offerings from strangers. My friend Hassan felt the same way.

Isfahan was then the film capital of the country, with many feature films being shot there. Popular restaurants and hotels were frequented by actors, and we often joined them. One day after an evening at such a restaurant, we arrived at the office to find the file clerk warning us to be careful, as we were being watched closely. Shortly after, the human resources department requested a copy of Hassan's certificate, which he didn't have because of our professor in Germany failing him. I was fortunate to have passed, thanks to my lecturer, Mr. W. Now, we were in a bind. We could delay the certificate presentation for a few months, but the day was approaching. Hassan had completed all his studies and exams, and deserved his diploma, but a racist professor had unjustly denied him that right.

In the office, our work was constantly sabotaged - drawings disappeared, and documents were falsified. I felt helpless, as though we were being systematically intimidated. One day, while I was in Tehran, Gisela was on the phone with my mother. She passed the phone to me, and Mama asked how I was doing. I told her about our troubles in Isfahan. She advised me not to let anyone take away my rights and to stay independent, reminding me of my father's integrity. I promised her I would try.

Reassured, I called Hassan and told him I didn't want to stay in Isfahan. He left the final decision to me. When I returned to the office, I found a crowd of discontented, helpless people at the entrance, holding plastic bags full of files and papers. After sorting through my mail, I asked the elderly file clerk to let them in. We began processing the files, many of which concerned plots near designated biotopes or green areas from the German B-Plan, which wouldn't be developed for twenty years. Some plots crossed the boundary by only a few meters, and the owners were willing to donate the land, but they couldn't get building permits. I issued as many permits as possible according to the law, even photocopying documents for the owners so they could sell the land with the permit, even if they couldn't build on it immediately.

The file clerk was thrilled to see people finally getting what they needed. When I entrusted him with the files and money for photocopying, his eyes shone with joy. That evening, as we left the office, some people were still waiting to thank us.

The next day, Hassan and I were summoned to the Governor's office. He received us in his usual stern manner, berating us for our undisciplined attitude and ignorance. He gave us an ultimatum—one more misstep, and we'd be fired. As I stood there, my mother's words echoed in my mind. I responded by recounting our experiences—how people were tormented trying to obtain building permits, how we had been threatened, and how we were being prevented from doing the work we had been trained to do. I reminded him that we were here to serve our country, otherwise we would have stayed abroad.

The Governor was momentarily speechless, clearly not expecting such a response from a young man who could barely speak Persian properly. Perhaps because of my youth, my upbringing, or my time in Europe, I did not have much respect for him. I handed him our resignations, and his demeanor suddenly changed. He became friendly, summoned his secretary, and offered to issue appropriate certificates of dismissal, paying our salary until the end of the month. He even expressed regret at our decision to resign. I suspect that he was concerned that we would share our experiences in Isfahan with the authorities in Teheran.

Returning to the office, we were once again greeted warmly by the people at the entrance. But I couldn't take it anymore—I wanted nothing more to do with the situation. We packed our important documents and books, said our goodbyes to the employees and colleagues, and left. The file clerk embraced me, blessing me as I departed. His sad voice asked for God's blessings for me and for my parents who had raised me this way.

The house was eerily empty when we returned to pack our things, and the silence felt like a cemetery. The people who had been with us daily, attending to our every need, were gone. Word had spread quickly, and we had been abandoned just as swiftly.

Early the next morning, we left for Tehran under a bright blue sky. The sun was shining, as usual, and the weather was predictably pleasant—no need for a weather forecast here, unlike in Germany. If it did rain, which was rare, the sun would shine all the brighter afterward. We felt a mixture of relief and happiness. Despite the good experiences and the high-paying jobs we had, the cost of staying would have been too high. The nightmare of the last few weeks was finally over, and we could now look forward to a future where we didn't have to compromise our principles or integrity.

46

THE CORONATION

Mohammad Reza Pahlavi, Shah of Persia, was crowned on his 40th birthday after reigning for 26 years. For the first time in Persia's history, Farah Diba was also crowned as Shahbanu, or Empress, during the ceremony. We watched the entire event on television, but I found it personally strange. I had anticipated that the coronation would be a joyous occasion for all, a celebration that would resonate with the people. Instead, the ceremony felt oddly formal and disconnected. The Shah placing the crown on his own head and then on the Empress's head was particularly striking. The dissatisfaction among the people was palpable, echoing throughout the country.

The coronation, coupled with my recent experiences in Isfahan, left me deeply disillusioned. I had returned from Germany with high hopes of contributing to the development and modernization of our country. My father had done his part, ensuring that his sons were educated abroad, and now it was our turn to contribute. I initially thought that Isfahan's challenges might be an isolated case, a result of the inevitable mix of good and bad people found everywhere. However, the reality was more complex. The stark divide between rich and poor, the clash

242

between old traditions and modern ways, and the deficiencies in the school system were all contributing to significant conflicts that were felt nationwide.

A culture shock was brewing, and it needed to be addressed with care and patience. Unfortunately, the coronation only widened the gap between the regime and the people, missing a crucial opportunity to foster unity. As a young and inexperienced observer, I found it baffling that the country's politicians and rulers failed to recognize the widespread discontent. It was evident everywhere I went. Although the Shah's powers were limited by the constitution, which was democratic and modern, modeled after the Belgian Constitution and fought for over a century ago, the disconnect between the monarchy and the populace was alarming.

MY FRIEND HASSAN'S father owned a small civil engineering company with construction machinery like trucks, bulldozers, and excavators. Hassan explained that his father took on small jobs and occasionally rented out his equipment. This inspired us to start our own business together. It had long been my dream to run a well-structured construction company based on the German model, with satisfied and financially secure employees. Throughout my studies, I envisioned this company and aspired to make it a reality.

At home, everything was going well. Gisela's mother decided to return to Germany, but she knew she was welcome anytime, and we promised to visit her every year. My mother had grown very fond of her, loving her dearly, and the two mothers got along splendidly despite the language barrier. Gisela wasn't homesick; with so many siblings around, how could she be? She had endeared herself to everyone with her kindness. Throughout all these years, she never asked or inquired about what I was doing or how things would turn out, trusting completely in our shared journey.

47

BIRTH OF OUR SON, KAMBIZ

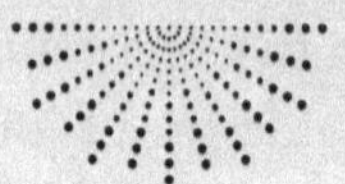

Gisela was now pregnant with our second child and suddenly developed a craving for German sausage, along with other foods she didn't usually eat. We had been hoping for a son and were confident that our wish would come true. While it couldn't be determined medically at the time, my mother, with her experience of giving birth to ten children, was certain it would be a boy based on Gisela's abdominal girth. I had no reason to doubt her intuition.

It was now Tir, the first month of summer in Persia. On June 28, 1968, while I was watching the movie *On the Run* with Richard Kimble, Gisela was calmly packing her suitcase for the hospital. A short time later, she told me it was time to go. She was so serene that I asked if we could wait until the movie was over, especially since my brother had borrowed the car. However, within minutes, my sister arrived and drove us to the hospital.

I brought along a gold coin, as it was customary to reward the nurse who brought the good news of the birth. Gisela was taken to the delivery room, and while I was still filling out the admittance forms, a nurse told me that Gisela had given birth to a beautiful baby boy. I joyfully gave her the gold coin, astonished that it had all happened within 15 minutes of our arrival. It was an easy birth, and sure enough, we had a son whom we named Kambiz, meaning "gifted" in Persian. Gisela had trusted that everything would go smoothly, and indeed, God had been with her.

The wonderful news quickly spread through the family, and when my mother heard the story, she gently scolded me, saying, "My son, you promised to take care of her just as you did for me. What would have happened if your sister hadn't arrived in time?"

A few days later, Gisela and Kambiz were discharged from the hospital, and we were given a photo of his first moments on Earth as a keepsake. We now had two children: a beautiful daughter and a splendid son. My sister and her maid had prepared everything for our arrival. The apartment was spotless, food was ready on the stove, and the refrigerator was fully stocked. I immediately sent a telegram to Mutti to let her know she was a grandmother once again. That evening, we had a big celebration at our place. My mother had come from Tabriz, but Father, as usual, stayed home.

While Gisela cared for our two babies, I was busy setting up the construction company with Hassan. There was much to do: my certificates had to be translated and evaluated, permits obtained, and the company name registered. We needed capital, so I asked Mother to speak to Father about it. It had always been this way—when we wanted something from Father, we would go through Mother first. A few days later, our brother-in-law (also Father's business partner), brought us a check and congratulated us on the establishment of our company, which we named "Iranlibelle."

Our office was conveniently located a short distance from our apartment, allowing me to return home every noon. Our daily routine was pleasant: I went to the office at 9 a.m., returned home for lunch at 1 p.m., rested until teatime at 4 p.m., and enjoyed Persian pastries, tea from the samovar, and fruit. I then went back to work from 5 p.m. to 8 p.m.

After my years in Germany, life in Tehran felt like a vacation. Stores stayed open until midnight, and the streets were bustling with people. Over the past decade, the country had undergone a dramatic transformation, with new factories opening every day. Iran was producing and even exporting household appliances, air conditioners, cars, and electronic devices. Elephant Shoes was a successful product, gaining international fame. New industrial developments included a steel plant in Isfahan and refineries in Tabriz, Tehran, and Kermanshah. I found it all exhilarating and was proud to be part of the progress in my homeland.

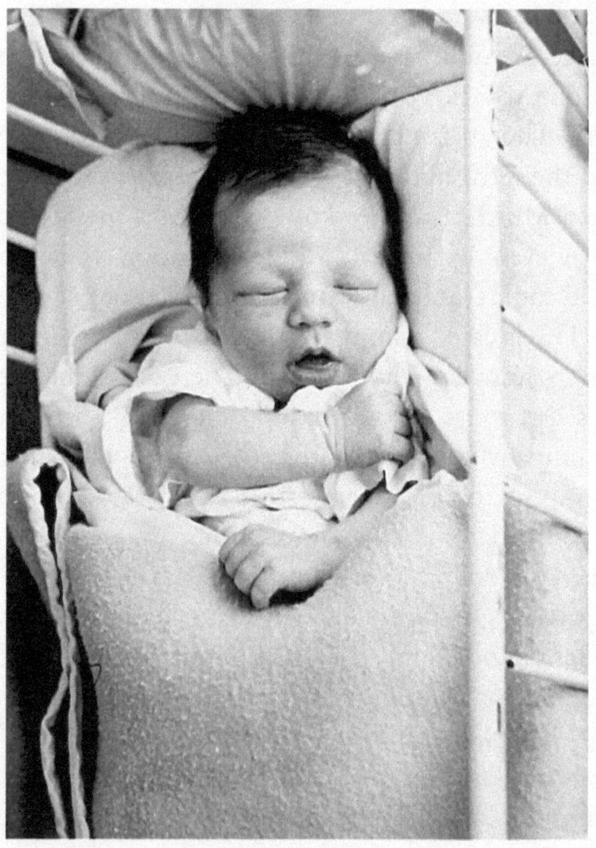

Our beautiful baby boy, Kambiz, was born on June 28, 1968, in Tehran. Minou was excited to have a brother now!

Four generations of resilient women sitting at Mutti's place.
Starting from left: Gisela holding Minou, Mutti, great grandma
Elise with Kambiz on her lap.

48

CITY OF ARAK - OUR FIRST ORDER

It took some time before we received our first order, which was a public tender for road construction in the city of Arak. Situated in the Markazi province in central Iran, Arak is known for its mountainous, barren, and remote terrain. The area often suffers from low-quality water supplies, which has historically kept it from being a major target for Persian conquerors. As a result, the Aryan population in this region has remained especially pure, with many of the locals having light skin, blue eyes, and blond hair. The city is about 250 kilometers from Tehran, with a well-built road passing through the Holy City of Qom.

The construction site itself was an unparalleled adventure. We had to position an asphalt machine with its accessories and a large tank holding about 30,000 liters of tar and bitumen close to the city. We also transported and set up a quarry machine to crush rock from the nearby mountains, which we used as gravel. Additional materials were sourced from Germany. We had to produce everything ourselves, from concrete to asphalt, which required the appropriate machinery and specialists. This was a great opportunity to learn from the local workers—mostly technicians who, despite having limited formal education, were highly skilled in their trades. While many of the machines were rented, we purchased the asphalt machine, making it our first major investment. It was a large mixer that sorted broken stones and mixed them with hot bitumen to produce asphalt. Although locally manufactured, it consumed almost all of our capital. We also needed rollers, trucks, tanks for water and fuel, and many other items.

Except for weekends, I commuted daily to Arak—a journey of approximately 280 kilometers. This meant many hours spent in the car each day. I would leave at 5 a.m. while Tehran was still asleep. If I left later, the journey would have taken much longer due to traffic. I enjoyed listening to the morning program on the radio during the drive, which began with prayers in Persian that touched my soul. I arrived at the construction site each day with great joy and confidence. My partner, who excelled at surveying despite having failed the subject in university, handled the surveying work. He also managed the office and was responsible for securing new orders.

Once the construction site was organized, I tried to implement the work practices I had learned in Germany—regular working hours, fair wages, safety gear, and clean, hygienic accommodations. Of course, it was challenging to achieve all these goals for about 80 workers, especially since safety gear was expensive, but I made the effort.

Road construction can be hazardous. The asphalt machine itself posed significant risks, as it involved constantly pouring boiling tar into large truck-sized tanks. If hot tar touches the skin, it burns down to the bone and cannot be cooled with water or any other means. Without electronic or automatic instruments, the hot tar had to be manually ladled from the tank using buckets. Apart from a few mechanics and professionals, most of our workforce consisted of farmers who took on side jobs until the harvest season.

We established a camp to provide food and hygiene facilities for the workers, and with perseverance and God's help, everything was arranged. It took about a month before the first truckload of asphalt made its way toward the city. I will never forget that day. I arrived in the city around 8 a.m. and saw steam and dust rising in the distance—it was our asphalt machine in action. My joy was immense. I prayed from my heart, thanking God that we had come this far.

Some days, I stayed longer at the construction site, trying to teach the younger workers a few things. They showed a strong interest in learning, and I told them that if they paid attention, they could become full-time employees. I also offered to send some of them to night school to learn to read and write. They often shared stories with me about their families and their worries. On some evenings, I returned home very late—exhausted, but happy.

Fortunately, everything was going well, and we hadn't had any accidents so far. I made it a point to introduce myself to the city administration, and word quickly spread that the contractor from Tehran treated his workers well and did quality work. In our country, such things do not go unnoticed.

CORRUPT OFFICIALS

My disenchantment only deepened in Arak, even more than it had in Isfahan. Several city councilors had expressed their displeasure over my delay in formally introducing myself, something I couldn't quite comprehend. Why was it necessary for me to personally present myself to these council members? I was asked if I had reported to a member of the city council or to the farmandar, the governor's representative in Arak, but I didn't even know who the farmandar was. When I asked for his address, the room erupted in laughter—it seemed everyone but me knew him. Confused and feeling out of place, I left the building, realizing no one had prepared me for navigating the maze of bureaucracy.

Our accountant led me to an old building, where a crowd of people stood in a shady courtyard, clutching their files—an all-too-familiar scene reminiscent of Isfahan. After reporting to the secretary, I waited an hour before being allowed into the farmandar's office. Inside, I found a slim, well-dressed gentleman seated behind a large desk. I greeted him politely and extended my hand, but he ignored me, pulling open a desk drawer and continuing to write without even acknowledging my presence.

Unsure of what to do, I stood there awkwardly until, after some time, he finally dismissed me. I left his office drenched in sweat, feeling humiliated.

When I met our accountant outside, he looked embarrassed. "I've already fetched the necessary money," he told me.

Puzzled, I asked, "For what?"

He explained that without the farmandar's permit, nothing could proceed, and I realized the envelope in his hand contained a bribe. Speechless and deflated, I felt a profound sadness.

Reluctantly, I followed his instructions. We went back inside, and I told the secretary, "Tell your boss I'm back."

This time, I had no respect for the man but knew I had no choice. The farmandar let me in immediately, and I placed the envelope on his desk before he could open his drawer again. He picked it up, threw it into the drawer, and asked my name without ever looking at me. After answering, I rushed out of his office, my disillusionment with my countrymen growing.

That evening, as I drove home, my sense of trust in my homeland was shattered. Things worsened when my partner revealed how many other officials would also demand money. He explained that his father's experience had taught him that nearly all government officials were corrupt, and we needed to factor bribery into our budget. Though I couldn't understand or accept it, I had no choice but to go along. Not everyone was corrupt, of course—I met a few honest government workers over the years—but I was now caught in the system and couldn't simply stop.

We continued bidding for public works advertised in state newspapers, submitting quotes to win contracts. The process was always complicated - finding the right documents, identifying the correct officials, and determining who to bribe. My partner's uncle, an experienced contractor, handled these tasks, while I tried to distance myself from the corruption, though I couldn't avoid being involved.

We eventually submitted our first invoice for the road work, as much of the construction had been completed. Our financial situation was tight—we had loans to pay, not only to banks but also to wealthy merchants who, despite being devout Muslims, charged us 30% interest.

About a week later, I went to the town hall to follow up, as we desperately needed funds. Mr. R. greeted me cautiously and asked, "How much have you brought?" When I asked him directly what he meant, he responded, "For our cooperation."

At that point, I realized I had no option but to comply. After hours of negotiation, we agreed on a fixed amount for the councilors' share of the profit. Only then was I able to collect the checks from the accounting department. It was a Thursday, and the banks would soon close for the weekend. The clerk, moving painfully slowly, spilled tea on one of the checks, forcing him to void it and start over. Frustrated, I pleaded with him to finish quickly, as my workers were waiting for their wages. Finally, we cashed the checks, paid the workers, and gave the councilors their cut. I went home feeling somewhat satisfied, though the whole process left a bitter taste.

Our company bank account was held at a branch of the National Bank, conveniently located across the street from our office. The bank director, a kind and pleasant man, often invited me for tea. As our company grew and financial demands increased, we applied for a loan, which was approved after the bank reviewed our information. However, our business was still young, and the pressure on our finances continued, leading to more frequent visits to the bank.

One day, the director introduced me to Dr. Shafii, a former minister who had served as the Telecommunications Minister during the administration of Prime Minister Ali Mansour. Dr. Shafii, a cultured and well-educated man who spoke several languages, had resigned after Mansour's assassination in 1965, when Amir Abbas Hoveyda became Prime Minister. Dr. Shafii and I quickly developed a friendship, and I was captivated by his knowledge of politics and culture. In time, he became our business partner and advisor, using his connections to help our fledgling company. Though Hassan was cautious and preferred a slow, steady growth for the business, I had grander ambitions. I wanted to expand quickly, help others as my parents had done, and be socially useful. To do that, I knew we had to become strong and independent.

Despite a few challenges, the Arak project progressed well. Sometimes I took Gisela with me, as we wanted to explore the country and find a place for our future home. We visited nearby villages, caravanserais, and ruins, meeting locals along the way and gaining a deeper connection to the land and its history.

50

CITY OF MAHALLAT AND AMLASH
ON THE CASPIAN SEA

We soon received several new orders, one of which involved constructing the city hall in the city of Mahallat, the birthplace of Karim Aga Khan, the leader of the Ismaili sect. My partner took charge of that project, while I oversaw another assignment in the village of Amlash, located in the Gilan province near the Caspian Sea. It was a refreshing change to see the stunning landscape surrounding this vast lake.

The Caspian Sea, the largest lake in the world, spans an area of about 371,000 square kilometers. It stretches approximately 1,200 kilometers in length, 400 kilometers in width, and has a depth of 1,000 meters. This immense body of water, which is larger in area than Germany, is called a sea despite being enclosed and not connected to the world's oceans. The Persian side of the Caspian is lush and verdant, teeming with plant life. Along its coastline are hundreds of picturesque cities and towns with white sandy beaches —something I would never have imagined existed in our country.

The fertile land along the Caspian is separated from the mainland by the Alborz mountain range, which boasts dense, green forests reminiscent of Switzerland. The region is dotted with massive rice fields, magnificent tea plantations, and orchards full of orange trees—a visual feast for any visitor. Even Germany's artificial forests, which I admired greatly, seemed like small parks compared to this expansive, breathtaking landscape.

HAVING COMPLETED several contracts over the past few months, I quickly set up the site in Amlash, and everything ran smoothly. I even felt comfortable working with the mayor at the small, cozy town hall. The mayor was a pleasant man, and I assured him that everyone would be paid their due once I cleared a profit. At home, our parents had raised us to be honest, with lying and deception being foreign concepts. But the society I now lived and worked in had taught me otherwise. My parents would never believe the changes I had undergone.

During my time in Amlash, I was fortunate to have a reliable driver named Abbas. He was about forty years old, slim, serious, and not very talkative. He came highly recommended by an acquaintance as trustworthy and dependable. Abbas quickly earned my trust, and we became friends. His knowledge of the local dialect and language proved invaluable, as I was still far more familiar with Germany—my adopted homeland—than with my own fatherland, despite having been back in the country for three years. Life in Tabriz felt like a distant memory, a lost paradise, and I often felt like a stranger in my own country.

Abbas opened my eyes to a different side of Persia. He introduced me to the forgotten people—those living in poverty, struggling to adapt to the rapid development in the country. Workers who used to enjoy simple lunches of bread, cheese, and grapes at the local markets or small shops were now forced to navigate modern department stores. These people, unfamiliar with the new shopping environment, were often ridiculed by the nouveau riche and the heartless. While Dr. Shafii had introduced me to the upper class, Abbas showed me the true face of our society, one marked by inequality and hardship.

257

51

OUR NEW HOME

As the children grew, so did our social obligations, and our apartment had become too small. We decided to buy a house in Vanak, located in the northern part of Tehran. It was a beautiful two-story home with a marble facade—bright and spacious, a world apart from our small apartment in Mettmann, where we had spent some of the best years of our lives. I acquired the house with the help of my acquaintance, Dr. Shafii, on very favorable terms. I must admit, the generosity of some Persians knows no bounds.

Dr. Shafii had shared my life story with his friend, a builder, who sent us the key to view the house. We were told that if we liked it, it would be ours, and we could pay the bill whenever we were able. Although we could have declined this offer if the house wasn't suitable, doing so would have been considered an insult to the builder's generosity.

The house had a large living area on the first floor, complete with a beautiful atrium. The upper floor consisted of several bedrooms and bathrooms, and there was modern accommodation for the staff. A spacious terrace overlooked a meticulously landscaped garden, which featured a water basin and fountain. While the house was well-equipped, there was one major drawback—we had no direct water supply. The surrounding area was still being developed, so for a while, we had to rely on water from a reservoir located beneath the garden.

When my mother visited our new home for the first time, she was overjoyed. To her, it was a sign of divine intervention, proof of her faith, righteousness, and Gisela's pure heart, that I had become so successful so quickly with God's help. She had no understanding of the corruption and injustice that plagued our country, and I didn't enlighten her. I preferred to see her laughing and happy in her own idealized world.

Gisela was happy too. She decorated the house beautifully, despite our limited furniture, blending modern European style with traditional Persian elements she had learned from our old house in Tabriz. Our visitors marveled at her impeccable taste.

Our driver, Abbas, became part of the family, moving into the house and only returning to his own family on weekends. He was a kind and caring individual of slight build with a wide, friendly smile that showed some gold teeth. On evenings when we went out, he watched over both the children and the house, always making sure that everything was in order. We were so lucky to find such a decent, trustworthy friend.

Shortly after we moved in, Gisela met Krista, a young German woman married to a Persian chemist. The two crossed paths at a hair salon in Tehran, where Gisela was reading a German magazine while Minou, dressed in a traditional Bavarian Dirndl, hopped around playfully. Krista noticed Minou and, intrigued, started a conversation with Gisela. This led to an invitation for Kaffee & Kuchen at Krista's home. As it turned out, Krista was also from Düsseldorf, and it wasn't long before she and her husband, Behzad, became our closest friends. We spent nearly every weekend together, the bond growing naturally from shared roots and mutual affection.

Gisela, my dear friend Behzad with his wife Krista, and myself
at an event in Tehran.

52

OUR SOCIETY

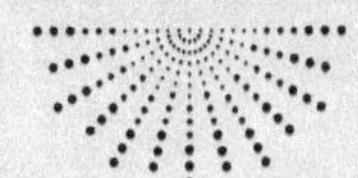

Through Dr. Shafii, I gradually became acquainted with the upper echelon of society, from businessmen, bankers, manufacturers, and entrepreneurs to ministers, high-ranking officials, and even princes and princesses. I also met people of remarkable character who had accomplished great things through diligence, perseverance, and patience. Many had started as mechanics and had risen to become factory owners. However, there were others, born into wealth, who had never worked a day in their lives. They spent their days in foreign countries, indulging in affluence, yet were perpetually bored and never satisfied.

One of our acquaintances was an elderly Jewish antique dealer who specialized in collectible jewelry, antique books, and artifacts, selling them through his store in France. Many of his items fetched millions at auction houses. He had done very well for himself and was incredibly generous with his fortune. So generous, in fact, that he paid for my airfare and accommodation at the Hilton Hotel in Paris. There, I met around fifty other people who were also his guests. One evening, during our week-long stay, we arrived at a cabaret only to find it entirely empty—he had reserved the entire venue for us to enjoy a private dinner and show. It was an extraordinary experience! Before we left for home, he invited us to his store on the famous Champs-Élysées, where he lavished us with gifts for our wives. He was a remarkably generous man.

Many others, too, had become overnight millionaires by buying and selling property and land. The nouveau riche, with their sudden wealth, threw money around as if they had no idea what to do with it. They drove expensive cars, flew to Europe on extravagant shopping sprees, and generally cared little for anyone else—it was atrocious.

MEANWHILE, Hassan had completed his project, and the contract in Arak was finished. Our work in the north was progressing well. I often traveled there alone while Abbas stayed behind to watch over the house. I lived in an apartment at a charming motel in the village, perched on the edge of a forest and surrounded by orchards and rice plantations. In the early mornings, as I stepped out of my room to go to work, the smell of orange blossoms and damp earth filled the air, making me feel at home. I thought to myself, this must be one of the most beautiful places on Earth.

There are many aesthetically pleasing places in the world— deserts, forests, mountains, steppes, beaches, and valleys, but Persia offers a remarkable combination of all these elements, creating landscapes that are breathtakingly beautiful. The country is so diverse that one can swim and ski in the same season, hunt in dense forests, or draw water from an oasis in the desert.

IT TOOK TIME, but I eventually came to understand the language and desires of the local officials. Sometimes, I would simply leave bribe money on the table for them to divide among themselves.

Despite that unpleasant reality, I always strove to do my work properly and professionally.

Working on the construction site allowed me to explore the region. From the extreme west at the Port of Astara to the eastern border with Turkmenistan, there were nearly 1,000 kilometers of long, white sandy beaches. Dense forests lined the well-developed roads, leading high up into the mountains. I drove along the beach road through many beautiful towns, where modern hotels and the palatial homes of the wealthy were built in perfect harmony with the natural landscape. The highlight of my journey was Ramsar.

This stunning city, blending European culture and architecture with avenues of palm trees, was impeccably maintained and clean. Ramsar was also home to the famous Hotel Ramsar & Casino, complete with its own private beach. The hotel and casino, built during the reign of Reza Shah in the early 20th century, reminded me of the grandeur of the casino in Baden-Baden, Germany. The artistic stucco work—an ancient Persian architectural tradition—was masterfully combined with glass and mirrors, decorating the vast walls and ceilings of the hotel. It had long been one of the most popular cities for tourists.

53
DREAMS

On February 2, 1971, the Ramsar Convention—one of the oldest international treaties on environmental protection—was adopted. Many of our friends had splendid villas with extensive gardens, full of palm trees and orange orchards. During the summer, when time permitted, I took Gisela and our two children with me to visit Ramsar. We had become well-acquainted with the northern part of the country, and between Krista and Behzad, and several other German-Persian families, we had built a wonderful circle of friends. We often gathered and shared many happy moments together.

Abbas had become more than just my driver; he was part of our family. He not only drove us but also handled the shopping and tended to the garden. When needed, he would also help my siblings, which kept him constantly on the move.

Our company's administration director was a retired major who, like many others, still needed to work. He took a particular liking to me, and over time, we developed a close friendship. He, along with Abbas, remains fondly in my memory.

One day, Dr. Shafii approached me with a proposal to participate in a tender for the city of Tehran. The contract was for the renovation and renewal of sections of the old city. Hassan was against the idea, believing our small company could not handle such a large project. Despite his reservations, we began discussions with the authorities and were praised from all sides. Dr. Shafii established connections with foreign banks, while I reached out to German companies, including Beton und Monier Bau AG, where I had interned. After arranging meetings, we flew to Germany - where I would also be able to see my brothers again!

When we sat down with the director of Beton und Monier and his team, he immediately recognized me. He was visibly pleased to see that one of his former apprentices, at the young age of 26, was now managing his own construction company. After the successful meeting, he took me to the office where I had worked years earlier. Not much had changed, and most of the technicians and engineers were still there, standing behind their drawing boards. They greeted me with wide eyes as I thanked each of them for their guidance and support during my early years.

After a brief visit with my brothers, we flew to Paris for more meetings. We stayed at the Hotel Napoleon—not the finest, but centrally located and close to the banks. Our meeting at the Bank de France was well-organized and took place in a large conference room. Dr. Shafii introduced me as the owner of my company, and though some found it hard to believe they were negotiating with someone so young, we had another successful meeting. We achieved almost all our goals with the construction companies and investors, securing reasonable terms.

Upon our return to Tehran, we had numerous discussions with the authorities, armed with documentation from our overseas trip. Despite the high-level talks and favorable terms of our offer, something—or someone—blocked our progress. After weeks of time and money spent, our proposal was rejected in the end.

〜

THE PACE of development in the country had become frantic. The desire for a modern and comfortable life grew, and many began to adopt Western living and dining habits as models. The old Persian culture I had known growing up in Tabriz gradually faded away. Beautiful, cozy houses with lush gardens and old trees were replaced by residential blocks with small apartments, which had little in common with our traditional lifestyle. In the past, generations lived under one roof, sharing in both joy and sorrow. The old and young alike were involved in the struggles of life. In these new, modern apartments, such a way of living was no longer possible. Families began to grow distant, and a sense of alienation took hold.

While the wealthy built ever-larger villas and palaces, these displays of opulence became a source of envy and resentment among ordinary citizens. The growing divide between rich and poor fueled feelings of hatred. Drive-in cinemas, car washes for flashy street cruisers, American fast-food chains, cabarets, and dance halls began to spring up everywhere. The country was industrializing, but perhaps too quickly.

Steel mills, machinery construction, car factories, and petrochemical plants were established at a rapid pace. Products like Elephant Shoes were being exported across the globe. Locally made furniture adorned many oriental homes, and factories were churning out household appliances and televisions. It seemed a new, modern factory opened every day.

All of this was driven by private investors and businessmen, as the state failed to pave the way for industrialization through proper legislation and socially just regulation. An industrial revolution had begun.

In Europe, the industrial revolution had been accompanied by laws protecting workers' rights, such as limits on working hours, minimum wages, health and accident insurance, vacation time, and retirement benefits. In our country, however, it was left to the discretion of investors and factory owners. They ran their operations as they saw fit, often disregarding the rights of their employees. This led to growing discontent among the working class. As the economic boom created a demand for labor, many peasants left their villages and moved to the cities for work. High rent and living costs forced many to live in temporary housing on the outskirts of the cities. As a result, uncontrolled satellite towns sprang up outside major urban centers, often without even proper names.

My friend Behzad, like me, was an immigrant from Baku. His parents had emigrated to Germany years ago before returning to Persia, where his father established one of the country's first paint factories. After his parents passed away, Behzad and his brothers took over the business, gradually modernizing it. Their factory was well-organized and equipped with safety measures, offering regular working hours, free meals in the company canteen, and transportation for the workers. It was one of the few socially just and humane companies in the country at that time, and the workers were satisfied. I had great respect for Behzad, and we became close friends.

When I traveled to Amlash to finalize a contract and settle our services, I learned that a new governor had been appointed for Gilan province. To my astonishment, it was the former farmandar of Arak—the same man who had received several thousand from me. He had been well rewarded for his corrupt nature and promoted. My disillusionment with the corruption in my homeland grew deeper, and I returned to Arak to clear the site.

54

A NEAR TRAGEDY

On the way from Arak to Tehran, I spotted a bus parked on the side of the road. There were no other vehicles in sight on that endless stretch of black desert road, but I slowed down instinctively. Just as I neared the bus, a little girl suddenly darted across the road. I swerved to the left toward the embankment to avoid hitting her, but the right fender of my car still struck her. The girl, with blonde hair and about the same age as my daughter, was thrown through the air. My entire body shook as the horrifying scene unfolded. In a split second, memories of the well construction accident in Tabriz, when the workers were buried alive, flashed through my mind. I shifted into reverse and drove out of the embankment with a jolt.

A crowd had already gathered around the girl, and her mother was wailing in anguish. Some invisible force seemed to guide me through the people. Thankfully, there was no blood, and the child appeared unharmed, at least on the surface. I gently pushed the distraught mother into the back seat of my car, then carefully lifted the child into her arms. Without wasting another moment, I sped off toward the nearest hospital. The mother cried uncontrollably, while the child sobbed from the pain. Tears streamed down my face as well.

As the sun set, marking the usual time for prayers, I silently prayed to God for help, begging Him not to let any serious harm come to the little girl. A few moments later, my prayers were answered. The girl spoke up, saying she was hungry. Her mother screamed with joy, her tears turning into cries of relief.

We reached the hospital twenty minutes later. I rushed inside, carrying the child, and promised the doctor a substantial reward if she was well taken care of. Naturally, I covered all the expenses. The initial examination revealed only some bruises on her arm, but she was admitted for further observation. I went back to the entrance to bring in her mother, who had not been allowed in earlier, and took her to her daughter's side. By the time everything was settled, it was midnight. Exhausted and emotionally drained, I resumed my journey, driving through the darkness toward Tehran.

CITY OF HAMADAN

$\mathcal{I}$n the following months, we secured contracts in Malayer, a city near the border with Iraq, as well as in Tuyserkan, located in the same province. The landscape was particularly charming, with pristine, picturesque views, warm days, and cold nights. The climate was perfect for growing poppies, which were cultivated under state supervision for medicinal purposes.

Our third project was in Hamadan, a city west of Malayer and about 300 kilometers from Tehran. Once known as Ecbatana in its heyday, about 2,500 years ago, Hamadan had been destroyed and rebuilt several times since its founding around 750 BC. It later became the summer residence of Cyrus the Great, the Persian king. The city was rich in historical sights, dotted with fully irrigated fruit orchards. It was also said to be the place from which the Magi set out for Bethlehem. I was eager to explore this part of my homeland and get to know its people.

I settled into the 5-star Bu-Ali Hotel, named after Abu Ali bin Sina, better known in the West as Avicenna. He was a renowned Persian physician, philosopher, physicist, jurist, mathematician, astronomer, and alchemist of the 10th century. Our project involved building roads and renovating the tomb monument of Avicenna himself.

When I studied in Germany, most students hadn't even heard of him, and some assumed he was Arab. In fact, Avicenna was Persian and never left the country. He had written his books in Arabic because, during the rule of the Arab caliphs, it was forbidden to write or speak in Persian.

It was an honor for me to work on something related to Ibn Sina. In my free time, I delved deeper into his works and philosophy. Among his many writings, his most famous work is *Al-Shifa*, or *The Book of Healing*. Avicenna also founded the first hospital in Isfahan, which was comparable to modern hospitals today. His books were later translated into Latin by Spanish Muslims and distributed throughout European universities. During the tolerant period of Al-Andalus under Abd al-Rahman III, many Arabic texts were translated into Latin, transmitting knowledge and new scientific discoveries from the Orient to Europe. Avicenna's works, such as *The Book of Healing* and *The Canon of Medicine*, became some of the most sought-after translations at that time.

I often took Gisela and the children to visit the construction sites. Whenever possible, we would explore the countryside, getting to know the area and its people. I drove about 300 kilometers each day from one site to another without ever feeling fatigued. Krista and Behzad often accompanied us, and together, we enjoyed visiting historical buildings, Jewish shrines, and tombs.

For nearly four years, I had worked tirelessly, driven by the hope of achieving my dreams. Yet, in that short time, I had also faced many disappointments and injustices. I had only been able to visit Tabriz a few times. My father, always proud of me, never complained. On the contrary, he gave me encouragement and hope, always eager to hear about my work.

Meanwhile, my eldest brother had returned from Germany with his wife and three children and settled in Tehran. He opened his medical practice, which I helped furnish in a modern style. Our youngest sister was studying biology at Tehran University, leaving our parents alone in Tabriz. To fill the void, my mother adopted two young boys from our maid and took responsibility for their education.

My younger brother, who had just completed his military service, had also experienced his share of injustice. I recall the time when he clashed with his superior officer, leading to his transfer to Torbat, a remote town on the Afghan border. There, in a large garrison, he endured the strict and inhumane treatment of his superior, which soon made him ill. We had to intervene.

My mother was deeply concerned. My younger brother-in-law arranged for me to meet a high-ranking general who could take up our cause, and Dr. Shafii secured a letter from the Ministry of Defense. Armed with both, I set out to meet the general.

Entering the Ministry of Defense, I felt a strange unease as the gates closed behind me. After some waiting, I was led into a large room filled with tables and seating areas. Unsure of where to go, I stood there until a tall, elderly gentleman called me over. His friendly face put me at ease as he asked for my name in a calm voice. I introduced myself and handed him the letter of recommendation.

After a brief pause, he asked why my brother should be exempt from service like other soldiers. I explained that my mother had raised six sons, but now she and my father were alone in Tabriz. I also mentioned that my father had sent us abroad for the best education so that we could return to serve our country, which I was doing. The general listened attentively, and when I finished, he directed his secretary to give me a letter.

Standing up, he shook my hand and said, "Go and take your brother back to his mother, and greet her for me. I, too, have a mother like yours, and remember, I'm doing this because of her."

Overjoyed, I returned home and immediately called my mother, assuring her that everything would be fine. I promised her that I would personally fly to Torbat to bring my brother back.

56

ADVENTURE ON THE BORDER OF AFGHANISTAN

I flew to Mashhad, where I would continue my journey by bus to Torbat. After arriving, I immediately visited the shrine of Imam Reza—my second time. Pushing through the crowds to the tomb, I made my way directly to the shrine, clutching the massive silver grate and asking God for His help.

The following morning, I took a cab to the bus terminal outside the city. Numerous modern buses offered service to various cities, but for Torbat, I noticed a dilapidated old bus, reminiscent of those in Indian films. Among the travelers were people carrying live chickens, mattresses, cooking pots, and even a small lamb! In contrast, I stood there in a suit, tie, and leather shoes, with only a briefcase and a light raincoat.

After a long wait, the bus finally filled up, and we departed at noon for the five-hour journey to Torbat. The road was mountainous, winding, and poorly constructed, with treacherous passes. Whenever the road narrowed, we all prayed together. As we climbed higher, snow began to fall, and by the time we arrived just before sunset, there was half a meter of snow on the ground.

The bus stopped in front of a rundown garage. I disembarked and walked to an old shack that served as an office. Inside, an elderly man sat alone next to an oil stove. I greeted him and asked for a cab. He stared at me, wide-eyed, and said, "There are no cabs here!"

I told him I needed to get to the barracks. He stepped outside, pointed into the distance, and said, "There, where the faint lights are." He then showed me a footpath. Not a soul was in sight, and with no other option, I set off on foot toward the distant lights. My light patent leather shoes quickly became soaked and cold, as did my suit.

As I trudged up the wet slope, I could hear dogs howling in the distance, but it didn't worry me. I reassured myself that my heavy briefcase would serve as a weapon if needed. After about forty minutes, I reached the perimeter wall of the barracks. Suddenly, a loud voice commanded me to stop, and I complied.

A soldier on the other side of the wall shouted, "Who goes there?"

"I'm from Tehran," I replied, "and I have an important message for your commander."

"Stand against the wall," he said, "and don't be afraid if you hear wolves howling. I'm right behind you, and I'm armed. Help is on the way." He then blew his whistle several times to summon his comrades.

While we waited, the soldier expressed his concern about me traveling alone, saying that the locals would never do such a thing, as the area was crawling with wolves. Every night, packs of them roamed, attacking stables and livestock. The soldiers had to go out frequently to protect people and their cattle. Hearing this, my legs nearly gave out from under me. Thankfully, a military police jeep soon arrived to drive me to the barracks.

A large steel gate opened, and we entered a vast complex, driving for several minutes along well-maintained roads until we reached the base headquarters. Inside, I introduced myself to the officer on duty, explaining that I had come from Tehran to see the commander.

After a brief wait, the commander appeared—a man my brother often referred to as a nightmare. He greeted me with a formal military manner, one I had seen from some of my professors in Germany. Sitting down, he asked what I could possibly want at such a late hour. I told him plainly, "I've come to get my brother."

He chuckled at first, but his demeanor changed when I placed the letter from the high general on his desk. Upon recognizing the sender, he stood up immediately, adopting a rigid military posture. After reading the letter, he ordered an officer to retrieve my brother.

I quickly interrupted, insisting that I wanted to surprise my brother and retrieve him myself. The commander hesitated, but I met his gaze firmly, fueled by the memory of my brother's description of him as an authoritarian. At that moment, all the stress and exhaustion from the past two days came to a head, and I snapped. My fury startled him, and he finally understood my frustration. Although he didn't respond directly, his ashen face gave him away, and he ordered the military police to take me to my brother.

I followed the police officer into one of the barracks, where everyone appeared to be sleeping. He called out loudly for my brother in the dark, smelly room. When I saw him, I rushed over, and his cry of joy at seeing me is something I will never forget. We embraced warmly, as my mother's wish and my prayers had finally been fulfilled. After packing up his belongings, the military police drove us overnight to Mashhad.

Early the next morning, just before sunrise, we found ourselves at the shrine of Imam Reza, offering thanks to God for His help and mercy. The good Lord had once again watched over us.

Back in Tehran, my brother found a job as a medic at a military hospital, and after completing his service, he went on to study civil engineering at the same university where I had studied.

57

SNOW IN AUTUMN

When I arrived back in Hamadan, I was met with an unexpected situation. The hotel manager informed me that I needed to vacate my room, as the Shah was scheduled to visit the city. In preparation for his stay, the entire hotel was undergoing renovations, including the installation of new bathrooms, and had to be completely empty during His Majesty's visit. I was told I could return once he had left. With no other choice, I complied and moved to a different hotel.

When I moved back in, I was appalled by the shoddy and tasteless renovations done in preparation for the Shah's visit. It was clearly a waste of time and money, and I was sure the monarch remained completely unaware of these so-called "upgrades."

WE HAD SET up camp with all our heavy construction equipment outside the city of Hamadan, at a desolate caravanserai—once a resting place in the Middle Ages for caravans. These square, two-story buildings with large courtyards had also served as fortresses. At night, gates would be closed, offering travelers safe accommodation, along with fresh water and food if needed.

Sometimes I spent the night there. In the evenings, as the workers returned to camp after washing their clothes and eating supper, I would sit in my room, gazing at the old walls still stained with soot from long-extinguished fires. In the middle of the courtyard, where merchants and travelers once fed their animals, now stood our massive asphalt machine, alongside several tar and oil tanks. The surrounding rooms, mostly decayed, were used to house our crew.

I often sat with my cousin Nader, who accompanied me everywhere. A skilled mechanic, Nader had some construction equipment for rent and, more importantly, was both my friend and confidant. We spoke about everything. He often questioned my goals, asking why I was chasing dreams in the desert. I tried to explain my vision to him, telling him this desert was our home, and it was our duty to build for the future. Nader, being a patriot and a pioneer, was undoubtedly testing me.

It was early autumn, and we were near the end of our contract, with only three or four days of work remaining. One morning, when I woke up, I couldn't believe my eyes—half a meter of snow had fallen overnight. Though rare, it was said to happen once every decade when a cold wind blows at the beginning of September, signaling the sudden onset of winter.

I dressed quickly and went to our camp, where Nader had already arrived, having gotten up earlier. The entire site, including all the construction equipment, lay under a thick blanket of snow, like a colossal white giant. We went into our room to discuss how to proceed. In the meantime, the workers gathered outside our door, making the room dark with their presence. They were agitated, nervous—much like a herd of thirsty horses catching the scent of water. The situation grew serious, as the workers wanted to be paid immediately and return to their families before dark.

Neither Nader nor I knew what to do. Paying wages for almost

200 people was a huge burden, especially since we were still waiting on payment from our client. Though unprepared, we understood the workers' anxiety. The crowd outside grew louder, pushing toward the door. Nader scolded them loudly, reminding them that after all this time working with me, they should know I would take care of them. He suggested we go to the mayor's office to sort things out.

The workers calmed down, and with our accountant leading the way, we walked towards town. As we made our way to city hall, I wondered to myself why everything seemed to be going horribly wrong. Locals watched with wide eyes, not understanding what was happening, and some even joined our procession.

Once at the city hall, I went directly to Maleki, the mayor. He was an honest, helpful man, with little formality. He quickly organized the necessary payment, allowing us to pay all our employees. However, when we left for Tehran later that evening—tired and disappointed—we didn't even have enough money to buy a pack of cigarettes.

A FEW MONTHS LATER, Dr. Shafii brought good news: we had secured another road construction contract from the Ministry of Transport, this time in the city of Malayer. The contract involved asphalting a ten-kilometer stretch of road. While Hassan was skeptical about the order, I was pleased, as I was familiar with the city and the surrounding area. Within a month, the contract was signed and sealed.

Malayer, located southeast of Hamadan in the Zagros Mountains, has a warm, dry summer and a cold, snowy winter. The contract was to be completed in six months, with work beginning in early spring. We set up our construction site halfway along the ten-kilometer route, ensuring the shortest distance for transporting supplies. We needed to produce the asphalt mixture, as well as source crushed gravel and stones.

We debated whether to blast stones from the nearby mountains and crush them with machines, or extract gravel from a dry riverbed. The mountains were too far, so we searched for a suitable riverbed. After days of scouting, often in areas untouched by humans, we found one. With the site established, work could finally begin.

We invested nearly all our capital in this project. Heavy machinery had to be bought or rented, and raw materials like tar, gasoline, drinking water, and food were constant challenges. Nevertheless, the construction site and camp were well-organized, reflecting our German efficiency. Many even thought we were a German company. Everything was going well, and I was grateful to God, reminding myself to keep this in mind when dealing with the workers.

∼

MEANWHILE, Gisela had just returned from a visit to Germany, having also stopped in Tabriz to see my parents with our children. Everyone there was doing well, except my mother, who was lonely and wanted to move to Tehran. My father, however, preferred to stay in Tabriz.

By now, we had many friends and acquaintances, as the German community in Persia had grown significantly. Families from different nations, often in mixed marriages, lived and worked together. Our friendship with Krista and Behzad deepened, and we frequently helped each other out. Behzad was a generous, loving man, never speaking ill of others and always willing to lend a hand.

Once, due to a technical problem at his factory, I went to help. His factory was run like a well-oiled machine—very German. The floor was well-lit and ventilated, the workers wore safety gear, and they kept regular hours. At his request, I stayed for lunch. We ate together with the workers in the canteen, a warm atmosphere I had rarely experienced.

In recent years, telephone connections had improved, allowing me to stay in touch with my parents in Tabriz and the construction site when I was home. This made life much easier.

Though the drive was long, I regularly visited the construction site. I enjoyed the early morning drives through the desert, stopping in small villages or at green oases to eat local dishes and chat with the people. My mother had advised me to avoid rest stop food, but if necessary, to eat a raw onion and yogurt with my meal. I must admit, the food in these old, rundown houses often tasted better than in the nicest city restaurants.

Spring was coming to an end, the weather was warming, and air conditioners were humming again. Though the electricity would occasionally cut out, it was improving daily, thanks to the completion of several large dams.

Celebrating Minou's third birthday at home in Tabriz. From left: Mom, Minou, Kambiz, and Gisela.

58

GOD IS OUR PROTECTOR

One evening, during our weekly gentlemen's meeting—which I attended whenever possible—one of my friends asked me to drive his new American car to his villa in Ramsar. Dr. Shafii suggested I take the weekend off, and we could drive there together, and Abbas would then pick us up on Sunday. While I would have preferred to spend the weekend with my wife and children, I had to accept the offer. As the German proverb goes, *Friendship must be cultivated.*

After gathering some gifts, we set off, heading north via the newly completed highway to Karaj, about 40 kilometers from Tehran. From there, we continued toward Qazvin, once known as Caspian, before crossing the Alborz Mountains and arriving in Rasht, the capital of Gilan province. (Many years ago, my parents had sailed into this beautiful port city from Baku.) We followed the stunning coastline all the way to Ramsar.

At one point, we stopped at a tea plantation where a group of dervishes sat peacefully in the shade of a large tree. We got out of the car and were warmly greeted. We spent a pleasant time talking with them, their conversation gentle and wise. As we prepared to leave, I offered them some money, but they refused.

"Why would we need money?" they asked. "We have everything we need. We sleep beneath the Lord's blue sky, and food is provided by generous people like you."

I insisted they accept the money and asked that, if they didn't need it, they give it to someone who did. Finally, they agreed, saying, "God bless you, and drive carefully!"

We said our goodbyes, and Dr. Shafii took over the driving. It had begun to rain, but the road was nearly empty, so we weren't worried. We were deep in conversation as we drove along, and Dr. Shafii, unaccustomed to the weight of the new car, was going a bit too fast. As we rounded a curve, the car began to swerve. He hit the brakes, trying to regain control, but the car was too heavy and unfamiliar. Suddenly, we veered off the road and the car flipped, rolling several times.

It all happened so quickly that I barely registered what was going on. Before fear or pain could take hold, the car landed upside down on an embankment, and everything went dark.

I remember feeling each roll of the car, as if I could count how many times we turned over. In that moment, I saw faces flashing before me—my mother, Gisela, my children, my father, my siblings, and so many others. The front windshield had popped out entirely without breaking, and the roof was crushed down to the point that we were nearly pinned in our seats.

Dr. Shafii called out to me, desperately reaching for me with his hands, repeatedly asking if I was alright. I felt no pain, just confusion. I didn't know where we were or what had happened. Were we still alive? Were we in heaven?

At some point, I heard voices outside the car. People were trying to flip the car over. How they managed, I don't know, but with a loud crash, the car was suddenly back on all four wheels. I still couldn't move. The doors had been crushed in, but the men worked tirelessly to tear them off, and suddenly, light poured into the wreckage. I found myself lying on my stomach on the roof of the car, with Dr. Shafii's feet right in front of my face. The men carefully pulled us out, with no small effort, and finally, we were free.

I stood up, moving slowly, checking my body for any injuries. Miraculously, I had no visible wounds—no cuts, no bruises. We were both in shock, but somehow, neither of us was hurt. The people who had come to our rescue looked at us in disbelief. They didn't know whether to laugh or cry. One elderly woman told me we must have had a guardian angel watching over us. The kindness of these strangers overwhelmed me—one brought us water, another tea. Everyone wanted to help.

The car was a wreck and had to be towed, so we rented another vehicle to complete our trip to the villa, still about an hour away. When we arrived, disheveled and in torn, dirty clothes, our friends were understandably concerned. Once we assured them that we were unharmed, they were relieved. Our friend, to whom the car belonged, didn't care at all about the damage. He was simply grateful that we were alive.

I had survived two accidents in a short span of time. In our country, there's a saying: *There are no twos without a third.* I prayed that God would spare me from the third.

THE MISFORTUNE

The summer season had begun, and the average temperature at the construction site soared above 40 degrees in the shade. Despite the heat, the project was progressing well, and we had already started asphalting. One evening, however, Dr. Shafii called to inform me that I was expected to attend a meeting with the Ministry of Transport the next day. He didn't know the reason for the sudden summons, but I wasn't concerned. The work was on schedule, and I thought, perhaps, we might even receive our first payment.

Abbas drove me into town for the meeting, and upon arrival, I was led to the minister without much delay. His name was Shalzian, if I recall correctly. After the usual formalities, he got to the point: His Majesty, the Shahanshah, would be visiting the area in a week's time, and our section of the road needed to be completed before then.

I remained calm and replied, "That's impossible. There's simply not enough time. According to the contract, we have until the end of summer—about five more weeks, which is plenty to finish the job. We've already begun asphalting, the most difficult and costly part of the project. But finishing in just one week is out of the question."

"That won't work," he said. "A large construction company, Firme Beta, has a site nearby. They'll transport asphalt from their facility and complete the road before His Majesty's arrival."

"What about us?" I asked. "Our site and equipment have cost us a fortune, and none of that is covered in the contract."

"Correct," he replied. "That portion will be settled after the asphalting is done."

Suddenly, I felt a sharp pain in my chest, and my hand instinctively moved to the spot. It was the first time I had experienced anything like it. The minister noticed and asked, somewhat indifferently, if I needed a glass of water. But I wasn't really listening anymore—my thoughts were racing: *It's all over.*

A few moments later, I gathered myself enough to continue. "This is unfair. You can't do this. We've invested everything here, and we're on track to finish the contract within four weeks."

The minister, now visibly irritated, responded, "There's nothing more to be done. I'm sorry. Maybe you'll have better luck with the next project."

I glared at him, stunned by how easily he had dismantled everything we had built. There was nothing left to say. I left his office and found Dr. Shafii waiting for me outside. I explained everything and asked if there was anything we could do. Before he could answer, I blurted out, "I'll get a lawyer!"

He quickly warned me, "No—if you do that, you'll have to deal with Savak," (the intelligence service.)

I walked back to the car, my shoulders slumped, where Abbas was waiting for me. He could see from my posture how defeated I felt. I was disappointed in myself and everyone involved. Nearly a hundred workers would need to be laid off and sent home. They were entitled to their wages—it was their right—but I couldn't pay them. I wondered how their families would react. What would they think of me? Shame coursed through my body, making me tremble.

As we drove through the streets of Tehran, my mind was consumed with thoughts of the construction site. The tanks were full, nearly 100,000 liters of asphalt and bitumen, which would be left to waste in the desert. No one would bother to pump them out, except perhaps the villagers. The cost of removing the heavy machinery and paying for rentals would be astronomical. Clearing the site would cost far more than setting it up.

Lost in these calculations, I turned to Abbas and instructed him to drive to a car dealership so I could sell the car.

The sale happened quickly, and when I returned to Abbas in the parking lot, he automatically opened the door for me. I told him I had sold the car and handed him the money. "Take your salary," I said, "and leave the rest with the accountant. The oldest and neediest workers are to be paid first."

I embraced him, saying goodbye. He looked at me with tear-filled eyes, unable to comprehend how his boss had lost everything in a single afternoon. If he had known, he wouldn't have let me sell the car. Whether he fully understood the gravity of the situation, I didn't know. What I knew for sure was that life was no longer worth anything to me, and I no longer believed in anyone anymore.

I took a cab home. Gisela was in the kitchen, but I went straight upstairs to the bedroom to write my will. I felt sorry for her and my two small children. What would happen to Gisela? My father would take care of her and the children, so I wrote that request in my will. I felt like I was in a hypnotic trance and felt totally spent. I stood before God for the last time and prayed for forgiveness.

Then I took several sleeping pills and got into bed. The pills started to take effect quite quickly. I became calm and felt like I was born again, with no worries and no heartache. The bright sun shone into the room, but the glare disturbed my eyes. I closed them and my whole life played out before me like a movie. Then I heard the joyful voice of Gisela downstairs in the living room. She was chatting to someone on the phone and laughing so heartily—when she is really happy, she laughs with all her heart, like my mother.

I woke up briefly and suddenly realized the situation I had gotten myself into. My brain began to work. I'm going to kill myself, I thought. I saw the empty bottle in a blur. I am almost dead, I thought. Then I thought of my mother. How would she react and do when she heard that her happy son had taken his own life at the young age of 26? What would Gisela do when our children called for their dad? No, I must not do it.

I dragged myself to the stairwell with the last of my strength and called for Gisela. My voice was strained as I felt too weak to call any louder. A nearby flowerpot was my salvation. With the last of my strength, I pushed it down the staircase. After that, I blacked out.

A CLOSE CALL

When I woke up, I found myself lying in bed, feeling weak and disoriented. I couldn't remember anything that had happened recently. Gisela and my oldest sister were standing beside me, their faces filled with relief and joy. I had returned from the dead.

Later, Gisela explained what had happened. She told me she had heard the flowerpot crashing down the stairs and rushed to find me passed out on the floor. Despite her attempts, she couldn't wake me. In a panic, she ran across the street to Krista for help. Fortunately, Behzad had just come home early from work. Realizing the seriousness of the situation, he wasted no time dragging me to his car and driving me to the nearest hospital.

As she spoke, bits of memory started to return. I recalled my stomach being pumped and a doctor inserting a tube with a ball-shaped end into my mouth and down my throat. I could still hear the doctor's words, repeating over and over, "I will not let you die, my son."

The cuts and bruises on my feet and legs were from when Behzad dragged me down the stairs. He hadn't waited for help—if he had, I might not have made it. After my stomach was cleared, I was taken to my sister's house, where I remained unconscious for three days before waking up again. It took several weeks before I could sit or walk normally. My actions were never openly discussed, and I still don't know if my parents ever found out.

When I eventually returned to the office, the nightmare resumed. Creditors were coming in droves, demanding the money we owed them. Hassan did his best to calm everyone, and some, having heard about my ordeal, showed compassion and understanding. But it made me feel worse. I was appalled with myself. Despite his best efforts, Dr. Shafii, having no official obligation to our company, could only do so much. Ultimately, the responsibility fell on Hassan and me.

At Gisela's insistence, we sold our house and moved in with my second oldest sister, taking a single room upstairs that served as both our living room and bedroom.

One morning, as I was leaving the house for the office, I was arrested. A good acquaintance, from whom we had purchased some small construction equipment, had cashed one of our checks, which had bounced. He demanded immediate payment and took me to the police station. There, they confiscated everything I had— glasses, wallet, belt—and logged it all. I was then led to a filthy cell in the basement, just three meters square.

Dressed in a suit, tie, cashmere coat, and polished shoes, I stood out among the other prisoners, who looked at me with wide eyes. I greeted them and stood quietly in a corner. They told me I'd be taken before a judge who would set the terms for my release. But if I didn't pay my debt, I would be sent to a real prison. In my heart, I pleaded with God, asking over and over, *Why?*

I remembered my mother's words: *Always be a good person, and nothing bad will happen to you.* Had I not been a good person? Hadn't I given everything I had? How could the Shah's visit bring disaster upon me and my helpless workers instead of blessings? Why were we, of all people, suffering such injustice?

After several hours, I was finally released, thanks to my father's partner, Mr. Rawaie, who had settled the payment and signed the necessary documents. He hugged me and, trying to lift my spirits, said, "Cheer up, it could happen to anyone."

We left the prison and went to a tearoom to talk. Over tea, he advised me to go into hiding for a while. My father had entrusted him with handling the creditors. There were too many checks and drafts in circulation, and he needed time to sort through the books. The legal side of the situation also had to be addressed, and he informed me that we would have to declare bankruptcy. Iranlibelle Construction, my company, was finished.

I understood that he couldn't keep bailing me out of police custody every day, so I went into hiding while he negotiated with the creditors. Mr. Rawaie was a good man.

IN THE COMPANY OF THE DERVISHES

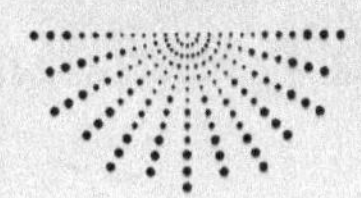

A hymn says:

"Guide me, you dear light,
You support my step,
I do not desire to see the distant land,
For me, one step is enough."

I asked Dr. Shafii to help me disappear. Afterward, I called Gisela to say goodbye to her and our dear children. To the family, it was thought that I had traveled abroad.

The doctor took me to a beautiful house in an exclusive neighborhood in the northern part of Teheran. It was modern, well-kept, and surrounded by a big garden. The owner, a well-dressed middle-aged woman, tried to keep me entertained but nothing interested me anymore. I was advised not to leave the house, if possible, but I felt so listless that I mostly stayed in my pleasant room, lying in bed, and reading books. I had no idea how long this would last, and I worried about what would happen if someone betrayed me. Most evenings, people visited to play cards, eat, and drink while the friendly owner played host —I'm sure she got a cut of the profits. I recognized some of the guests, and they often asked me to join them, but I had lost my spirit for such games. I always found an excuse to avoid them and was relieved when the nights came to an end.

I soon heard that our other construction projects had come to a standstill, meaning we couldn't get paid for those jobs either. It was all becoming too much for me, and I couldn't take it any longer. I craved peace and solitude. I called Dr. Shafii and asked him to move me to quieter accommodation where I wouldn't be disturbed.

A few days later, he picked me up, driving south of the city without telling me where we were going. After a long drive, we arrived in a part of town I had never seen before, seemingly poorer than the areas I knew. I saw young children carrying heavy containers of clay in a brickyard. There were tiny workshops, old grocery stores, and street vendors with wooden carts selling fruit and herbs. Cars crowded the dusty, narrow streets and alleys—it was a stark contrast to the northern part of the city.

We drove through narrow, stony streets until we arrived at an old house with its front door wide open. Walking through a small courtyard, we entered a two-story building. Up a stone staircase, we came into a room where a frail man with long gray-white hair and a mustache sat on a worn Persian rug. He greeted us by name and, to my surprise, suddenly stood up with agility. Hugging me, he said, "Our Lord is generous, my son. Come, sit with me."

After this introduction, Dr. Shafii left. I sat there, nervous and at a loss for words, unsure of what was happening. I felt utterly alone, abandoned by everything and everyone. But to my surprise, I began to calm down. I no longer cared about anything—I had lost my courage and my will to live. I never forgot that feeling.

Throughout the evening, several men visited the old man, while a few women went downstairs to see his wife. I didn't understand why people came by, but they had tea or water while the old man quietly conversed with each guest before moving on to the next.

Later, when everyone had left, he asked me to join him for a walk through the town's dusty alleys. Passersby greeted him respectfully as we made our way to an old house. Announcing our presence with a loud cough and a shout of "Ya Allah," a veiled woman appeared and led us to a small room. On a mattress lay a sick girl, about ten years old. The old man sat by her, speaking softly and stroking her hair. After a few minutes, we left the room, and he pressed a handful of money into the woman's hand without a word.

As we walked back, I noticed how tears streamed down his ashen face and into his beard. An elderly man approached us, and though it was a cold autumn evening, he asked if I truly needed my coat. Without hesitation, I took it off and handed it to him. The old man, with sad but kind eyes, looked at me and gave the coat to the stranger.

When we returned to the house, he showed me a corner of the room where I was to sleep. Later, I learned he was a Sufi—someone who loved others more than himself. As I lay on a thin blanket on the hard floor, I heard his quiet voice reciting *zikr*, the rhythmic remembrance of God, the heart of Sufi practice.

The following evening, after dinner, some visitors gathered in a circle, and Adieb, as he was called, began leading the *zikr*. It started with communal chants of "Hoo," a name of God in Islam, after which a man with a strange but pleasant voice began chanting alongside the others. The rhythmic movements of the Sufis gradually pulled me into a state of peace and relief—feelings I hadn't experienced in a long time. Adieb is an old Persian word for *scholar* or *teacher*, and Adieb did indeed become like a father to me, a guide and confidant.

In the mornings, we ate simple breakfasts of fresh bread, cheese, and tea. He never shopped for supplies; friends and students brought everything to the house. His wife, whom I rarely saw, prepared the meals with great care. Adieb himself ate and slept little, depriving himself of many comforts. After breakfast, he read old books for about an hour before we went out together to visit the sick and needy.

He distributed money that had been given to him the previous evening, helping people in different ways according to their needs —some with money, others with advice, and even healing the sick. I observed carefully and believed psychology played a role, though he admitted there were people even he couldn't help.

As we walked back each day, he would tell me who or what awaited us at home. It all seemed unbelievable to me at first, but over time, I grew accustomed to his ways. Eventually, he allowed me to participate in the meditations and sessions.

Sufism is independent of any particular religious affiliation and is older than Islam itself. However, most famous Sufis believe that only with the Prophet Muhammad and Islam did Sufism develop fully. We wore simple white cotton clothing, and after *wudu* (ritual washing), we always asked for *rukhsat*—permission to proceed. Cleanliness, purity, and *adab* (spiritual etiquette) were emphasized.

He explained that every person has a divine spark hidden deep within their heart, but it is veiled by worldly distractions and forgetfulness. Through prayer and *zikr*, we sought to rediscover God within ourselves. "The *zikr* of the tongue, we practice together," he said. "The *zikr* of the heart, you must do alone."

WINTER ARRIVED EARLIER and colder than usual. I didn't have any winter clothes with me, and for two months I had worn the same pants and jacket. Though my shirts and underwear were washed daily, my crumpled suit had become unwearable. Adieb chuckled, saying I now fit in more than ever. It wasn't about money, he said, but the art of austerity. Sufism wasn't theoretical— it had to be lived through one's actions.

I often told him stories about my past in Tabriz with my parents and siblings, as well as about my wife and children in Tehran. He would sometimes contribute, even reminding me of accidents I hadn't mentioned. He praised both my mother and Gisela, expressing a wish to meet them one day.

Dr. Shafii came to update me on various meetings that had taken place over the past few months. My father, through his partner, assured all creditors that their claims would be settled as soon as the totals were finalized. It was a complicated task, with grocers, suppliers, camp providers, hotels, and even bathhouses needing to be accounted for. Until the final settlements were reached, I remained in Adieb's house.

PERFECT SYMMETRY

One day, Adieb received an invitation from the north and asked me to accompany him. I accepted eagerly, filled with anticipation. One of his students, a merchant, drove us to the city of Rasht, located on the Caspian Sea. From there, we continued to Lahijan, a city known for its rice and tea plantations, where our host resided.

The house we arrived at was a charming, old structure nestled in a large garden filled with orange trees. The beauty of the setting was matched by the warmth of our welcome. Our host greeted us with great enthusiasm, and I noticed that the other guests came from all walks of life—civil servants, doctors, engineers, lawyers, and laborers. Almost all of them knew Adieb as their revered Master, and before long, he disappeared into the crowd as groups formed on the exquisite Persian carpets spread across the large rooms.

Dinner was wonderful. We were served noodle stew along with freshly baked bread, cheese, nuts, dates, and an array of fruit. The tables were beautifully set, adorned with fresh flowers, and the atmosphere was one of quiet reverence and community. After the meal and a brief rest, we were taken to a washroom and changing area, where we were given white shirts and pants to change into.

Once we were dressed, we were led to a large room and instructed to sit on the floor and wait. Adieb invited me to sit beside him, and as the fifty or so guests settled into their places, the candles in ornate stands were lit, casting a soft glow around the room. The lights were then turned off, leaving the space illuminated only by the flickering candlelight. From my position next to Adieb, I had a clear view of the gathering, and the scene was enchanting.

Our host stood and greeted everyone, expressing his gratitude to the Master for returning to the community after so many years. He then respectfully requested that Adieb lead the gathering. I later learned that the Sufi leading the group must be the highest order bearer.

Adieb began to pray, his voice gentle yet powerful, invoking the Creator in the name of Allah. The room fell into a deep silence, the only sounds being the rhythmic hum of his voice and the soft crackling of the candles:

> *"Torat, e Musa (Old Testament of Prophet Moses),*
> *Enjil, e Issa (Bible of Prophet Jesus),*
> *Zaboor, e Dawod (holy book of Prophet David),*
> *Goran, e Mohammed (Quran of Prophet Mohammed),*
> *May the session succeed.*
> *May God Almighty free our hearts from hatred and envy,*
> *So that we purify our souls and forget our egos for a while."*

He explained that the purification of the soul was the core of the Sufi path, closely tied to the *Zikr* we were about to perform. As the *Zikr* began, an electric sensation ran through me, and I felt my hair stand on end. Adieb held my hand firmly, guiding me through every movement with a gentle pull. The ritual and meditative exercise started with the invocation of divine names, repeatedly chanting "Ya Hu."

He had already explained the stages of *Zikr* to me: "In the first stage, you recite the name of God with your voice, though your mind may wander. The heart might not yet be in harmony. But if you persist, you'll reach a point where the voice continues, the mind begins to focus, and the heart slowly attunes to the practice.

"In the next stage, everything aligns: the voice chants, the mind concentrates, and the heart resonates in unity. Once you reach this level, you stop vocal recitation and return to daily life, but your heart continues the *Zikr*. At this stage, you gain an unshakable conviction."

For the first time, I felt I had reached that stage, though part of me wondered if it was just an illusion. Still, the state I entered was beyond description, a feeling of transcending everything I had ever known.

He spoke again, saying, "We live on the surface of life, but through meditation, we can access deeper realms—even within our physical being, through the electromagnetic field we call the aura. Beyond that, we tap into our psychic levels of consciousness, transcending the limitations of our ego."

Eventually, I was gently awakened from the trance. For a moment, I had no idea where I was or what had happened. The candles had burned out, and the room was bathed in silence. New candles were lit, casting a soft glow around the room. I glanced at Adieb, and his face was pale, almost chalk white. But I felt calm and relieved, a sense of peace I had not experienced in a long time. He reminded me that after each session, it was important not to rush back into reality. The feeling of having touched something beautiful leaves you sensitive and vulnerable.

A few days later, we returned to Tehran. The experience had been transformative for me. I felt I had gained a deeper understanding of myself and the world, and the challenges I faced no longer seemed catastrophic. I had glimpsed a purer, more beautiful way of living—something far beyond what I had ever experienced.

As the Master continued to guide me, he led me deeper into the mysteries of life. Every night, we held sessions, and I met many good people. It no longer surprised me to learn that others—Christians, Jews, and Zoroastrians—had joined our meditations and chosen him as their Master as well.

As Christmas approached, Adieb told me it was time to return home. Before I left, he said, "The wrong done to you could have brought misfortune to many others if your father had not been so generous in settling the debts. Now, your duty is to take care of your wife and children. Your wife wishes to celebrate her Christian feast with you. For now, don't worry—everything will be fine. Soon, things will be different and better than they are now."

Though I was sad to leave him, I was also excited at the thought of being with my family again. I longed to hear my children's voices, to take a shower in my own bathroom, and to sleep in a real bed. I knew I was not yet a true Sufi—I was still thinking about my own comfort. It is a difficult path, to be a true Sufi.

Before leaving, I asked him one more question, "What will happen next?"

"Nothing bad will happen to your health," he replied. "Don't worry, and please, no more questions."

With that, he pressed a handful of money into my pocket and gave me a fatherly hug. Following the custom of Sufis, I kissed his shoulder and, after nearly half a year, said goodbye to my master. A car with a driver waited outside the house. As I stepped into the car, my thoughts drifted to Abbas, my faithful friend and driver from my past.

RETURN TO REALITY

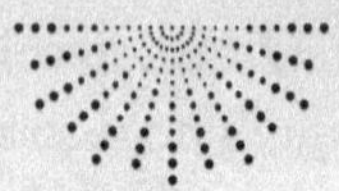

There was great joy at my sister's home when I returned. Everyone was told I had come back from abroad. The children had grown so much over the past few months—Minou was almost three and a half, and Kambiz was two. They were ecstatic to see me and clung to me, refusing to let go. Gisela handled it all with a composed grace, much like my mother would have. To explain my appearance and weight loss, I told a few white lies, saying I had driven back from Europe and encountered many difficulties along the way. Life seemed to resume its normal rhythm, with visitors coming and going, and everyone appeared happy.

Yet Gisela was quieter than usual, and I couldn't blame her. Despite her big heart and understanding, she had lost her home, the place where her children had once lived happily. But she knew my father stood behind us, a solid, unwavering presence like Mount Damavand in the Alborz range. The events that had unfolded were unexpected and beyond our control. It was not our fault, but we were still the ones who suffered the consequences. I had started my company with such hope, not just for myself, but because I believed in my compatriots.

That night, as we went to bed, I learned that Gisela had been suffering from a toothache for days. She had been too ashamed to tell anyone because she hadn't had enough money to go to the dentist. Hearing this broke my heart. I had lost everything—our house, our car, my business—and my wife couldn't even afford a simple visit to the dentist. I couldn't bear to look her in the eye. It was a maddening situation, and I felt utterly helpless. The Shah's visit had come at the worst possible time, and I hadn't been able to send the workers home without pay. I'd also been forced to give money to right others' wrongs, neglecting my own family in the process. Who would believe such a story?

Desperate, I got out of bed, poured a glass of water, and closed my eyes. I thought of Adieb, imagining him holding my hand as I gripped the glass. I opened my eyes to find Gisela and the children sitting next to me, watching. I handed her the glass of water and asked her to drink it, telling her it would ease her pain. We went back to bed.

The next morning, I asked if the water had helped. Gisela gave me a curious look but said it had eased the pain somewhat, though she would still need to visit the dentist soon.

It HAD BEEN a long time since I had been to Tabriz, and I felt a deep longing to see my parents again. I also wanted to thank my father for stepping in to help. But I had a problem—during past visits, I had always brought gifts for the family and given money to my mother to help with household expenses. This time, however, I had nothing.

My older sister was the only one who knew the full extent of my situation. She understood that while I was not overly attached to money, I would need her help—discreetly. After packing our suitcases, I felt a wave of desperation, so I retreated to one of her guest rooms for a secret *Zikr* session, locking the door. There was much misunderstanding and prejudice around Sufism, which made sense since very little was known or read about it at the time in our country.

As we were about to leave the house, a messenger arrived with a package from the Master. Inside was a substantial sum of money and a note. His wish was for me to distribute and donate portions of the money during my time in Tabriz. Once again, I was reminded of the generosity of the Creator.

When we arrived in Tabriz, my parents greeted us at the airport. The reunion was filled with joy, and I had tears in my eyes —not only from happiness but from the weight of everything that had happened over the past few months.

The atmosphere at home was different now. It no longer had the same cozy warmth I remembered. My mother seemed listless, feeling abandoned, while my father had aged significantly.

When we were alone, my father asked why I was so downhearted. I expressed my regret over everything that had happened. He laughed and said, "My son, things like this happen in business. Thank God we were able to repair the damage. Don't worry, I sold one of our houses and have settled everything. Hold your head high and continue on your path."

I was speechless. My father's kindness and generosity knew no bounds.

Later that night, as my mother and I sat alone drinking tea, I asked if everything was alright and whether she had enough for her expenses. Standing by her usual window, smoking, she replied, "No, my son. There is so much misery, and we can't handle it all by ourselves." Her sadness weighed heavily on me, and I regretted bringing it up.

I hugged her and handed her the money from the Master. She was shocked but overjoyed to accept it. "Do you have enough for your trip?" she asked, concerned. I assured her that I did—God is always gracious and generous.

After a few days, I returned to Tehran. The company was

declared bankrupt, and the sign was removed, though we kept the office open. I felt deep sorrow for Hassan, my dear partner and friend. He never blamed me; instead, he did his best to calm my worries. Meanwhile, the good Dr. Shafii had his own dreams and was already planning his next venture, having emerged from the debacle unscathed.

64

2500TH ANNIVERSARY CELEBRATION

In 1971, the country was bustling in preparation for the 2500th anniversary of the Persian Empire, set to be held in Persepolis, the ancient capital of Persia. A massive tent hotel was constructed near the tomb of Cyrus the Great (Kourosh in Persian). Leaders from around the world were gathering for the celebration. In Tehran, hotel chains like Hilton, Sheraton, and Hyatt sprang up, highways were built, and parks and large dams were completed. The country was on an upswing, brimming with optimism.

Yet, I remained deeply pessimistic. Corrupt officials like the *farmandar* in Arak or the Minister of Transport, whose arrogance had contributed to the downfall of my company, cast a shadow over the nation's future. I believed that if the country was to truly prosper, people like them should be in prison, not holding office.

Thankfully, I knew several wealthy merchants. One of them, an antique dealer, and his partner wanted to fund the construction of 250 schools to commemorate the anniversary and donate them to the state. It was an enormous task, but one I gladly took on. The work brought joy back into my life, providing a good income. These two men were fair and generous.

We rented a new apartment, and Gisela was in her element once more, joyfully furnishing it with love and care. Even with modest means, she managed to create a warm, inviting space. Surrounded by friends, family, and steady work, our life began to feel bearable again.

~

I CONTINUED my sessions with the Master, Adieb, deepening my meditation practice. Over time, he began to trust me more and shared some of his personal insights. Once, when my mother was visiting us in Tehran, I asked if she would like to attend a session being held at our home. At first, she was skeptical. Dervishes and Sufis in Persia had always been the subject of much debate and prejudice. People often accused them of being beggars, sorcerers, or even non-Muslims. But my mother, curious, agreed to see it for herself.

To help her understand, I explained the meaning of *Dervish* (originally *Darvish*). In Persian, "darvis" means "poor" or "religious mendicant," while "khish" means "oneself" or "wish." So, a *Dervish* is someone who thinks of others. Conversely, "Dar khish" means thinking only of oneself—in Latin, "egoist." Adieb had once told me that Jesus Christ himself was a *Dervish* and a great Sufi.

As Adieb explained, "The causes of many problems are not material but psychological. The teaching of Sufism offers an answer to the deeper needs of the human soul."

My mother sat with Gisela and other women in the adjacent room (meditations are always held separately by gender). The Master led the session, and though I tried to concentrate, I found myself distracted. Knowing that my mother and Gisela were nearby filled me with restlessness. I couldn't free myself from worldly concerns and distractions. Adieb must have sensed this, as he ended the session after about an hour. I felt like a man dying of thirst but deprived of water. Yet, to my surprise, both women were deeply moved by the experience. Gisela, in particular, spoke of an inner awakening that had touched her profoundly. Though I had always seen her as pure and just, it seemed she had reached a new level of spiritual awareness.

~

WINTER HAD RETURNED, and once again, I traveled with Adieb —this time to Arak. We had a meeting with the deputy, Mr. R., who had helped us in the past. The meeting ran late, so we ended up staying the night at his home. He refused to let us go to a hotel, instead inviting us to his large, traditional Persian house. The rooms were spacious and comfortable, and a wooden fireplace filled the space with warmth. Mr. R. was clearly captivated by Adieb.

At breakfast the next morning, Mr. R. proudly introduced us to his son, a handsome young man of about twenty. The moment Adieb saw him, something changed in his expression. His eyes widened in shock, and I saw tears welling up behind his thick glasses. His reaction startled me, though I didn't ask about it at the time.

Later, as we said our goodbyes, we took the young man with us on the drive to Hamadan. During the journey, I tried to understand what had troubled Adieb so much, but he remained silent. We eventually dropped the young man off at his home in Tehran, where he asked if I would be going back to Arak soon. I told him it wouldn't be anytime soon but promised to take him with me the next time.

Several months passed, and one day the phone rang. Gisela answered it, her hands trembling as she passed the receiver to me. It was the brother of Mr. R, and his voice was choked with grief. Mr. R's son had crashed the new car he'd been given, and he had died in his fathers' arms. The news hit me like a blow to the chest. I felt sick, consumed by the pain of it.

Without hesitation, I went to Adieb's house. He was already waiting for me, sensing the urgency of the situation. Together, we embarked on the difficult overnight journey to comfort my brother, Mr. R. For a Sufi, helping others without being asked is a sacred duty.

Persepolis

65

NEW BEGINNINGS

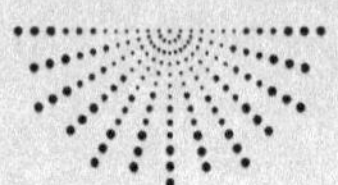

An old friend of Dr. Shafii, an agricultural engineer, owned a modern orchid farm in the north of the country, near Rasht by the Caspian Sea. He cultivated rare orchids and tropical flowers, having studied agriculture in Belgium some 40 years ago. A true farmer at heart, he had even attempted to start a farm in the south, near the Persian Gulf, where the winters were milder, but the land was barren and dry. He invested much time, effort, and money in cultivating the land, growing northern fruits and vegetables, and transporting them across more than three thousand kilometers to the south. It was a labor of love and perseverance.

I had known him for many years, and one day he spoke to me about the challenges in Hormozgan province. Professionals, he said, avoided working there because it was one of the poorest and least developed regions in the country. His best friend, the governor of the province, was trying to gather a group of skilled individuals to help him on his journey to develop the region. He spoke of the enchanting landscape, the climate, and the people with such passion that I was captivated. Being from Azerbaijan in the far north, I could only dream of traveling so far southeast, to the edge of the Persian Gulf.

We invited him for dinner one evening, and over tea, he asked me if I had ever considered working in Hormozgan province. The question caught me off guard. He explained that if I wanted to truly serve my country, I would find the greatest opportunity there. While I wouldn't become wealthy, I would receive the highest civil servant salary. If the Ministry of Interior approved, I could begin work soon.

A few days later, I met with Adieb. Before I could even ask him for advice, he said, "Your wife wants what's best for you. Leave this city with its empty glamour, bright nights, and gray days. Go to Hormozgan—there you'll find honest and simple people, much like those you knew in Tabriz. You'll serve your country and find peace within yourself."

When I told Gisela about my conversation with Adieb, she was thrilled by the idea. She had already seen many parts of our homeland, but neither of us had ever ventured so far south. It would be a new adventure, far from family and familiarity. Bandar Abbas had a reputation as a place of exile for prisoners and misfits. I joked with Adieb, "People will think I've been exiled because of my business problems."

He just laughed and said, "Those who know you will understand. You won't harm your family's reputation. In fact, they'll admire you for this. Just take care of your health." With that, he gave me his blessing.

At the time, we had recently enrolled our children in a good school in Tehran—Minou had just started first grade, and Kambiz was in preschool. Our rented home, complete with a small garden and swimming pool, had been beautifully furnished by Gisela. Moving south would mean starting over again, from scratch.

Before making a final decision, I flew to Tabriz to seek my parents' blessing. My mother was thrilled by the idea. With my youngest sister preparing to graduate from high school and my youngest brother still at home, she was slowly adjusting to the quiet house. My father, despite his old age, continued working diligently.

I visited my uncle and aunt at their leather factory, which was still in operation. But the factory seemed stuck in time—there was no modernization, and everything felt old and worn, like a forgotten flower wilting away. The country might have been on the upswing, but my uncle's business had stalled.

I also visited Mr. Jawadi, who had stayed with us in Germany and suffered from asthma. When I mentioned my plans to move to Bandar Abbas, his reaction surprised me—he was overjoyed. Despite his illness, he worked as a freelancer and headed the Red Cross in Azerbaijan. He spoke of the desperate need for professionals in the country. While many preferred to stay in Tehran, he believed my decision to move south would be a great act of service. He even gave me a recommendation letter, should I need it.

Later that evening, as my father and I sat together, he shared how proud he was of my decision. His friends had congratulated him, and it filled him with joy. However, he wanted to ensure Gisela was on board with the idea, so I reassured him that she was fully supportive.

I returned to Tehran with my mother for a visit. During the drive, she told me about my oldest brother, who had emigrated to the United States with his wife and children. He had planned to become a specialist surgeon, but the language barrier and American laws had made it difficult. Now he wanted to return home, and Mother was looking for a house or apartment for him.

When I shared this news with Gisela, she immediately said, "We're moving to Bandar Abbas for a few years—our house is big enough and fully furnished. If he and his family want it, they can take it over, even temporarily."

And so, our adventure in the Persian Gulf began.

Gisela and the kids on their usual afternoon stroll through the city of Tehran.

66

THE PERSIAN GULF

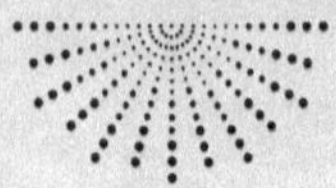

One morning, I said goodbye to my wife and children and began my journey south to the Persian Gulf with Dr. Shafii and Mr. Gezelayag. It was a cold winter's day, but the sun shone brightly, gradually warming the barren and dry landscape. We drove through the holy city of Qom, passing Kashan, and continued toward Isfahan. By the time we reached Yazd, perched on the edge of the salt desert, it was time to spend the night.

Early the next morning, we set off again, driving through Kerman, along the salt desert to Sirjan, and finally to Bandar Abbas. Darkness had already fallen by the time we arrived, but the air remained warm enough for us to sit outside and take in the quiet, unfamiliar landscape. I felt uneasy as I surveyed the surroundings—date palms, small houses, and huts known as *kapars*. A part of me scolded myself for diving into this adventure, questioning whether I had made the right decision.

But the next morning, everything looked different. We ate breakfast under a cloudless blue sky that stretched to the horizon, where the sea shimmered in the distance. The light was so bright we had to wear sunglasses. In the distance, I could see the high mountains of Qeshm Island. The air felt smooth like silk. The exotic plants basking under the sun made us feel like tourists, far removed from our everyday lives. The people we met were simple, friendly, and easygoing, reminding me of my childhood in Tabriz.

After breakfast, we visited the orchid farm, about an hour's drive through barren land. As we approached the coastline, the terrain transformed into lush greenery. When we arrived, the farm revealed itself as a square building with water wells and a few tractors scattered about. The farm's owner greeted us enthusiastically, diving straight into a passionate discussion about his work and his hopes that I could lend a hand.

Later that afternoon, we went to meet the governor, who received us warmly. I handed him the reference letter from Mr. Jawadi, which he read with a calm, steady demeanor.

"Would you like to stay here or return to Tehran?" he asked. "I only ask because many who come here leave shortly after. They can't get used to this kind of life—salty water, limited access to fresh food and fruit, unreliable electricity, poor phone connections with Tehran, and scarce modern apartments."

"So, what are the benefits of living here?" I asked.

"A clean environment, and those who deserve it can build a better life," he replied.

Without hesitation, I answered, "If I'm given the freedom to work, I'd like to stay, no matter how difficult it is."

The governor seemed visibly relieved and pleased. He introduced me to an agricultural specialist he knew well and promised to support me however he could.

MY TEMPORARY ACCOMMODATION measured just 2.5 meters by 6 meters, but it had a cooler mounted in the window above my head—though it rattled noisily day and night. I was given an office, which I began furnishing to my taste, along with a Jeep and a driver named Avazpoor. I took an immediate liking to him. He was wise and kind, and I could sense he would be invaluable to me in this unfamiliar place.

The governor introduced me to various department heads and directors. Bandar Abbas was slated to become a naval base, so I was constantly dealing with the military. However, the governor left it up to me to manage relations and resolve any conflicts that arose.

Deputy Governor Mr. Hadjian was a no-nonsense man with extensive knowledge of the country and its people. His American wife, Linda, added to his worldly demeanor. I also met Mr. Montazam, the director of the Ministry of Water and Electricity. Having studied in Germany, he was an electrical engineer from a distinguished Persian family and was married to a German woman. Many of the other generals and officers also had foreign wives, making it seem even more likely that Gisela could adapt to life here.

Over the next few months, I built valuable relationships. Avazpoor, my driver, taught me countless things: what to eat and avoid, whom to trust, and how to navigate the local customs. He became like a father figure to me. I felt grateful to God that I never encountered any harm—instead, I found joy in the company of these people and learned so much from them.

The State Chancellery had ambitious plans for the region, and the government provided significant funds for various projects: roads, refrigeration plants, freshwater facilities, warehouses, silos, airports, hospitals, and even a dam in Minab, the second-largest city in the province.

A few weeks later, I flew back to Tehran for the first time, my suitcases packed with gifts for everyone. Avazpoor took me to the airport, whose terminal was still under construction. He handled everything for me, and everywhere I went, I was treated with great respect. I was surprised by the authority I wielded, even in Tehran, where my official ID card allowed me to bypass security easily.

At home, my siblings and my faithful cousin Nader organized a party to welcome me back, but my parents were notably absent.

Despite the poor phone connections, I had spoken to my mother almost every evening, so she knew about my return.

Later that night, I told Gisela everything about Bandar Abbas. She was thrilled by the possibilities, and we agreed that we could live there permanently. It felt like a new beginning, a unique challenge for us both.

I RETURNED to Bandar Abbas and dove straight into work. There was much to do in terms of urban planning, and every project seemed more interesting than the last. I began with the construction of a large boulevard connecting the airport to the far west of the city. The avenue, which stretched 45 meters wide, would later be lined with trees and feature separate paths for pedestrians and cyclists. I put my all into the project, though there were, of course, many challenges.

The state had paid large sums for sections of land, but it took years to settle disputes with adjacent landowners. One day, I needed to demolish a section of a wall that obstructed the construction, but the owner of an ice factory refused to allow it. Though he had been paid, he claimed the electrical boxes mounted on the wall supplied ice to the entire city, essentially blackmailing us. I went ahead and tore the wall down, watching him frantically save the fuse box. Word of the incident spread quickly, and we began making faster progress.

I also demolished the high garden wall of the winter palace belonging to a sheik from the Gulf Emirates. My superior had reservations, fearing it might spark diplomatic tension, but I bore the responsibility and went ahead without their knowledge. Fortunately, there were no repercussions, and I even reached out to the ruler across the Gulf, advising him on how to rebuild the wall in harmony with the new cityscape.

Every morning at six o'clock sharp, my superior would drive his black Mercedes through the construction site. According to his driver, he was pleased with our progress.

After a few months, I grew accustomed to the harsh conditions and wildlife. I encountered scorpions, snakes, and large spiders, but none ever attacked me. One evening, while sitting on the beach wall watching the sunset, I noticed a scorpion right next to my hand. It seemed to be basking in the last rays of sunlight. I slowly pulled my hand back, and in a flash, it disappeared. It was a close call, but one that left me marveling at the strange beauty of this place.

A typical gathering with colleagues working at the boulevard construction zone.

Behzad and Krista visited us in Bandar Abbas.

MEMBER OF THE REGIONAL
SECURITY COUNCIL

One morning, I was summoned to the boss' office. Mr. Avazpoor advised me not to go directly from the construction site, but to change into white pants and a white shirt. "You must look neat and tidy," he said, and I wholeheartedly agreed.

When I arrived, the secretary led me into a large meeting room I had never seen before. Around the table sat directors and officers from every department: military, air force, navy, infantry, health services, economy, transport, customs, police, among others. I was momentarily taken aback when all eyes turned toward me. At just 28, I was the youngest member in the room, now seated at the Regional Security Council. My boss pointed to a chair on his left for me to sit, while Mr. Hadjian, his deputy, sat on his right.

After I sat down, my boss introduced me to the others. Now everyone who had influence in the province knew my name, and I knew theirs. They also knew I was from Tabriz. Some of them, I'm sure, wondered what I was doing in such an important role at my age.

By the end of the meeting, I had been assigned to oversee the construction on the islands in the Persian Gulf, particularly Abu

Musa and the Tunb islands, which Persia had recently regained from the British. The scope of the work was unclear to me, as I had never been to these islands. I asked myself, *Where exactly is Abu Musa?*

Mr. Hadjian. and Mr. Montazam., both nationalists and idealists from prominent families, consistently encouraged me to bring my family south so that I could work in peace. Despite having ample opportunities to work in Tehran, they chose to serve in Bandar Abbas, one of the country's poorest provinces, and it was clear they wanted me to do the same.

When I flew back to Tehran, my heart was filled with joy. I was now the technical director of the entire province! Gisela already knew about my promotion and my state of mind—or *hal* as we called it in Sufi tradition. *Hal,* or state of mind, is one of the most significant concepts in Sufi teachings. It refers to the subtle, spiritual wandering that can change in an instant, like a bolt of lightning, from despair to euphoria—if it is anchored deep within the heart. To others in my family, who had moved to Tehran seeking a more comfortable life, our decision to relocate to one of the poorest regions was perplexing. But Gisela and I knew what we were doing.

Upon my return to Bandar Abbas, I began searching for a new apartment. It would be another farewell to friends and family, but I had done that several times before.

The project was moving along well, and most of the boulevard was complete. One evening, I was invited to the governor's house for dinner. Arriving a little early, I wandered through his magnificent garden, filled with indigenous trees and plants. The old gardener knew every tree intimately, having spent his life tending to this lush oasis. He explained that the garden was overgrown and many trees needed to be relocated. The timing couldn't have been better, as I realized that some of these plants could find new life in the boulevard.

I rushed to the governor, who was entertaining his guests in a large, impressive hall where all kinds of delicacies and refreshments were being served. Though I interrupted him, he listened attentively. When I asked if he would allow some of his trees to be replanted on the boulevard, he enthusiastically agreed. Without wasting time, I left to set the plan in motion.

My driver, who had accompanied me to the dinner, was astonished when I asked him to take me back to the office immediately. "But everyone is just sitting down for dinner!" he exclaimed. But we had work to do.

A few days later, the plan materialized. The center island of the boulevard was completed, and the cityscape had been transformed. What had once been a narrow, barren road was now a kilometer-long avenue lined with beautiful trees and plants, running through the heart of the city. The people were delighted to stroll along the avenue, and it became a source of pride for the community.

The director of water and electricity had his hands full providing utilities for the project, but he made it happen. With the progress going so well, the governor and others insisted on keeping me in Bandar Abbas for a longer period. Eventually, I found a suitable house for my family, one of the best available, and began renovating it immediately.

One evening, while enjoying a meal at the Hotel Gambron, where I dined most nights, I received a phone call. I was informed that the following day, a naval officer would take me to Abu Musa, an island in the Persian Gulf near the Arab Emirates. My task was to audit the invoices of the contractors working there.

That night, my driver took me home and stayed with me. He often did this when he sensed I was unwell or homesick. This time, however, he was worried about my upcoming assignment. He had heard through the governor's driver that the construction company on the island belonged to the navy chief's brother—or was somehow connected to him. The company had been awarded several multi-million-dollar contracts, and previous auditors had failed their inspections, resulting in them losing their jobs.

The next morning, I arrived at the naval base, where they were already expecting me. I was taken aboard a destroyer, greeted by the commander and captain, and shown to my cabin. Later, as I sat in the ship's canteen, I marveled at the discipline and professionalism of the crew. The officers were impeccably dressed, and many spoke multiple languages. It was hard to believe this was the same navy that had been destroyed when the British occupied Persia during World War II. Now, here I was, aboard a state-of-the-art ship, working with some of the best-trained personnel in the country.

As I wandered through the ship, I found the library filled with rare books. Everything about the ship was impressive, and it filled me with pride. I promised myself that I would do my job thoroughly and honorably.

THE ISLAND OF ABU MUSA

The island, with its single peak, Mount Halva, was visible from afar—a dry and barren place in the eastern Persian Gulf. Since the port was still under construction, large ships had to anchor offshore. After arriving close to the island, I climbed down a long ladder—about 50 steps—to board a small motorboat that would take me ashore. I clung tightly to the rope, struggling to keep my balance as rough waves rocked the boat. It was a miracle I didn't fall into the sea!

After a high-speed, bumpy ride in the motorboat, we reached the island, wet and a bit shaken. The boat's driver cut the engine a few meters from the shore as the harbor wasn't finished. He instructed me to step out and wade through the water. Nervous, I grabbed my briefcase and gingerly stepped into the sea, uncertain of the depth, especially since I wasn't a good swimmer. Thankfully, two men from the island jumped in to assist me. After a few difficult minutes of wading, we reached dry land.

I slumped onto a rock, exhausted. Soaked with sweat from both humidity and nerves, I couldn't help but think what a risky adventure this had been. Surely, it would have been safer—and cheaper—to use a helicopter instead of a warship! "It wasn't properly organized," the Germans would say.

The site manager greeted me and took me to his office, which was essentially a container with a generator powering the lights and a refrigerator. As I looked around, the only signs of civilization were the large steel water tanks, tents for the fifty workers, and various pieces of construction equipment.

Later, when it cooled down, I ventured out to speak with the workers. They gathered in a circle and began sharing their concerns. Almost all of them spoke Azari, my native language. These were tough men, doing hard work, and they were eager to pour their hearts out to someone from Tabriz. I listened carefully, as my master had taught me, and assured them they could speak openly and freely.

As I wandered through the camp, I noticed the terrible working and living conditions. The accommodation, food, and hygiene was inadequate. Many of the workers looked pale and unhealthy. The site manager explained that due to the extreme heat and humidity, some of the men would sneak into the sea to cool off, despite it being forbidden. However, the salty water left salt crystals on their skin, and since fresh water had to be transported from the mainland, it was only available for drinking and cooking, not for rinsing off.

Although I wanted to help the workers, my primary task was to audit the contractor's invoices, which was no small feat given the complexity of the construction. For instance, a breakwater was being built to create a calm water basin for ships. This involved blasting rock from the island's lone mountain, which was then transported by trucks to the sea, forming a pyramid-shaped wall beneath the water. The contractor claimed that the strong currents at the 20-meter depth widened the wall more than expected, requiring more rocks than originally calculated.

When it cooled down further, I went up the mountain with a team of Indian engineers to inspect the depot. The road was treacherously steep, and at one point, the front tires of our jeep lifted off the ground! Nonetheless, we made it safely. The blasters, who were from Azerbaijan, explained their work in detail to me in Azari, which could not be understood by the Indians and Persians there. They shared key information: the number of holes drilled, the quantity of explosives used, the number of daily blasts, and the trips made to transport the rocks down to the sea. This data was reliable, as the blasters were paid per blast, and it would aid my survey. Still, I needed hard proof and precise measurements for my report, so I also performed my own calculations so that I would have all the documents necessary to address the inaccuracies that might be presented by both sides.

That evening, the workers built a large campfire using driftwood from whole sections of wrecked ships that had accumulated on the deserted shores over the centuries and now lay half-buried in the sand. The island had no vegetation or animals, aside from a few goats (brought in as livestock) that chewed on cement bags and drank saltwater. The atmosphere was quiet and almost melancholic. In the distance, we could see the burning oil rigs of the Arab Emirates, and the sea whispered ancient stories. The workers shared their grievances about the poor living conditions, although their demands were simple and reasonable. The Indian workers, being vegetarians, seemed content with their provisions. I felt sympathy for the men and resolved to help.

Over the next few days, with help from the Indian engineers, I completed my audit. I compiled a list of the workers' needs, along with my own recommendations—such as building a runway for small planes or a ramp for hovercrafts, which would provide quicker and cheaper access to the island. I doubted the planners had ever set foot on the island or understood the dire conditions here. Through our military connections in Bandar Abbas, I requested fresh food and better supplies for the workers.

Surprisingly, my requests were approved without delay. The workers received everything I had asked for, and I promised to return and check on their progress. After saying my goodbyes at sunset, I returned to Bandar Abbas, where my driver greeted me, noticing how much weight I had lost.

I filed my report, complete with survey documents, calculations, and the workers' demands, handing it to the governor. Without reading it, he sealed the envelope and asked if I stood by my findings. When I offered to explain further, he stopped me, saying he didn't want to know—I alone was responsible for the report. Later, I learned that the project was viewed with skepticism in Tehran due to the involvement of the navy chief's brother. This might explain why other inspectors had refused to file reports. However, I knew my report was solid, backed by verifiable technical arguments, just as I had learned in Germany.

A few days later, the Rear Admiral's brother visited my office to thank me warmly. I took the opportunity to suggest he focus more on improving conditions for his workers.

As time passed, I received more contracts, and with them came new responsibilities. I was even provided with a twin-engine Cessna to cover long distances and visit the outlying islands. Meanwhile, Gisela was preparing to move to Bandar Abbas, and my brother's family was set to move into our old apartment in Tehran. The navy offered to enroll our children in a well-regarded school for navy families, and we were invited to numerous events by Mr. Hadjian, Mr. Montazam, and others who were thrilled to meet Gisela. A friendly, collegial connection developed which exists to this day. We helped each other with daily life and shared specialties from Tehran and Germany which arrived in care packages from time to time.

Our rented house featured a natural ventilation system called a *badgir*, or wind-catcher, which are a traditional Persian architectural element that had been used for centuries to cool buildings. The badgir is solidly built tower that extends from the lowest room of the building to a point above the roof. It is divided into four vertical ventilation ducts that open in all four directions at the top, and which can be closed individually for control. The height of the tower enables a chimney effect based on heat flow, the supply of fresh air and the unhindered action of the wind. If the temperature inside is higher than outside, with no wind, then the chimney effect takes place. This occurs frequently at night, the cold night air flowing through the building and cooling the walls that act as a heat buffer. The hot air rises through the badgir and escapes. If the outside temperature rises than the air sinks and a reverse-chimney effect occurs. The air cools on the walls and ventilates the interior. The circulation and cooling was impressive but it had its drawbacks—animals often found their way inside. Scorpions and other poisonous creatures were a daily concern, so we placed our bedposts in cans filled with kerosene to keep them out of the beds. Despite our efforts, we found several dead scorpions every morning.

Every day started early. By 6 a.m., I was at the construction site, where my boss would drive by in his black limousine to check on us. At 9 a.m., I briefly returned home for breakfast before heading back to the office or flying to inspect projects on the islands. Sometimes when we flew back to the mainland, we would circle above the hotel Gambron where I could see Gisela and the children at the pool. It was my way of signaling my arrival to them, and to my driver, who would then pick me up at the airport, before the plane returned to Shiraz.

In the evenings, work took on a different pace, with meetings usually starting around 6 p.m. and often extending late into the night, especially when security matters were involved. Many of these meetings concluded with dinner, further fostering relationships with local officials.

One day, I received a call from the head of the secret service, Savak. A good man with fine manners and always well-dressed, he invited me for coffee at his office, where he expressed admiration for my work and praised my contributions. He was well-informed about my family and past and seemed particularly impressed with my efforts on the islands. I assured him I was committed to staying in the region to continue helping the country. As we concluded our meeting, he asked if I had anything to report from the islands, but I explained that I had already shared everything with the governor. That was the last I heard from Savak.

We continued building runways and expanding infrastructure, allowing us to fly more frequently between the islands. We didn't have a co-pilot due to budget constraints, so over time, the pilots taught me how to fly and co-pilot. This skill came in handy when we were planning an airstrip on the island of Siri. The military was instructed to build a landing strip, but they were endlessly delayed and so, with the pilot's guidance, I surveyed the island from above at a height of 30 meters. We then proceeded to land in what appeared to be a suitable area and marked out the future runway with rocks gathered from nearby. We had landed on soft ground, and the wheels had made deep ruts, so we tried to smooth them out with our shoes before taking off again. It was a hot afternoon, 40 degrees in the shade. That translated into a cockpit temperature of 60 degrees (140 Fahrenheit) which was higher than the permissible temperature. As we tightened our seatbelts, I called on the good Lord to help us, and the pilot recalled his mother's words, "Fly carefully and slowly, my son."

We started to taxi, the wheels bouncing through the ruts, and pulled up into the air just as we ran out of runway. The plane rose and then dropped immediately as we started out over the water. It was terrifying to face the possibility of crashing on a deserted island where nobody would even know to come to our aid, but we were lucky enough to stay just a few feet above the water before finally ascending to a safe height. I will never forget how wonderful it felt to circle above the hotel that day and announce our safe return.

The rapid development brought new challenges. Although the

city and islands now had modern housing, hotels, and utilities, the ports were overwhelmed with cargo, causing extended delays, and the infrastructure struggled to keep up with the demand. Refrigerated warehousing was extremely limited. Suppliers were unable to meet all the demand and building materials like cement had to be imported in large quantities, adding to the delays. Discontent among the population grew as the pace of development outstripped the capacity to manage it. The country was transforming quickly, and many struggled to keep up.

Kambiz and Minou at Hotel Gambron in Bandar Abbas in their school uniform which was mandatory for social equality.

69

ROYAL VISIT OF EMPRESS FARAH

When Empress Farah was scheduled to visit Bandar Abbas, special funds were made available to the governor for projects and upgrades. One such project involved constructing a modern clubhouse and facilities for visiting officials near the new boulevard. However, the path connecting it to the boulevard was rocky and muddy. I proposed upgrading the path to a proper road, suggesting it would benefit the city and leave a positive impression on the empress. Everyone agreed enthusiastically, but there was concern—we had only two weeks to complete it. All eyes turned to me, knowing I had already planned and scheduled the project before my arrival.

Fortunately, the contractor who had built the boulevard was still on-site, with the asphalt machine and other equipment ready to go. The main challenge was soil replacement and building the road base, but I estimated it could be done in two to three days, with the remaining work completed at night. I laid out the proposal and explained the timeline. Everyone agreed to cooperate, and by midnight, excavations began. The once-sleepy city came to life as residents, awakened by the commotion, came out to see what was happening.

I oversaw the construction day and night for a week. Whenever time allowed, I'd go home for a brief break to play with my children, who hugged me with joy, giving me renewed energy. Gisela's confidence and optimism, combined with my trust in the good Lord, gave me the strength to work for a week without proper sleep.

As the asphalt machine roared and the rollers smoothed the road, I drove to my boss's residence to select trees from his garden for the newly built road. My boss, excited and invested in the project, often drove by on his motorcycle, disguised under a helmet. For him, this was a matter of prestige; for me, it was about doing good for the city and leaving a lasting memory. I wished my mother could see it—she would have been proud.

Once the road was complete, the median was planted with beautiful trees and plants. The residents, however, couldn't understand the lengths we went to for the empress's visit, and some even insulted me! When the work was finished, and the street cleaned, I finally went home for a long, well-deserved sleep. By the time I woke, the reception had passed, and the royal party had departed.

A few days later, in the governor's meeting room, I encountered a group of unhappy young people. I listened to their concerns, then introduced myself, explaining that I was only in the province temporarily. I shared that the road built for the empress was not for personal gain; I had received no extra payment for the project. While some accepted my explanation, there was still an air of distrust among others.

During the regular state security commissions, held in the governor's office, I always sat to the left of my boss. As the youngest and least experienced in the room, I sometimes couldn't help but speak my mind, voicing the discontent I'd heard from the locals. The department heads and officials often looked at me with wide eyes, surprised that someone so young would openly criticize his government. At times, the governor had to intervene, explaining that I was young and, as an Azari, prone to passionate outbursts. Still, I believed constructive criticism would only benefit the country.

~

OVER THE PAST SEVERAL MONTHS, much had been accomplished. The island of Abu Musa and other smaller islands now had airstrips for small aircraft, freshwater plants were constructed by the German company Krupp, and large cold storage warehouses were built. In Bandar Abbas, we began constructing 2,500 houses. To the east, in Minab, progress was made laying thick concrete pipes to transport water along the road to Bandar Abbas, demonstrating to the population that water shortages would soon be resolved. The work demanded great perseverance, not only in construction but also in navigating bureaucracy and laws.

One major challenge was the budget cycle. Provincial ministries received funds at the beginning of the Persian year (April), which had to be spent by year's end or returned to the treasury. However, the timing created problems. While Tehran experienced winter, the south had summer, and vice versa, making it difficult to utilize the budget efficiently. By February, the best working month in Bandar Abbas, unspent funds had to be sent back to Tehran.

I suggested a workaround: we would declare projects as "completed" and issue final invoices, even if the work wasn't finished. The money would be deposited in an escrow account, supervised by the Ministry of Finance, and then disbursed to contractors as work progressed. Though not strictly legal, it was a practical solution. I took responsibility for signing the fictitious invoices, despite the governor's warning that I could face jail time for fraud if the invoices were ever audited. I took the risk, knowing it would enable progress on vital projects.

70

OUR DAILY LIFE IN THE PERSIAN GULF

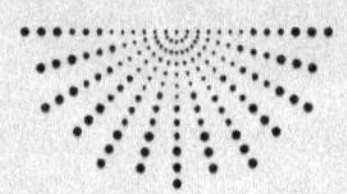

Our children had settled into their new school, which, though a strange environment for them, made them content. Gisela, too, developed good friendships and was happy with our life in Bandar Abbas. I called my parents every evening, often speaking at length with my mother. She was lonely, with my youngest sister studying at Tehran University and my youngest brother in Dallas, Texas, for his education. The long winter nights, alone with my aging father in the big house, were hard for her. The adopted children were all she had left for company. Sometimes, she cried on the phone, pouring out her heart, and it pained me deeply to hear her sadness. I often wondered if leaving my parents had been a mistake—perhaps being with them would have been more important than anything I was doing. Yet, Father always reminded me, "The country needs you," and was proud of my work.

I flew daily to supervise construction on the islands and mainland, where skilled labor was scarce, but with the help of qualified engineers and technicians, we made progress. Family and friends who visited us from time to time were amazed at how much had changed in the province over the past two years. Beyond the construction, my friend's orchards had thrived so much that he was harvesting strawberries and vegetables to be shipped to Tehran.

Over time, the province became a vacation destination. The winter months brought pleasantly warm weather and exotic landscapes, attracting tourists, some of whom built villas and vacation homes. However, water and electricity plants struggled to meet the rising demand. Although several power plants were completed, the load increased with development. The telephone network had improved, and long-distance calls were now possible. The country had essentially become one vast construction site.

I brought my old friend and partner, Hassan, to Bandar Abbas. Despite having a decent job and a family of his own—he had married our old company's secretary and settled in Minab—I felt it was my duty to help him. As a good surveying engineer, his skills were valuable, and I could use his help on our many projects.

One evening, my driver reported that a gentleman from Tehran had come to visit. It was Mr. P., an Armenian businessman whose company in Tehran supplied water pumps and motors. I was glad to see a familiar face, though he didn't look well. He reminded me of myself during the worst of times.

Once we were alone, he confided his woes. He had been forced to declare bankruptcy, leaving his wife and children behind. Struggling to get paid and drowning in debt, he found himself hiding from creditors. Like me, he sought refuge in prayer but didn't know what to do next. That's when he thought of me.

Hearing his story saddened me, especially because Armenians are known for their reliability and integrity. In Tabriz, many Armenians are skilled mechanics, engineers, and doctors. Their contributions to the arts and culture—ballet, cinema—are deeply valued in our country. I listened, thinking of ways to help. One thing was certain: the road through the Persian Gulf desert had to be his salvation. I reassured him and promised my help, trusting that it would work out. As Sufis say, "The Lord is generous—trust Him!"

The next morning, we shared breakfast under a clear blue sky, the cool air soothing our spirits. But inside, I wasn't calm. I felt the weight of his situation. Fortunately, it didn't take long to find a solution. I knew an Armenian entrepreneur who worked at a shipping company, clearing ships at the port. I had met him several times and knew his company was always busy—he would likely welcome the help.

I took Mr. P. to meet him, and after introductions, I asked if he needed an honest, reliable man. The entrepreneur confirmed he was looking for someone, so I vouched for Mr. P., adding, "He's Armenian, like you." To my relief, the entrepreneur hired him, and within months, Mr. P. held a leading position in the company, his life beginning to return to normal.

MANY OF OUR construction projects were based at ports and on islands off the mainland, and soon there was a need for a boat to serve as our mobile office. We found a large yacht, once owned by the actor who played Richard Kimble in *The Fugitive*. The yacht was luxurious, with a spacious living/dining room, bedrooms, and modern comforts. Though serviced and piloted by the Navy, it was ours to use. However, locals viewed it as a symbol of luxury for our pleasure, while for us, it was a necessary mode of transportation.

By this time, almost all the islands, cities, and larger towns had airports or at least airstrips. Warehouses, factories, cold storage facilities, modern schools, and colleges had also been completed. Given that much of our work was limited to six months of the year due to extreme heat and humidity, the speed of progress was impressive.

During the hot summer months, we worked mostly at night, stopping early in the morning before the heat returned. When summer vacation started in May, Gisela and the children stayed in Tehran or visited her mother in Germany, while I remained behind in the sweltering heat. My faithful driver kept me company, but my free time was limited as there was much to catch up on, despite the challenging conditions.

Off to work in the Cessna.

My other job was co-pilot!

A trip in the mountains close to Bandar Abbas.

Kambiz trying to catch fish at the hot spring.

The yacht provided by the Ostandari (office of the governor) to access the islands for work in Bandar Abbas, Persian Gulf.

Christmas in Bandar Abbas. The tree was a gift
from Behzad who sent it to us by airplane!

With my children Minou and Kambiz

SHORTAGES AND CONSEQUENCES

Cement was supplied by domestic factories, but the demand far exceeded the supply, requiring large quantities to be imported. Despite these efforts, we still had to ration it, which led to frequent complaints from representatives of major construction companies.

One day, I overheard loud voices coming from the adjacent room. A young American engineer was angrily protesting the cement shortage and had gone so far as to insult the official in charge. I stepped in and tried to explain that we were facing numerous challenges—overloaded ports, a shortage of trucks for transport, and other logistical issues. I reminded him that, as a guest in our country, he should behave accordingly. After that, I had him removed from my office. Though I knew he worked for a major foreign company with connections to the imperial family, their complaints could have serious repercussions. However, no consequences followed. Both the young engineer and his boss apologized to me several times before they received their allotted cement again.

I frequently visited the island of Abu Musa, where many projects had reached completion, such as the harbor basin, landing strip, freshwater plant, and a large cold storage facility. Road construction and housing developments were also well underway. The emperor himself had visited the navy stationed on the island and was highly pleased with the progress, which only increased the pressure on me, as I was responsible for overseeing all construction activities on the islands.

To the south of Abu Musa was a small village inhabited by Arab fishermen who had lived there since the time of the Ottoman Empire. Their circumstances had improved over the years, as they were now supplied with fresh water and food by the Emirate. When branches of the Iranian National Bank, Bank Melli, opened on the island, I met their sheikh. We reached an agreement to set up trade facilities for the islanders. The Arabs supplied daily provisions such as fresh bread, fish, and groceries, which they received from the mainland, and in exchange, our workers were allowed to shop there.

From the island, we could see the burning gas towers of the oil fields in the Arab Emirates, which were not far away. Electrical appliances and luxury items were imported from Dubai via domestic ships, and by selling them to our workers and visitors, the locals created a new source of income. This small trade also provided a diversion for our workers on the once lonely island and helped foster acceptance among the locals. Historically, Arabs have not been fond of Persians, even though it was through them that we were Islamized. However, Persians had followed the path of Ali, the son-in-law of the Prophet, and his descendants, the Twelve Imams, which created a significant cultural and religious divide.

Much had changed at the construction site over time. I worked with the site manager and engineers to modernize the camp, improving accommodations for the workers and installing a new kitchen. Hygiene standards were raised, and we adjusted the working hours to better suit the local climate. I even developed a healthier menu with the help of an experienced cook from Tabriz, ensuring the workers had more nutritious meals. I regularly ate with the crew and often stayed until sunset, fostering a bond with them. Despite the occasional oppressive silence at the dinner table, I made efforts to engage them in conversation.

After dinner, I would walk through the bunkhouses to ensure the well-being of the workers, always accompanied by strong men from the crew. My presence was necessary to prevent any misconduct, especially among men who had been away from their families for months. We also installed televisions in the camps, and by 1973, the range of sports and news broadcasts had improved significantly, helping to lift the overall atmosphere.

Significant global events during this time included the end of the Vietnam War, with the signing of the Agreement for the Restoration of Peace in Paris. Egypt and Syria launched an attack on Israel on Yom Kippur, scoring their first victory, albeit limited. OPEC countries, including Iran, cut oil supplies by 25%, creating the first oil crisis and driving up prices. Iran, however, strategically continued to supply oil to various nations depending on its national interests. Other major developments included the military coup in Chile, which led to the death of President Salvador Allende, and Juan Peron's election as president of Argentina. Additionally, the USA and USSR signed an agreement to prevent nuclear war.

With the oil crisis escalating, the government pushed for faster progress in modernization efforts. Tehran placed immense pressure on us to accelerate construction projects. In a bid to assist the poor, a directive was issued to minimize the use of machinery for road construction, creating manual labor jobs for the locals. Most of these workers were simple farmers who had little experience with such work. Nonetheless, they collected their wages at the end of the month. This initiative opened the door to false payrolls and corruption. Countless people—some of whom didn't work or even exist—were paid monthly, contributing to widespread inefficiency.

Moreover, goods were being imported in an attempt to lower prices, yet inflation continued to rise, exacerbating the already strained transportation and administrative systems. This led to growing discontent and disappointment among the population.

At the harbor, ships queued for miles, waiting to be unloaded. Perishable goods such as wheat and sugar, along with building materials, were left rotting due to the high humidity. The warehouses were overflowing, and many supplies had to be stored in the open air. With the public unable to grasp the complexities of the situation, the widespread dissatisfaction deepened. Decades of censorship and lack of free speech only fueled mistrust in the government.

The people were largely unaware of the vast foreign investments being made to reduce Iran's dependency on oil. These investments included stakes in major corporations such as the German company Krupp, Pan American Airlines, and an oil refinery in South Africa. Iran had also invested in the French nuclear industry to secure fuel for its own nuclear power plants, which German companies were already operating in Bushehr. Further investments were made in India and the United States. Iran Air had become one of the safest and most respected airlines in the world, and the Iranian currency ranked among the top ten globally.

72

GRATEFUL ARMENIANS

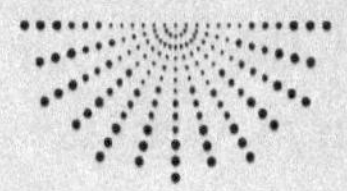

One day, we had an unexpected visit from my brother-in-law, who was also my father's business partner, arriving from Tehran. I had always been fond of him, as he was a dear and positive person, both about our work and life in general. His visit concerned a shipment of butter that had arrived from Denmark, which, like many others, was waiting to be unloaded and cleared through customs. The problem was that the ship's refrigeration system was malfunctioning, and if the container wasn't unloaded within the next few days, the entire load would become inedible. He came to me in desperation, asking if I could do anything to help, as the office in Tehran had written it off as a lost cause. I couldn't refuse; he was honest, straightforward, and well-loved by our family, especially by our mother, whom he had accompanied on her pilgrimage to Mecca. I had to try.

The following day, I went to see the governor and explained the situation. I didn't want to take advantage of my position, but this was a legitimate emergency—wasting food on such a scale would be disastrous and could even lead to protests. After a brief consideration, the governor granted immediate approval to unload the goods, leaving the organization to me.

I informed the head of the port and the customs office; both of whom assured me they would assist as soon as possible. However, we still needed enough refrigerated trucks to transport the cargo to Tehran. That's when I thought of my old Armenian friend, Mr. P., who had established himself as an entrepreneur over the past year. As I moved from office to office, my brother-in-law stayed by my side, amazed and proud of how I handled the situation. I called Mr. P. to my office, explained the issue, and without hesitation, he began planning the necessary logistics.

Within 24 hours, and with the help of dozens of capable workers, the ship was unloaded, and the butter was on its way to Tehran in refrigerated trucks. Mr. P. had come a long way, rising from a low point in his life to become a successful entrepreneur. His willingness to help me was a gesture of gratitude for the support I had given him in the past, and together, we managed to save both the shipment and my family's business partner. As my master Adieb would say, "The Lord is indeed generous."

With the crisis behind us, I decided to take a few days off. My younger brother had completed his university studies in Wuppertal, Germany, and was writing his thesis. He was about to get married, so Gisela and I, along with our children, flew to Germany for the wedding celebration. It had been our parents' wish that we represent the family at the event, and by this point, my mother had accepted that she would likely never see her sons marry in their homeland. She had come to terms with the fact that those who studied abroad would probably settle there and find partners far from home.

We stayed with Gisela's mother in her cozy, familiar apartment, which brought back many memories. As a student, I spent a lot of time there, swapping stories about our respective countries. Her mother had visited us many times by now and knew my family well. It was hard to believe that nearly seven years had passed since our own beautiful wedding.

My other two brothers and their families also came for the

wedding, and with a few friends, we Persians were not in the minority. The bride's family was warm and welcoming, doing everything they could to make our stay as pleasant as possible. After a few wonderful days, we returned to Tehran, stopping in Tabriz to visit my parents before heading back to Bandar Abbas.

The cityscape of Tabriz had changed dramatically. It was noisy, crowded, and uncomfortable. Our house, in contrast, felt quiet and empty. My father could no longer walk to the store, so he was picked up by a cab each day. Mother was happy to see us, but the loneliness weighed heavily on her. With all her children grown and gone, she longed to move to Tehran, where she could be closer to her grandchildren. My father readily agreed, so we planned to celebrate the Persian New Year in Tehran and begin searching for a suitable house for them.

Once we returned to Bandar Abbas, I went straight back to work. The job was becoming increasingly difficult as daily requests poured in from Tehran. I wrote one letter of complaint after another, which my boss forwarded to the Ministry of the Interior, but we received no replies, and the bottlenecks persisted.

One day, we were informed that an imperial revision group was coming to visit, and we had to provide them with suitable accommodations. This group consisted of retired military generals, confidants of the emperor, whose mission was to combat corruption. Their arrival annoyed me greatly. Our engineers and technicians were already stretched thin, and now I had to vacate their quarters to accommodate these well-paid generals. Since Bandar Abbas had become a vacation spot, hotel rooms were scarce, so I had to make room in our home as well. I asked Gisela to fly to Tehran for a few days, as there was no other option.

Frustrated, I asked my boss, "What are these gentlemen even coming here for?"

"They're here to inspect the bottlenecks and issues on-site," he said.

I couldn't help but laugh. "That's absurd! Everyone knows

there's a shortage of fresh produce, meat, and basic necessities here. Why subject themselves to such a long journey? We report these issues regularly, but there's never any response."

My boss simply chuckled and told me to let it go.

The first meeting with the group included all the directors, ministry heads, and high-ranking officials. The head of the commission, an elderly general, introduced himself and outlined their mission: to assist us in addressing the problems. After a lengthy speech, he asked if anyone had questions. I immediately raised my hand, despite a painful nudge from my boss under the table. I stood up and reiterated the concerns I had expressed in my numerous letters, all of which had gone unanswered.

When I finished, the room fell into an eerie silence. The general looked at me closely and asked for my name and position. After I introduced myself, he promised to visit my office and asked that I prepare a list of requirements.

The next day, several officials conveniently called in sick, creating an oppressive atmosphere in the office. Despite this tension, our guests at the house were treated well. With the help of my driver, we did everything we could to make their stay as comfortable as possible.

After about a week, we heard that the group had completed their inspections and were preparing to leave. I was disappointed, having prepared extensive proposals that I was eager to present. I went to the governor's office, entered unannounced, and found the governor sitting with the head of the commission. Feeling I had intruded at the wrong moment, I quickly moved to leave, but the general surprised me by inviting me to join them.

He asked me to sit down and began by saying he knew my father. When he inquired about him, I informed him that I had recently visited and that he was doing well. The conversation seemed lighthearted, and I relaxed—until he told me that he was there to oversee a complete audit of the books and payroll, which would be reported directly to His Majesty. I suddenly felt like a schoolboy, anxiously awaiting the results of the audit.

My brother-in-law, Agha Rahimi, in Dad's office. He was a one of our dearest family members and a helping hand whenever it was needed.

73

A RIDE IN THE HEAVENS

Dark clouds gathered ominously as we flew from Kish Island to Bandar Abbas. The sky's rapid change was alarming, and the worsening weather reduced visibility to nearly nothing. Air traffic control were unable to assist us. Lacking proper instruments to guide us, we were truly at the mercy of the storm. The pilot, growing increasingly anxious, took us down to 200 feet, hoping to fly beneath the thick cloud cover, but still, nothing was visible. We circled in desperation, climbing and descending in search of any sign of the ground, as our fuel supply dwindled.

The tension in the cockpit was palpable as the captain turned to me, unsure of what to do next. My mind raced, and in my confusion, I instinctively called out to Adieb for help, eyes shut tight as I kept repeating his name. I asked the pilot how much lower we could safely go, and he estimated about 100 feet—approximately 30 meters above sea level. He explained that at that altitude, the air resistance would almost act as a natural runway, allowing the plane to skim the surface of the humidity. Desperate, I agreed this was our best option.

The pilot carefully descended, and I kept my eyes fixed on the altimeter, the numbers ticking down in rhythm with the pounding of my heart. The plane groaned under the strain, sounding like a weary beast of burden, but at last, we broke through the clouds. Beneath us lay the serene, blue ocean, and in the distance, the mainland shimmered on the horizon.

When we finally landed safely, the relief was overwhelming. Our situation had been far more dire than we had realized—unbeknownst to us, the Navy had been placed on high alert, deploying search teams to find us. Word had spread quickly throughout the town: the engineer from Tabriz and his pilot were missing. My driver recounted the wild rumors circulating in the city. That evening, as the news of our safe return spread, many visitors, including the governor, came to check on us. Gisela and I were busy entertaining guests until midnight, grateful to be home.

In the aftermath of this harrowing experience, we pushed ahead with even larger projects: the construction of a new harbor and shipbuilding basin, a railroad connecting Bandar Abbas to Kerman with links to the national railway network, and the expansion of power plants to meet the growing demand. However, a major issue persisted—the shortage of skilled labor and housing for workers and contractors. The city was bursting at the seams, with no free rooms and skyrocketing rental prices.

I proposed to the National Security Commission that contractors should be responsible for arranging their own accommodations for their teams. Some of the officials laughed, looking at me as though I had lost my mind. But I pointed out that we had major contracts with large international companies; these companies could house their workers on ships, much like they did in Europe. It seemed a viable solution to our housing crisis.

To my satisfaction, the idea took hold. Soon, workers were brought in from overseas and housed on residential ships anchored nearby. Supplies and provisions for the personnel were sourced from the Emirates, across the Gulf. This arrangement eased the burden on the city's infrastructure, keeping rental prices stable and avoiding further strain on local resources.

Shortly thereafter, the Prime Minister visited the region and decided to hold a trade exhibition. With the Arab Emirates growing wealthy from oil revenues, the market presented a significant opportunity for Persia. Dubai, once an isolated oasis in the desert, was transforming into a thriving free port zone. Many of the region's influential families had Persian ancestry, and they sought to improve relations with the government, lobbying for better diplomatic ties. However, the Shah remained largely uninterested, often making the sheikhs wait months before granting them an audience.

Despite the Shah's indifference, preparations for the trade fair moved forward. We built the fairgrounds and exhibition halls, determined to showcase Persian industry to the growing market across the Gulf. Within a few months, the halls were completed. The exhibition drew participants from various sectors of engineering, construction, petrochemicals, household appliances, textiles, etc. Each proudly presented their products, eager to tap into the opportunities presented by the expanding market.

Opening ceremony of a Construction Trade Show
where I am walking with the governor of the
province, and ministers from Tehran. Two days
later, a major earthquake took place in that region.

74

EARTHQUAKE

We were hard at work constructing an access road, with heavy machinery in full operation. The vibratory rollers, capable of delivering 40 tons of impact force, moved steadily over the road, shaking the ground beneath. I stood in the middle, overseeing the process and giving instructions when suddenly, I noticed something unsettling—the roller had stopped, yet the earth continued to tremble. Turning around, I saw the concrete poles supporting the power lines swaying unnaturally, bending from top to bottom like writhing serpents. It was a sight I could hardly comprehend. How could these solid concrete columns, so sturdy, be moving like that? Power lines were snapping up and down violently, accompanied by a deafening noise, like hundreds of helicopters hovering overhead.

People began flooding out of the nearby bank, their faces filled with terror. Screaming and crying, they scattered in every direction, running with no clear destination—just desperate to escape. I stood frozen, as if caught in a surreal nightmare. It dawned on me then: this was no ordinary disturbance—it was an earthquake, and a powerful one at that. My thoughts immediately raced to my family. Our house was old; I feared it would not survive such violent tremors. What if something had happened to them?

Panic overtook me, and I ran without thinking. My mind was blank, my body driven only by the desperate need to do something, though I didn't know what. Just then, my driver came speeding toward me, the car skidding to a halt in front of me. The doors flew open, and out jumped Gisela and the children. Relief flooded over me as I embraced them tightly, thanking God for their safety. We quickly piled into the car and made our way to the hotel, a more modern and sturdy building compared to our home. Despite being near the coast, I figured we'd be safe as long as a tsunami didn't follow the quake.

Once at the hotel, I ran through the halls to assess the situation. It had to be evacuated immediately; after a major earthquake, the risk of fire due to broken electric and gas lines is always high. The elevators and escalators had already stopped working, making the stairwells the only viable escape route. The hotel featured grand mahogany staircases, rarely used, but now they posed a serious risk. If a fire broke out, those stairs could become death traps for hundreds of guests. The director was already organizing the staff to set up tents on the hotel lawn, providing food and music to calm the guests as they gathered outside.

With the hotel under control, I headed to the office to meet with the governor. He was unavailable, busy trying to establish contact with other cities and villages. The air force and navy were out in full force, offering aid where they could. That night, we were invited to stay with the chief of the waterworks at his modern, earthquake-resistant home located on a small hill outside the city. As we settled in, the small TV on the table wobbled each time an aftershock hit. The dogs, sensing the tremors before they arrived, would howl loudly, then suddenly fall silent moments before the ground shook once more. It was a deeply unsettling and frightening experience for all of us.

A few days later, we flew to Tehran, but the trauma lingered.

The shock of the earthquake was still with us, ingrained deep in our bones. Every sound, every slight movement sent waves of fear through us. Gisela and the children were taken to Tabriz to stay with my mother. In her nurturing way, she did everything in her power to care for them, offering emotional support and calming their nerves. Psychics were consulted, and other women gave advice —each with their own remedies and reassurances that helped restore their spirits. After about a week, Gisela and the children returned, noticeably calmer and more collected. Perhaps the fresh mountain air of Tabriz and my mother's loving care had played a part in their recovery.

But before long, Gisela and the children traveled to Germany to stay with her mother. I, however, had to return to Bandar Abbas, as my responsibilities were far from over. There was still so much to do in the aftermath of the quake.

The earthquake had measured 7.1 on the Richter scale, claiming 100 lives and injuring many more. Though it had caused devastation, we had been fortunate. Luck had been on our side this time.

75

LAST NEW YEAR'S FESTIVAL WITH MOTHER

In the spring of 1975, we spent the Nowruz Festival in Tehran. Mother joined us, but as usual, Father stayed behind, perfectly content at home. It would be our last New Year's festival celebrated on such a grand scale. With the exception of my two brothers—one in the US and the other in Germany—we were all together again, just like the happy times we had in Tabriz. After the celebrations, Mother flew back to Tabriz, and we returned to Bandar Abbas. My faithful driver greeted us at the airport, and after dropping Gisela and the children at home, he drove me to the office. I exchanged New Year greetings with the staff, sorted through some correspondence, and then headed home, expecting a peaceful evening. But fate had other plans.

During the drive home, a strange trembling began to take over my body. By the time we reached the house, my entire frame was shaking uncontrollably. My driver had to help me to my bed, but even lying down did nothing to stop the tremors. The shaking intensified, and soon I was in the throes of what felt like a seizure. He sat on my feet, trying to hold me still, but I remained clear-headed and felt no pain—yet something inside me seemed desperate to escape, though I couldn't understand what. My teeth chattered so violently that the sound filled the room. I became gripped with fear for my wife and children, convinced that my time had come. God had spared me so many times, guiding me through the worst situations, but now, it seemed, this was the end. I found some solace in the thought that I had seen everyone once more in Tehran and even recently visited Adieb, who surely would have sensed if my death were imminent. And with that, I drifted into sleep.

When I awoke, the governor and his personal physician were standing by my bed. The doctor calmly informed me that I had suffered a severe nervous breakdown. Relief washed over me, and remarkably, I was able to get up later that same day, feeling completely normal as if nothing had happened.

The next day, I returned to the office, intent on resuming my routine. Yet as I sat at my desk, handling the usual administrative tasks, a sudden crushing pressure hit my chest, leaving me gasping for air. It only lasted a few seconds, but it drenched me in sweat. My mind raced through memories of my happy childhood, the gift of my loving parents, my studies abroad, my beautiful wife and children, and the challenges of the last seven years here. The attacks kept coming, and with each one, it became painfully clear that the demanding work I had been doing was no longer sustainable.

A few days later, my brothers took me to see a cardiologist in Tehran. After a series of tests, the doctor found no apparent physical issues. I was healthy in body, but he warned that these attacks would grow more frequent and severe if I didn't make serious changes to my high-stress life. I worried about the unfinished projects, about my colleagues who would be left to shoulder the burden. But as I reflected on my family, it became obvious—no work could ever be more important than them. I had to close this chapter of my life and start anew.

I returned to the office one last time to say my farewells. It was a deeply emotional moment, and everyone was saddened by my departure, especially the governor, my dear driver, and my two close friends from the waterworks. These were people who had become like family during my time in Bandar Abbas, and parting ways was harder than I had anticipated.

76

A NEW BEGINNING, AGAIN

I traveled to Germany to seek treatment from a well-known alternative practitioner, the father-in-law of my friend Behzad, the man who owned the paint factory in Tehran. Using acupuncture and sedatives, he treated me in his peaceful clinic, nestled in a small town on the Rhine near Düsseldorf. I longed to rediscover my inner peace, and this retreat seemed like the perfect opportunity. It's often the case that one only begins to search when something precious is lost.

The treatment, combined with the serene environment, worked wonders. After a few weeks, I felt much better and returned home alone. Gisela and the children were still staying with her mother, and I asked them to remain there a bit longer. I wanted to be alone and spare them any further worry.

However, during the flight back, I experienced the worst hours of my life. Seated at the back of the aircraft, the long aisle before me resembled a dark, narrow tunnel leading nowhere. Despite the sedatives, an overwhelming sense of anxiety gripped me, and my neck constricted as if I were choking. At times, the sensation became so intense that I wanted to lash out. The elderly lady beside me noticed my distress. With kindness and calm, she took my hand, massaging it gently and talking to me, offering reassurance. Her presence kept me grounded, and I shudder to think what might have happened had she not been there.

Upon arriving in Tehran, my dear sister went out of her way to ensure my comfort. The house was kept in complete silence—not even the radio or television was turned on—so I could rest in peace. Yet, despite her efforts, my condition didn't improve. So, my cousin Nader drove me to Tabriz to stay with my parents. I craved security and tranquility, and I knew I could find that at home with my mother.

Many of my old friends, including Said, came to visit me. I did my best to hide my condition during these meetings, but Father remained puzzled. He couldn't understand how a young man could be both healthy and sick at the same time. He lived in his own idealized world, unaware of the mounting problems in our country. But I preferred it that way. It was better for him to remain blissfully ignorant, and I found comfort in his contentment.

Mother, as always, was a saint. Despite her own worries and recent losses—her beloved sister and nephew, Ali Aga, who had tragically died in a car accident—she cared for me tirelessly. Separated from most of her children and grandchildren, she was burdened with many sorrows, yet she still found the strength to console me.

One day, she spoke to me in her simple, wise way: "No human can fully explain the mystery of the universe, or even the mystery of life. We are surrounded by things we cannot understand. The forces within our bodies are a mystery, just like the flowers growing in cracks in the wall or the green grass in the garden. What seems bad today may seem different tomorrow. Trust in God's justice, and you'll regain your health."

When it was time to return to my life and family, I hugged her tightly and wept. She hugged me back, whispering, "Don't cry. We'll see each other again soon. Karim has come home after finishing his studies in the US, and he's getting married soon. So, if God wills it, we'll all be together again before you know it."

Not long after, I received an offer from a construction company working on Abu Musa Island. They wanted me as their chief engineer. The chief of the navy had been deposed, and his brother—previously involved in the company—was now in trouble, leaving the project without the special privileges it once enjoyed. Despite my ongoing health concerns, I accepted the offer. It was generous, and I had to consider the future of my wife and children.

With my new role, I became responsible for overseeing all projects in the Persian Gulf. After I resigned from Bandar Abbas, my friend and partner Hassan had to leave as well, lacking the necessary engineering credentials. He had settled in Minab with his wife, and I arranged for him to manage the office there.

Shortly after starting the job, I received a large advance on my salary. I used it to buy a small, modern three-room apartment in the northern part of the city, not far from where we had once lived before our financial troubles. As Mother always said, "Stay true to yourself."

The company owners, who once doubted me, now respected and trusted me deeply because of my past work on the breakwater at Abu Musa. They had not believed that someone with no expectations of receiving additional under the table payments could complete such a thorough job, but I had done my duty with integrity.

When I visited the new apartment in Tehran for the first time, I brought with me the Holy Book and a mirror, as is customary. The Holy Book serves as a reminder that our time in any abode is allotted by God's will, temporary and unchangeable. The mirror symbolizes living a life of honesty—one should be able to look into it at any time without shame, because doing so with a clear conscience is no easy task.

My family helped me refurbish the apartment, and it was

reminiscent of the time Gisela had come from Germany with her mother and our children. But this time, things felt different. My illusions had faded after everything we'd been through. When Gisela returned from her trip, she had no idea about our new apartment. I drove her and the children there, surprising her with the new home. She was overjoyed. Finally, she had her own place again.

My parents visited us as well. Father hadn't been to Tehran in many years and was surprised by the size of the apartment. Though small, it had everything—a modern kitchen, two bedrooms, a large living room, and a bathroom. He couldn't understand how we managed in such a modest space, especially after the larger homes we'd lived in before. Standing on the balcony, looking out over the city, he shook his head, lost in thought. I could only guess at what was going through his mind. Perhaps it was the shock of seeing how much the capital had changed. Old, familiar families had been pushed aside, replaced by the new wealthy elite. Traditions were fading, and customs were being broken. The city was expanding rapidly, but some utilities still hadn't caught up. I couldn't help but wonder if this relentless development would eventually collapse under its own weight.

Meanwhile, my younger brother had been working on the Minab Dam with a large engineering company. After the project was completed, he conducted the final inspection, and the plant was successfully put into operation.

Despite my health concerns, I flew to Abu Musa Island, knowing it like the back of my hand by now. The island had slowly transformed into a modern town, with all the necessary infrastructure in place.

Our company also received a contract to build prefabricated halls in Bandar Abbas. The parts were imported from Norway, but we ran into issues with the steel components due to the extreme heat—it's a well-known fact that steel expands in high temperatures. Precision was key, or the cladding wouldn't fit. I clashed with the Norwegian technicians, insisting they submerge the steel measuring tape in cold water before measuring to counteract the expansion. The lead technician, confident in his European expertise, refused. It was always like this with Europeans and Americans. So, I sent him home on the first flight.

Once the halls were completed, I met the client—a well-groomed, pleasant man of about fifty. He was enthusiastic about the work we'd done, and after hearing my name, he guessed correctly that I was from Tabriz and knew of my father.

Shortly after, he spoke with my superiors, expressing his desire for me to manage various projects for his company. He was also a member of the Bank Iran o Arab board of directors. Once all the construction projects on Abu Musa were finished, and with the approval of my company, I accepted the offer of Dr. Shahib.

77

OUR NEW COMPANY

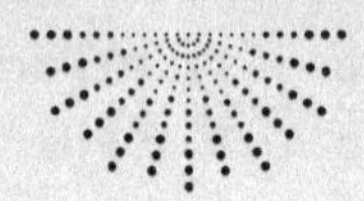

I became a director and partner in Dr. Shahib's construction company, and while reviewing the company registration documents, I was surprised to learn that Mahmoud Reza Pahlavi, a brother of the emperor, was also involved. I met him at several meetings and found him to be a very composed and meticulous person. Like my brother, he had also studied in the United States.

The company had several significant projects underway. One of the largest was the construction of a massive bread factory in Khash, a city in the extreme southeast of the country, bordering Pakistan. Situated about 1,350 meters above sea level in the Sistan-Baluchestan province, Khash was over 1,700 kilometers from Tehran. The population there was predominantly Baluch, and they spoke an Indo-European language.

The factory complex we were building in Khash was extensive, comprising wheat silos, bakeries, sales halls, and modern housing for the workers and staff. It was a project costing $2,000,000 and was completed with the cooperation of Werner & Pfleider Bakery Technologies – the international leader in the field. Most of the materials were sourced locally, with the exception of the ovens, which, naturally, were imported from Germany.

At the same time, we were constructing a brick factory in Ilam, a city close to the Iraqi border. This meant I was constantly traveling between the two locations. The summer heat was relentless, with little to no rainfall, but despite the harsh conditions, I found great satisfaction in my work. Gisela had no idea what kind of circumstances I was enduring, which, in hindsight, was probably for the best.

What I enjoyed most was the opportunity to explore every corner of my homeland. Each province had its own distinct character—different climates, people, languages, and cultures. Iran was, and still is, a land of diverse and often divided peoples. The Baluch, for example, are spread across Iran, Pakistan, and Afghanistan in the southeast. The Kurds are split between Iran, Turkey, and Iraq in the northwest. Azerbaijan is divided as well, with the northern section in Europe and the southern part in Iran. The Turkmen inhabit both the Republic of Turkmenistan and the northeastern part of Iran, while Arabs are scattered between Iran, Iraq, and the emirates along the Persian Gulf.

Beyond the ethnic divisions, Iran is home to many tribes, such as the Bakhtiari, Kurds, and Lurs. Despite the differences, these peoples had preserved their unique identities, which I saw as a positive thing. Forgetting or denying one's origins, customs, and traditions leads to the loss of identity, something I believed to be a grave mistake.

In Khash, which was one of the most underdeveloped areas in the country, we built another factory to produce bricks. Building materials were in high demand, and this new factory was meant to meet that need. However, constructing brick plants presented its own challenges, primarily the lack of raw materials. For example, producing clinker bricks required large quantities of high-quality clay, which was scarce in that arid region. I found myself working in one of the driest, harshest landscapes I had ever encountered.

The work was grueling, both physically and mentally, and it took a toll on my nerves. But eventually, that plant was also completed.

As the summer drew to a close, we gathered in Tehran for Karim's wedding. Karim was the eldest son of my dear sister Firuze, and had been educated in Texas, achieving a degree in Chemistry, and eventually becoming the director of the Tabriz oil refinery. He was tall, friendly, and handsome and we were delighted that our mother's long-held wish to see him married had finally come true! The celebration was beautiful and harmonious, bringing the whole family together for a joyous occasion. It lifted our spirits to be reunited, if only for a short time. But after just a few days, Mother was eager to return to Tabriz, worried about leaving Father alone for too long.

In the meantime, our eldest brother had moved his family to Tabriz. As the oldest son, he felt it was his duty to be close to our parents in their later years. He had a good job with the Air Force, overseeing the military hospital. In the evenings, he often cared for patients without charging them, even giving out medications for free. Thanks to his presence, our parents were no longer completely alone, which brought us all some comfort.

78

OUR MOTHER SLEPT FOREVER

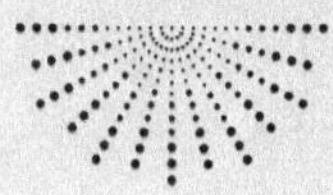

On a warm and sunny autumn day, we had been invited to a friend's house for a meal. The tables were set, and it promised to be a beautiful day—at least, that's what we thought. Soon after we arrived, the doorbell rang, and there at the front door stood my two brothers. They embraced me tightly, but neither spoke a word. Through their dark sunglasses, I could see tears streaming down their faces. Something terrible had happened. But what?

"Father?" I asked, my heart pounding.

"No... Mother," my favorite brother replied softly. "Our mother left us. Without the slightest sign, without even a goodbye. Quietly, and without a word."

He explained that it had been a Friday, a day off from work. As usual, Mother had prepared a meal. There were no complaints, nothing unusual—just a peaceful day. While the table was set for dinner and everyone was sitting together in a calm, Sunday-like mood, Mother had lain down on the couch in the next room. She had been chatting with our long-time house girl. When it was time for dinner, the house girl went to wake her, but she didn't wake up.

She was gone, having drifted into eternal sleep. She had left us without a word.

My brother, a doctor, had tried desperately to revive her, but it was useless. He must have lived through the worst hour of his life, watching helplessly as our mother slipped away.

When our beloved aunt had passed away, our uncle—the leather manufacturer—had purchased a double grave in Shah Abdol-Azim, a place of pilgrimage near Tehran. He had always intended for both sisters, who had loved each other deeply, to rest side by side in that grave. So, it was decided that Mother would be transferred to Tehran and laid to rest alongside her sister.

No one could believe what had happened. It seemed so surreal, so sudden. Many of my siblings immediately flew to Tabriz, but I couldn't. I was not well mentally, and I had anticipated that the news of Mother's passing would trigger a terrible nervous breakdown. I waited for it to come, but somehow, it didn't. It was as though the spirit of my dear mother helped me stay strong, keeping me on my feet when I thought I might crumble. During that time, I couldn't talk much about my family or see anyone. All I saw was the shadow of my beloved mother.

At the funeral, I stood in front of her open grave, waiting. Mother had yet to be brought from the medical office. There was a heavy silence all around—everyone present was waiting, just as we had waited for her in life. No one dared speak. Suddenly, I noticed movement in the distance. A group of people were coming toward us, carrying her coffin, which they brought to the graveside.

I sat on the ground, directly in front of her open grave, waiting for her arrival. How could I say goodbye? What could I possibly say to thank her for all her love, her sacrifices, her unwavering support? What would we do without her? What would our old father do? There were no words that could capture the depth of our loss. We had lost her at the age of 67, far too soon.

As I write these words, even after all these years, my eyes still fill with tears. I will try to finish this chapter quickly, but the pain of her absence remains as sharp as it was on that fateful day.

79

FAREWELL TO TABRIZ

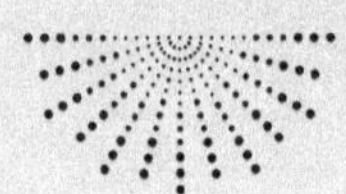

When I arrived in Tabriz a few days later, some friends were there to greet me at the airport and take me home. Said was among them, and he was crying as though he had lost his own mother. Our house, once full of life, now felt gray—no, black. There was a dead silence that hung heavy in the air. The high walls surrounding the house seemed to press down on me, suffocating me. I could hardly breathe; something was choking me. Even the cats howled in a way that was eerie and unsettling.

I saw our old father sitting quietly in a corner, well-dressed but staring into the void. It broke me. I lost my composure, just as my siblings had. We all cried, and though painful, the release of tears felt necessary, just as Adieb had once said.

By the evening, my tears had run dry. I was calm, even relieved, but utterly drained of any emotion. The house was full of people, all of them coming to pay their respects to my father. I had no idea who had organized everything, but food was being served on white tablecloths spread across the floor in several rooms. Everyone was busy, as if keeping occupied would help them forget the tragedy we were all living through. Strangers, too—many we didn't even know

—came to mourn. They had lost their protector and benefactor in my mother.

Old and young, students and shopkeepers alike, approached us with their worries. "Who will help us now? Who will pay for our medicine or care for the sick?" they asked, desperate. Some of the students wondered aloud how they would pay their school fees. Only then did we begin to understand the full extent of Mother's selfless devotion to others. She had been quietly helping so many for years, selling her jewelry to support them. Except for a few personal items—some clothing, shoes, and unimportant belongings—she had left nothing behind.

I wandered through the house with what little strength I had left, saying my silent goodbyes. (Our lives are filled with separations and goodbyes every day, though we rarely recognize them as such.) I made my way down to the basement, where we usually stored bread. But now, it was empty. There were no winter supplies, and the other rooms, too, were bare. This was no longer the house I had grown up in, yet in every corner, I saw memories from those Beautiful Past Times. I sat down on the cold floor and wept—not just for our lost mother, but for the paradise that had disappeared with her.

After a few days, my family sent me back to Tehran. The first thing I did was visit Adieb. He tried his best to comfort me, but I was in the same condition I had been all those years ago when I first came to him—only worse, because this time, I had lost something that I could never recover.

After our zikr session, he told me a story. "When our Creator sent us to this Earth," he began, "He gave us a protective suit, our body, which our soul and spirit need—like an astronaut needs a spacesuit. This protective suit is placed in the womb of the mother. On Earth, a day and night are divided into 24 hours, one full rotation of the planet on its axis. But there are much larger planets where the length of day and night is much longer. In the Holy Quran, it speaks of a planet where one day is equivalent to 50,000 times the length of a day on Earth. That means, one rotation on its axis lasts about 150 earthly years."

He paused, letting the idea sink in before continuing. "When our task on Earth is complete, we shed our protective garment and return to where we came from. If someone has lived 90 years on this Earth, they have only traveled a few hours in the time of origin. Your mother is now resting in her heavenly garden."

I was awestruck by his words. "How do you know this?" I asked, needing reassurance.

He smiled gently and explained, "There are three levels of knowledge. The first is the knowledge of the mind (AQL), which we gain through logical inference. The second is the knowledge of the states (AHWAL), which one can only access through direct experience. The third is the knowledge of secrets (ASRAR), and it is the knowledge that transcends the limitations of the mind."

Somehow, Adieb, with his kind heart and profound spiritual knowledge, was always able to shore me up and help me through the most difficult times.

80

THE MISFORTUNE CONTINUES

My brother, the senior physician at the Diakonie Hospital in Karlsruhe, Germany, had confided some troubling news to me shortly before Mother's death. His dear wife, whom we loved as our own sister, had fallen gravely ill. The doctors had discovered a brain tumor that required surgery. Fortunately, she was operated on by the renowned Persian brain surgeon, Prof. Sami, an old friend of my brother's. Wanting to shield Mother from further worry, we decided not to inform her about it at all.

During the mourning period for Mother, my brother called me with a voice filled with relief and joy. He announced that the surgery had been successful and that his wife was recovering well. But I had no good news for him in return. I had to break the news of Mother's passing, though my throat tightened at the thought. I can't even recall how I managed to tell him—at some point, someone had to take the phone from me. Thousands of kilometers away, our brother had to mourn Mother alone, without family around him.

In Tehran, we finally purchased the long-awaited house. It was a building with three separate apartments, providing space for my youngest sister and two younger brothers. Father stayed with our youngest sister, who took on the responsibility of caring for him. It was such a shame that Mother never got to see it. She would have loved the place. The only sibling unaware of Mother's passing was our youngest brother, still studying in Texas. Father wanted to tell him in person when he returned home.

I buried myself in work as a way to escape the overwhelming sadness. Often, out of habit, I found myself wanting to call Mother. A few times, I even dialed her number before reality struck me—she was no longer there to answer. My colleagues at the office noticed and gave me space to grieve in my own way.

One day, our chairman of the board, Dr. Sahib, who was also a banker, shared a story about our father. He told me that many people had initially distrusted the Persian National Bank, Bank Melli Iran, when it was first founded in 1927. It took time for them to entrust their money to the institution. Once, a wealthy and irate prince from Tabriz had demanded to withdraw a large sum from his account—millions in cash—as revenge against the bank director. Due to poor road conditions and unreliable telegraphic communication with the capital, the money had not arrived in time, and the bank couldn't fulfill the prince's request immediately.

Desperate, the bank director had sent a messenger to Father for help. According to the story, Father sent his accountant to the bazaar to ask the merchants for a short-term loan. Within no time, the necessary funds were provided, even exceeding the amount needed. Without Father's quick intervention, the National Bank would have suffered a serious embarrassment and lost credibility. Since that incident, whenever a new bank branch opened in Tabriz, an account with a substantial credit line was automatically opened in Father's name—but he never made use of it.

After forty sorrow-filled days, the official mourning period came to an end. Yet, our grief never truly subsided; it remained deep within us. In my everyday life, Mother's presence still lingered. In difficult situations, I found myself seeking her guidance. Whatever I did, whenever I looked back, I realized it was always in her spirit.

~

A FEW MONTHS PASSED, and spring arrived, along with our New Year, Nowruz. It was our first Nowruz without Mother, and despite the somber mood, our eldest sister tried to restore some semblance of normalcy. She set the Haft-Sin table as always, and we sat together, though our thoughts were elsewhere.

As visitors came and went, Father recited the New Year prayer, wishing us all the best. Then, in his usual way, he reminded us that we were still young, with many years ahead, but that our time would also come one day. He urged us not to dwell in sorrow, reminding us that Mother's soul would feel our sadness too. We had to return to our lives and work hard, always keeping family at the forefront, just as Mother had done.

In the year following Mother's passing, Father had been patient and stoic, remaining relatively healthy. But after the first anniversary of her death, his health began to decline. One day, after work, I was informed that an ambulance had come to take Father to the hospital. I rushed to be by his side and found him sitting calmly on the hospital bed. His first question was not about himself, but about me—he had always been selfless that way. He assured me he was feeling better and suggested we go home and have some fresh tea together. I didn't know why I was so worried. Father had never been sick in his entire life, had never even seen a doctor. But I couldn't hold back my tears. I told him I would take him home as soon as the doctors finished their tests.

Sadly, just two weeks later, on March 5th, 1976, Father left us. He passed away in a private clinic due to kidney failure. After 84 years of living a happy, fulfilling life, he was laid to rest in the family tomb at Shah Abdol-Azim, a place of pilgrimage.

Father had managed to achieve his greatest dream: to see all six of his sons and his daughter reach high academic achievements. Our youngest brother had just returned from Texas, having completed his studies in chemistry. Father had no more wishes left —except to be buried beside his faithful and beloved wife.

The funeral service took place on the same day in both Tehran and Tabriz. In Tabriz, the bazaar near Father's office closed in his honor. In Tehran, a large mosque overflowed with people wanting to pay their last respects to the man who had never said no, never lied, never complained, and had always remained hopeful.

Father's passing deeply affected our youngest sister. She became ill and couldn't continue her studies. We were all deeply worried about her. After Mother's death, our eldest sister, Firuzeh, took on the role of a surrogate mother. She had always been there to support and guide us, so, I turned to her for advice on how to help our little sister. Firuzeh suggested that Manije had known a young man, Ali Reza, for some time, and that perhaps marriage might help her find peace and stability. My siblings and I agreed.

Firuzeh, ever the organizer, somehow made it all happen. Not long after Father's death, Manije and Ali Reza were married. The celebration was small, with only close family attending. My good friend Ali hosted a dinner at the Hilton Hotel, and shortly after, the newlyweds flew to Spain for their honeymoon.

My sister, Manije's wedding day. From left to right: My nephew Karim, brother Parwiz, the groom Ali Reza, Manije, and myself.

81

IT CONTINUES

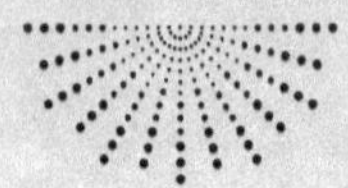

Death seemed to be an ever-present shadow looming over the Haj Bekoff family. We found ourselves attending funeral after funeral, almost monthly. It all began with the tragic loss of my cousin Ali in a car accident, followed closely by my aunt. And then, within what felt like mere moments, we lost both my mother and father.

Two weeks after my father's passing, the New Year's celebration arrived—a festival we had joyfully marked together for so many years in Tabriz. Now, however, it was a hollow occasion, stripped of its happiness. Instead of the traditional Haft-Sin table, with its display of sweets, new clothes, and dyed eggs, our table was bare, save for a bowl of dates and the Holy Quran. The house, usually vibrant with laughter and preparation for the new year, was now dark and filled with an indescribable sadness. Visitors came to offer their condolences, but they didn't linger. Grief had cast a heavy veil over our home, and it was as though no one knew what to say or how to ease the pain that had settled so deeply in our hearts.

Meanwhile, my brother in Germany was facing his own unimaginable heartache. His young wife, who had undergone a successful operation to remove a brain tumor, had relapsed. Upon hearing that her condition had worsened, I knew I had to be there for him, even though my own health was still fragile. My nerves were shot, and I often felt a dull ache in my heart. Yet, despite everything, I booked a flight and traveled to Germany, determined to support him in his time of need.

I stayed for as long as I could bear. It was agonizing to see his two children—his daughter, 11, and his son, 10—trying to make sense of the situation. They were so young, so innocent, and now on the brink of losing their mother. My brother, too, was utterly broken. Though a senior physician, with all the medical resources at his disposal, he could do nothing to save his wife. He had provided her with the best possible care, making sure she was as comfortable as possible in her final days, but the outcome was inevitable. She was terminal, and her remaining time with us was painfully short.

What made the situation even more heart-wrenching was that my sister-in-law remained blissfully unaware of her fate. My brother had gone to great lengths to shield her from the truth, even removing the mirror from her bathroom so she couldn't see the toll her illness and treatments had taken on her appearance. It was gut-wrenching to see her once-beautiful face swollen from medication, and to know that while she planned for the future, there would be none.

Sitting by her bedside, she asked me with such innocence about our parents, completely unaware that they too were gone. It was all I could do to keep from blurting out the truth. I had to maintain the lie for her sake, even though it felt like a betrayal.

In the evenings, while my brother sat vigil at the hospital, I stayed with her mother at their house. She was beside herself with grief, and understandably so. She kept asking me why this had happened to her daughter, who had always led such a healthy, pure life—never drinking, never smoking. What could I say to that? I had no answers, no words of comfort that could ease her anguish.

After a few days, my own condition worsened. My nerves,

already frayed, couldn't handle the stress any longer. I realized I had to leave before my health deteriorated further and added another burden to my already struggling brother. I knew his wife's remaining days were few, and soon he would have to make the unbearable decision to turn off her life-support. Before that terrible moment came, I bid my farewells and made my way back home.

The flight home was heavy with sadness. Though I had done my best to be there for my brother, I left feeling helpless, knowing that no words or actions could soften the blow of what was to come. As much as I had been through, witnessing the slow, inevitable decline of my sister-in-law had drained me completely. And yet, life would go on, as it always does, indifferent to the personal tragedies that mark our lives forever.

My brother Behruz with his dear wife Margot.

82

JERUSALEM, ISRAEL

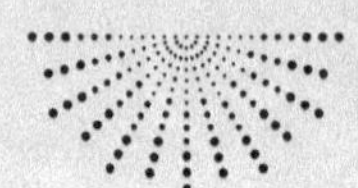

It had long been my dream to pray at the Al-Aqsa Mosque in Jerusalem. Coincidentally, my company had a business relationship with an international firm based in Israel, and I was selected for a business trip there. It felt like the perfect opportunity to explore something different and leave behind the troubling events of the past few months. On my way back from Germany, I arranged a stopover in Tel Aviv.

One of our business partners kindly picked me up from the airport and drove me to their headquarters. The meeting revolved around questions concerning the concrete pipes used in sewage systems, which had been manufactured using a special process. These pipes could also serve as bunkers in emergency situations, an intriguing concept that required my technical expertise. After addressing their inquiries, I was given a tour of the factory. The entire visit, conducted in German, lasted a few hours. While everyone spoke the language fluently, there was still a slight feeling of discomfort. However, they all knew I was Persian, and since Israel had strong relations with my country, the atmosphere remained cordial.

A room had been booked for me at the Hilton Tel Aviv, right

on the shores of the Mediterranean Sea. Before I left the office, the chairman advised me not to leave the hotel, warning that Arabs might see visitors from Islamic countries as traitors, which could be dangerous. This was an interesting observation as my visit to Jerusalem coincided with the visit made by Anwar Sadat, president of Egypt, for the peace talks. Sadat's visit with Menachem Begin and the Knesset set the stage for the subsequent negotiations that led to the Camp David Accords in 1978 and the eventual Egypt-Israel Peace Treaty in 1979. I felt a pang of disappointment when I heard the chairman's words as I had been eager to visit the old city of Jerusalem. With our next meeting not scheduled until the following evening, I had an entire day free. Sensing my enthusiasm, the chairman reassured me, promising to arrange a driver to take me on a day tour.

The next morning, I stepped out onto my hotel room's balcony, gazing over the Mediterranean and the vibrant city of Tel Aviv. Despite the visible rooftop water tanks, it struck me as a modern and beautiful place. At 9:00 a.m., a German-speaking driver arrived to take me on the coastal highway to Jerusalem.

Jerusalem, a city bearing one of history's saddest chapters, loomed in the distance. Over the centuries, much suffering had taken place here, often in the name of God. In 1099, Godfrey of Bouillon led the First Crusade, capturing Jerusalem in a massacre where at least twenty thousand were beheaded in just three days, establishing the Kingdom of Jerusalem. In 1118, Hugues de Payens co-founded the Knights Templar, turning the order into a military force to protect pilgrims. Years later, the Kurdish Sultan Saladin reclaimed Jerusalem for the Muslims. The city changed hands yet again in 1229 when Frederick II and al-Kamil signed the Treaty of Jaffa, ending the Sixth Crusade and returning Jerusalem to Christian rule.

As we drove, the German driver, who happened to come from the same region in Germany where I had studied, chatted amiably in our shared language. When he discovered I was Persian, he seemed to relax even more, sharing stories from the Torah, the Old Testament, and the Book of Chronicles. He spoke about Cyrus the Great, revered by some as a Messiah for allowing the Jewish return from Babylonian exile and being commanded by God to rebuild a house for Yahweh in Jerusalem. He even mentioned the "Cyrus Cylinder," an ancient clay decree now housed in the British Museum, which is often seen as an early declaration of human rights.

As we approached the city, remnants of past wars—abandoned military tanks and shattered machinery—served as stark reminders of the Six-Day War and the ongoing conflict. But when I caught sight of the golden dome of Al-Aqsa Mosque gleaming in the sunlight, my heart lifted. The driver dropped me off, and I entered the mosque, my spirit filled with anticipation. Its interior, while simple, radiated spiritual power. On the walls, steel rings used by Crusaders to tie their horses still hung, a testament to the past. In the center of the room, a glazed wooden box covered a sacred mountain, believed to be the spot where the Prophet Abraham prepared to sacrifice his son. The box also contained relics, including strands of hair from the Prophet Muhammad.

After visiting Al-Aqsa, we continued to the Wailing Wall, Judaism's most sacred site. At the entrance, I was given a paper yarmulke, which I placed on my head before walking toward the massive yellow stones of King Solomon's wall. Jews of various backgrounds prayed fervently at the wall, their bodies swaying rhythmically as they recited prayers. The sight was both profound and humbling. The driver suggested I could leave a note with my wishes between the stones, as was customary.

Our final stop was the Church of the Holy Sepulcher, believed to house the tomb of Jesus Christ. The dimly lit church, set below street level, had a cave-like atmosphere. The tomb itself was open to visitors, and people from all walks of life gathered to pray, light candles, and burn incense. The thick scent of incense mingled with the low murmur of prayers, creating an atmosphere of reverence.

As we drove back to Tel Aviv, I felt an overwhelming sense of gratitude for having visited three of the world's most sacred religious sites. I prayed not only for those who had passed but also for the world, with all its flaws and struggles.

The driver, after a moment of hesitation, asked me, "Which of the three religions do you belong to?"

I replied simply, "All three."

He looked at me, puzzled, through the rearview mirror.

"Religions are just paths leading to the same destination: faith in the one and only God. The goal is faith, not religion," I explained. "Each person must choose their own path."

I then asked him, "Do you know why Muslims always declare, 'La ilaha illallah,' which means, 'There is no god but God'?"

He remained silent, unsure of the answer.

"People often worship many gods—kings, caliphs, presidents, money, wealth, power. These become their idols. But a true believer," I said, "devotes themselves only to God, the Creator."

The driver nodded thoughtfully. Soon after, we arrived back at the hotel, and I prepared for the evening meeting.

83

OSLO, NORWAY

Instead of returning home from Jerusalem, the company sent me to Oslo, the capital of Norway. I was invited by the Tomberg Company to visit their factory, which specialized in manufacturing prefabricated warehouses. Upon arrival, I was immediately struck by the stark contrast in weather. The biting cold air of Oslo was jarring after the warmth of Tel Aviv. It was also incredibly dark, and I couldn't quite tell if it was noon or midnight—a disorienting sensation that only added to the feeling of unfamiliarity.

The chairman of Tomberg met me at the airport and drove me to a charming and cozy hotel. As he dropped me off, he mentioned that he would pick me up the next day at 1:00 p.m. Exhausted from the travel and the abrupt change in climate, I checked in and went straight to bed. However, my sleep was short-lived. A few hours later, I awoke feeling refreshed and wandered down to the hotel reception.

The front desk clerk looked at me quizzically and asked, "Is there anything I can assist you with?"

"No, thank you," I replied. "I'm just waiting to be collected for a meeting."

He raised an eyebrow. "In the middle of the night?!"

To my surprise, it was indeed midnight. Having only slept for a brief while, I returned to my room, realizing I had misjudged the time and promptly went back to bed.

The next day, the owner of the company arrived to take me to the factory. Though he spoke German fluently, he seemed reluctant to use it. When I inquired why, he explained that he had vowed never to speak German again. I understood his sentiment. I'd experienced something similar during a visit to Paris, where I had greeted a waiter in German, only to be completely ignored.

After touring the factory, I was invited to be a guest at his home. His residence was more akin to a castle, complete with luxurious amenities—a swimming pool, a sauna, and an elegant bar and dining area in the basement. One side of the room featured a breathtaking natural rock face, carved directly from the mountain, with polished stones gleaming under the lights.

Over dinner, he explained that in Norway, people generally preferred to entertain at home rather than dine in restaurants. He also noted that alcohol was prohibitively expensive, so it was customary to have a drink before the meal—usually gin. I couldn't help but compare this to Germany, where beer flows freely during meals, often followed by a schnapps. The French, of course, had their own tradition of wine with a baguette and cheese.

After a week in Norway, it was time for me to return home. Mr. Tomberg graciously drove me to the airport, and I thanked him for his warm hospitality, extending an invitation for him to visit me in Tehran, which he accepted. A few months later, he indeed visited as my guest.

During my time in Norway—a country that exemplifies democracy—I couldn't help but draw subconscious comparisons to my own homeland. In Norway, the connection between the people and their leaders seemed genuine and accessible. On certain days, any citizen could visit King Olaf and speak to him directly. In contrast, back home, even speaking to an ordinary civil servant required an intricate web of connections.

For over a year, the media had been filled with ceaseless praise for the fiftieth anniversary of the Pahlavi dynasty. The glorification was relentless and excessive. It was as if the entire country was caught in a constant loop of admiration for the monarchy. I often wondered why the Shah and Farah, both cultured and intelligent, didn't recognize how overdone it all seemed. Even my father, always thoughtful and humane, would quietly protest the constant glorification. He would often say, "If you do something good, don't boast about it endlessly! Yes, the Shah and his father have done much for our country, but they didn't do it alone. Thousands of people contributed to building and progressing our nation."

His words always stayed with me, a subtle reminder of the collective effort required to move a nation forward, and the humility that true leadership demands. As I reflected on my experiences in Norway, I saw more clearly the disparity between the democratic transparency of some nations and the exaggerated pageantry of others. The lessons from that week in Norway remained with me long after my return.

84

MOVING ONCE AGAIN

Our youngest sister had a nervous breakdown after our mother left us. I spoke with her doctor, who mentioned that her symptoms were strikingly similar to mine. It was clear that, without our parents to guide us, we were all struggling in our own ways. My eldest sister, feeling the weight of responsibility, tried to step into the role of mother. Even though our youngest sister was not in a stable mental state, she became engaged shortly after our father passed away. While the official year of mourning had not yet ended, my eldest sister insisted that the wedding take place sooner rather than later. So, we held a small celebration, catered once again in outstanding form by our friend, Ali, headwaiter at the Hilton Hotel. Despite the circumstances, it turned out to be a joyful event for everyone.

As our family continued to evolve, so did our living situation. The apartment in the Vanak district had become too small for our growing family, especially with two children needing more space. We decided it was time to move again. Gisela, with her usual flair for design, furnished our new home beautifully. It was something she excelled at, a reflection of her natural talent and keen eye for detail. In our new home, we made an effort to keep the family close, hosting gatherings on every occasion, hoping to maintain a sense of unity despite the challenges we faced.

Our eldest brother also moved to Tehran, no longer wanting to live in Tabriz. He set up a practice in the southern part of the city, where he treated patients in need, free of charge. His selfless nature and dedication to helping others were inspiring. My other brother, Parwiz, continued his work as well, running his own practice and teaching at Tehran University.

I rented out our old apartment in Vanak to the nephew of Dr. Saheb, the owner of our company. Unfortunately, the rent was never paid. It seemed that the upper class in our country had grown accustomed to taking without giving in return, a mindset that was becoming increasingly problematic. The simmering resentment towards this privileged class was steadily rising, and it was clear that such social disparities were becoming unsustainable.

As 1977 drew to a close, Gisela's mother came to visit us from Germany. Together, we visited my parents' graves. Mutti, as Gisela's mother was affectionately known, was heartbroken. It was as though she had lost her own sister. That Christmas, we celebrated what would be our last holiday together in our homeland, though none of us realized it at the time. The atmosphere was bittersweet, a mixture of nostalgia, grief, and a quiet anticipation of the changes yet to come.

Our apartment in Meydan-e Vanak district in Tehran.

UPHEAVAL APPROACHING 1978

$\mathcal{M}$eanwhile, our company was in dire straits. Meetings that were once held regularly had become infrequent, as many of the board members simply stopped showing up at the office. Dr. Saheb, who once exuded confidence, could seldom be found even though his large Mercedes was in the parking lot, a symbol of the uncertainty hanging over us. Many of our construction projects had slowed to a near halt, with engineers abandoning ship, emigrating in search of more stable opportunities abroad. This growing sense of instability pervaded not just our company, but the entire country.

The rapid economic growth driven by increased oil revenues and investments had triggered rampant inflation and severe supply shortages. The writing had been on the wall, yet few had prepared for the inevitable. In Bandar Abbas, hundreds of ships remained anchored for months, waiting for their cargo to be unloaded and transported. The country's infrastructure simply wasn't equipped to handle the flood of imports. Storage and transport systems buckled under the pressure, leaving goods stranded and further worsening the crisis.

By this time, the Shah's grand vision of a "Great Civilization" was well underway. His ambitious reforms, part of what he called the "White Revolution," had ushered in rapid industrial and military modernization, along with significant social and economic changes. Beginning in 1963, these reforms included compulsory education for both boys and girls aged six to thirteen and mandated Western-style clothing for men. In the referendum that followed in January of that year, an overwhelming 99 percent of voters endorsed the reforms.

Yet, despite this overwhelming support, the reforms weren't enough to silence the opposition. The powerful Shia clergy, feeling their influence threatened, especially resented the Shah's pro-Western policies. Among them was Ayatollah Khomeini, a cleric who had become the voice of the politically radicalized faction of the clergy. He called for nothing less than the abolition of the monarchy. While the Shah was modern and progressive in many respects, he had initially maintained good relations with the clergy. However, his reforms had shifted the balance, pushing him into conflict with a deeply entrenched religious establishment.

By the mid-1970s, Iran had made remarkable progress. Illiteracy rates had fallen, healthcare had improved, modern technology had been introduced, and the standard of living for much of the population had risen. But the critics were vocal. They argued that while the improvements were real, they were not enough, and that the country's vast oil wealth had been misused.

At the height of his power, the Shah of Iran ruled a nation of 35 million people, commanding the respect of global leaders from Washington to Moscow. Iran's oil billions fueled his ambitions, making its armed forces among the most powerful in the Middle East. Yet, for all his wealth and influence, he was ultimately a man without a country. As the revolution gathered force in January 1979, the Shah and his family were forced to flee, moving from one country to another in a desperate search for a secure place to call home.

Ayatollah Ruhollah Khomeini's rise to prominence had deep

roots. Born in 1900 in the town of Khomeyn, he began studying the Quran and Arabic as a young boy. By 1936, he had earned the title of Mujtahid, signifying his expertise in Sharia law. In Shi'ite Islam, this elevated him to the status of a jurist, capable of making legal determinations, including those regarding jihad. His political views were first laid out in his 1943 publication *Kashf al-Asrar* (*The Unveiling of Secrets*), where he called for the abolition of the monarchy.

For years, Khomeini taught Islamic law and philosophy in Qom, keeping a relatively low profile until 1963, when he first publicly denounced the Shah and called for his overthrow. The response was swift. In 1964, Khomeini was arrested and exiled, flown out of the country on a military plane to Turkey. From there, he relocated to Iraq, settling in Najaf, a holy city for Shiites. It was during his time in exile that Khomeini penned *The Islamic State*, his most significant work, which outlined his vision for an Islamic government.

Khomeini remained in Iraq until 1978 when Saddam Hussein, then president of Iraq, expelled him. His forced relocation came at a time when the revolution in Iran was beginning to simmer.

In January 1978, an article about Ayatollah Khomeini was published in an Iranian newspaper, breaking years of official silence about his existence. The article, written by Savak, the secret police, and the Ministry of Information, was meant to delegitimize him. Instead, it sparked a firestorm. The clergy in Qom organized a sympathy rally that quickly turned violent when the army intervened, leaving 300 injured and 80 dead. This event marked the beginning of a series of protests, which, held every 40 days in line with Shia mourning traditions, built momentum over the course of the year. By the end of 1978, these protests had become a national movement, signaling that the Shah's reign was rapidly approaching its end.

86

FINAL CELEBRATIONS OF 1978

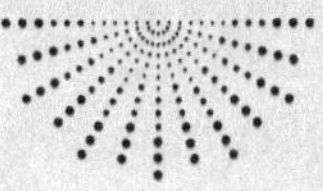

The 1978 Nowruz festival coincided with the Christian Easter holiday, and for the first time in years, all of my siblings and their families gathered together. We tried our best to celebrate both festivals, clinging to the happier memories of the past, even though they felt distant. My brother, Behruz, whose dear wife had recently passed away, flew in from Germany with his two children to stay with us for a while. We all mourned in silence, but the reunion revived some joy, rekindling the warmth of earlier times.

Our New Year, Easter, and my daughter's 11th birthday were celebrated in unison. The house was alive once again. Gisela had gone to great lengths to make everything as comfortable and pleasant as possible. The weather was perfect, allowing us to barbecue in the garden, and laughter briefly filled the air. But beneath the surface, our hearts were heavy. The country was in turmoil. Protest rallies had turned violent, businesses were set ablaze, cinemas torched, and banks attacked. None of this was mentioned in the newspapers, and television continued broadcasting movies as if the nation were not on the brink of revolution. The Shah attempted to salvage his monarchy by appointing a new prime minister, but it was already too late. His famous words, "I have heard the voice of the revolution," only deepened the growing divide.

Our new driver, a young man from Damavand, a small town nestled on the slopes of the mountain by the same name, became my constant companion. There wasn't much work to do, but perhaps he stayed close out of concern for my safety. We spent hours talking about the situation in the country. He confided that some people had seen the writing on the wall long ago. They had quietly sold their homes and belongings, moving overseas while it was still possible. Others simply packed a few bags and left, never to return. At that time, the Iranian rial was one of the ten most stable currencies in the world, and except for Israel and Switzerland, Iranians could travel to most countries without a visa. It seemed like a distant luxury as unrest simmered across the land.

As the summer heat intensified, so did the protests. Tehran and other major cities became flashpoints for demonstrations, and eventually, a military government took control. Many believed the new regime would restore order, but the situation worsened. A state of emergency was declared in Isfahan, followed by a strict curfew from 9:00 p.m. to 5:00 a.m. A few weeks later, Tabriz and Tehran were placed under curfew as well. Often, I stood on the terrace of our house, looking toward the city center, where plumes of smoke filled the sky. The streets below seemed surreal, filled with tension and uncertainty. I asked myself, *What will become of us?*

Meanwhile, our youngest brother's wedding was fast approaching. At Gisela's insistence, the ceremony was to be held at our house. She had just returned from Germany, where she had been caring for her ill mother, but made sure to be back in time for the celebration. The bride hailed from a well-regarded family in Tabriz, and both families had known each other for years. It was to be a small, intimate affair.

On a warm autumn day, beneath the blue skies, the wedding took place in our garden. All of our relatives and close family friends gathered, their spirits temporarily lifted by the occasion. After the cleric performed the ceremony, dinner was served, and the guests settled in for what should have been a joyful evening. But before the festivities could continue, I received a phone call. The message was clear: the celebration needed to end. The country was in the grip of unrest, and no event—not even a wedding— justified carrying on while clashes between demonstrators and the military raged nearby, with lives being lost. Reluctantly, we informed the guests, and they left quickly, hoping to reach home safely amid the chaos.

When the house finally grew quiet, I walked through the halls, checking on the children. Both were fast asleep, oblivious to the world outside. I sat down with Gisela in the dimly lit living room, our thoughts heavy with worry. The future had become uncertain. Every year, I had sent the children to Germany with Gisela, hoping they would learn the language and immerse themselves in the culture. Little did I know then that it was not merely a cultural experience—they would soon need to live their lives there, far from our homeland.

I took Gisela's hand, the weight of my decision pressing down on me. "I think it's best if you take the children to Germany," I said, trying to maintain my composure. "You'll be safe there."

She looked at me, eyes wide with anxiety. "What about you?"

"When things calm down, I'll join you. Or perhaps you'll come back. But right now, I can't leave, there's the company, and my family still needs me."

The very next day was Friday, September 8th, a day that would later be known as Black Friday. The streets of Tehran erupted in a frenzy of violence. Demonstrations turned into riots, and the military's response was brutal. The death toll climbed. In many ways, our family's situation mirrored that of my parents 50 years earlier, when they had fled Baku amidst similar chaos. History, it seemed, was repeating itself.

Last gathering of my brothers in 1978 in Tehran before the revolution started.

Gisela and I attending my brother Ayoub and Sima's wedding.

Our last home in Tehran before the riots and revolution started
in 1978.

87

THE END OF PARADISE AS WE KNEW IT

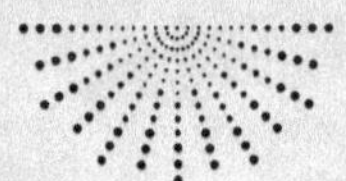

The 1978 Nowruz festival had been a subdued affair, one shadowed by the chaos engulfing the country. While this event took place in Iran, we heard of Gisela's mother falling ill once again in Germany. The climate, invariably rainy and damp, did not suit her health. Gisela had already set off with the children to be with her, and our farewell had been plain and simple. We assumed that, in no time, we would be reunited. But deep down, I wasn't sure.

The situation within my family mirrored the turmoil in the country. My eldest brother, Farokh, a doctor with a wife and three children, was helpless. In the southern part of the city where he ran his practice, wearing business attire like suits and ties had become dangerous. Many of his patients, the ones who needed him most, were being attacked. Parwiz, my brother who usually taught at the University of Tehran, was now performing surgeries on a daily basis for those injured in the protests. Yaghoub's wife, Liesel, was pregnant with their second child, while the uncertainty of his business weighed heavily on him. The youngest of us, Ayoub, newly married, was serving his military duty as an officer while desertions from the army grew rampant. As for me, I was a business partner with a brother of the emperor, a position that placed me in a precarious situation as the regime crumbled. Each of us faced a world turned upside down, with an uncertain future stretching out before us.

Unsure of what to do next, I asked my driver to take me to the office. He was a brave man, unfazed by the upheaval around him, perhaps because he had always been opposed to the regime. He had connections everywhere and assured me I was safe in his company, though I wasn't so certain of anything anymore.

One afternoon, Behzad, my dear friend and savior from past hardships, visited me at the office. He stood at the window, watching the endless stream of demonstrators flood the streets. After a while, he turned to me, his face serious. He said the outlook was grim. As we left the office together, we noticed that most of the offices were empty. The management, it seemed, had already begun packing and preparing to leave the country.

I returned home to a silent, deserted house. The rooms felt hollow, with only a few toys scattered across the children's room. Minou's new piano sat with the cover open, but the absence of her presence made it seem lifeless. As I walked through the house, the photographs on the living room wall caught my eye—memories of happier days: my parents, my siblings, our two children. They were just 10 and 11 years old, yet they had never known stability. They had changed schools more times than they could count, never having a real home. My thoughts wandered to our house in Tabriz, abandoned now, but once the setting of our happiest times.

Stepping out onto the terrace, I took in the cityscape. Smoke rose from fires scattered across Tehran, and the sky was a deep, choking black. The air had grown thick, making it difficult to breathe. Everything was falling apart, and I felt utterly powerless. Soon after, the situation worsened - workers went on strike. Power outages became frequent, and soon there was no gas for cooking, no kerosene for heating. The country seemed to be shutting down piece by piece.

The media, however, remained disconnected from reality. Television stations continued airing films, pretending the revolution wasn't unfolding on the streets. Newspapers ignored the chaos, leaving people to rely on whispered rumors circulating through the alleys and streets. BBC Radio out of London was the only reliable source of news. The fall of the Shah, it seemed, had already been decided by the powers that be. Persia, with its vast wealth—natural gas, oil, irrigation systems, and tourism—was unraveling.

My driver, always perceptive, had seen the signs for some time. Now, he suggested it was best that I visit my family in Germany. He pointed out that the company was no longer running, and the country was collapsing. He was right. I started packing, selecting only a few keepsakes, family heirlooms—precious memories of the life we had built.

At the Kuehne & Nagel forwarding agency, as I arranged to ship some of our belongings to Germany, I noticed a clerk sitting in the corner, sobbing. Concerned, I approached him, asking if he was hurt.

"No," he replied between sobs. "I'm not crying from pain. I'm crying for the absurdity of this situation. For months, we've been packing up houses for the wealthy. So much gold, silver, silk carpets, and precious objects—all being taken out of the country. Meanwhile, you are sending old pots, grubby carpets, and household goods of no value."

He didn't know that, as children, we had played on those grubby old carpets, that our parents had prayed on them. They were, in truth, the most valuable possessions we had, laden with memories and love.

On December 6, 1978, I flew to Germany with my sister-in-law, her 15-day-old son, and her little daughter. Before leaving for the airport, I wandered through our house one last time. The rooms, still filled with furniture, felt like a relic of a past life. The children's toys lay scattered as if waiting for them to return. It reminded me of my mother's farewell in Baku, 50 years earlier. When the driver came to collect me, I asked him to stop at the graveyard so I could bid my parents one final farewell.

As it turned out, it was indeed goodbye forever. The furnished house, our cars, our apartment in Vanak—I never saw them again. Everything was expropriated, and the company was nationalized. My father's hard-earned inheritance, the land, the buildings, everything he had worked for over 50 years, was taken from us. The work and commitment to our country that had spanned generations had been erased in a matter of months. Concessions made to the opposition came too late. We were left with nothing.

88

THAT (FATEFUL) YEAR 1979

As I mentioned earlier, the Shah's final attempts to salvage his reign were futile. His replacement of the Prime Minister could no longer turn the tide. The days of the Pahlavi dynasty were numbered. When Reza Pahlavi departed on January 16, 1979, at noon, he left behind a country irrevocably changed, with his parting words, "I am tired and need a break." It was not just a personal admission of exhaustion, but the end of an era. He left for exile, never to return, and the Islamic Revolution continued to gather momentum.

Merely two weeks later, on February 1, 1979, Ayatollah Khomeini returned to Iran, greeted like a messiah by throngs of supporters. His arrival signaled a decisive shift in the nation. Overnight, the country began to change, and for many of us, life worsened. The structure of power was swiftly dismantled, and the hopes of moderation and compromise disappeared. The revolution had fully arrived.

One of the earliest and most heartbreaking losses I suffered was my dear friend and lifesaver, Behzad. On April 5, 1979, just months into the revolution, Behzad was on his way home from his factory late one night. In the chaos of the revolution, it had become common for the newly established revolutionary committees to set up checkpoints. Behzad, perhaps distracted by the weight of the world around him, did not hear their command to halt. A bullet, fired without warning, struck him in the back of the head. He died instantly.

It felt like the soul of the country had also been executed that night. And that year, 1979, already stained by the deaths of my parents, became even more unbearable with the loss of Behzad and another dear friend, Hassan. Hassan had been battling cancer for months. Despite receiving treatment, it was not enough. I stood at his funeral, clutching his old father's trembling hand, and we wept together. It seemed that grief had become a constant companion.

By May 1979, the revolution was solidifying its control. I vividly remember the exiled Shah giving a defiant interview to *The Washington Post* from Cairo. He defended his reign with fervor, denying any corruption and proudly listing the accomplishments achieved under his leadership. "Eventually we went faster than some people could digest," he said, referring to the rapid pace of modernization. He spoke of the strides made in democratization and the dramatic increase in per capita income from $60 a year to $2,540. Yet, despite these claims of progress, he sounded like a man who had seen his dream unravel. "We were thinking of the great civilization," he lamented, "We were thinking life could be enriched by art and by spirit, by the blossoming of thought and spirit. And now it is all destroyed." Those words were heavy with a sense of irretrievable loss.

That same year, by November 1979, the newly formed Islamic Republic had cemented its rule with the adoption of a new constitution via a national referendum. Khomeini, now the *Supreme Leader*, was officially titled the *Leader of the Revolution*. His control was absolute, and with him at the helm, the direction of the country had irreversibly shifted.

Mohammad Reza Pahlavi, whose voice had once commanded an empire, passed away on July 27, 1980, in the Cairo Military

Hospital after a long battle with cancer. His death marked the final closing of a chapter. He was buried in the Al-Rifai Mosque in Cairo, next to King Farouk I, the penultimate Egyptian monarch. The Pahlavi dynasty was now a memory, and the "great civilization" that he had dreamed of lay in ruins, a casualty of the revolution that had torn through Iran and reshaped its destiny.

As I reflected on all that had transpired, I couldn't help but feel a deep sense of melancholy for the country we once knew, now irrevocably transformed. The passage of time had not dulled the pain of the upheaval, the losses, and the tragedies that came with the revolution. What was left behind were memories, and with them, the weight of a future that had been stolen.

89

NEW BEGINNING IN GERMANY

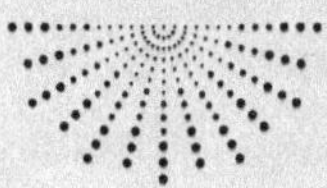

"A thousand half-loves must be forsaken to take one whole heart home."

— RUMI

On December 6, 1978, I arrived at Frankfurt airport, where my sister-in-law, Liesel, and her two young children were collected by her parents. I then continued my journey, flying on to Düsseldorf to reunite with Gisela and the children, who had been staying with Mutti.

Mutti lived in a small two-room apartment on the fifth floor. It was cozy but cramped: I slept on the front room sofa, Gisela shared the other sofa with Mutti, and the children slept on the floor, a notable change from the spacious comfort we were accustomed to. Aware of this, Mutti, with her loving care did everything possible to make us feel at home. She had visited us in Persia many times over the years and knew us well. During the day, she took the

405

children to the park or zoo, allowing Gisela and me time to discuss our uncertain future.

We didn't have much money—just a few thousand tomans I had kept for security and Gisela's savings from her old account at Deutsche Bank. Over the years, she had deposited money into it during her visits to Germany, but even that would only last for a short while. We kept in contact with friends and family in Persia, but the news was grim. There were more executions, looting was rampant, curfews and bans tightened, and homes were being expropriated. The military leadership was systematically eliminated. The country was spiraling into chaos, and we realized how fortunate we were to have left when we did.

Soon after I arrived in Düsseldorf, Gisela informed me that our funds were running low and urged me to start looking for work. I felt abandoned by God once again. Where was His guidance in this time of hardship? I asked Gisela to have patience, but even I couldn't shake the weight of our situation. I remember the day vividly when Gisela, overwhelmed, took the children to the zoo for some peace. Life felt unbearably heavy; we were struggling to adjust to a much humbler reality.

The next morning, I placed an ad in the local newspaper, advertising my desire for a position as a civil engineering director. I listed my credentials and waited.

A few days later, the phone rang. It was a Sunday morning. Curious, I quickly picked it up and heard a deep, confident voice say one word, "Götzen."

"Sorry, I don't understand," I responded.

"My name is Götzen. I'm calling about your ad. Are you Mr. Payandeh, and are you German by any chance?"

"No sir, I'm Persian," I replied.

"But your German accent is very good. I can clearly understand you!"

"I studied engineering in Germany, and my wife is German," I explained.

"Lovely," he responded. "Why don't you come over with your wife for a visit?" He gave me his address, and we eagerly prepared for the meeting.

We borrowed a car from Gisela's uncle the next day and drove to Mr. Heinrich Götzen's home. Both of us were curious to see what kind of opportunity awaited. Mr. Götzen, a small man with a big smile, greeted us warmly. He and his wife made us feel instantly welcome. As we settled in, I detailed my previous projects and responsibilities in Persia, recounting years of accomplishments in civil engineering and construction. They listened attentively, genuinely interested in our story.

To my amazement, Mr. Götzen offered me a position right there on the spot! Gisela and I could hardly believe it. We rushed home to share the incredible news with Minou and Kambiz. It felt like a fresh start—a new chapter. For the first time in a long while, I realized God had not abandoned me after all. He had been working at His own speed.

I later learned that Mr. Götzen was one of the most influential architects and businessmen in the region. He owned numerous buildings and ran a successful architectural firm from his home, employing about a dozen people.

For the first few months, I worked regular hours, but I felt as if I hadn't fully proven my value. I wasn't given direct tasks or orders, yet there was a mutual trust. I sensed that Mr. Götzen was waiting for an "ah-ha" moment to affirm my potential. Although I wasn't entirely satisfied with my work, I held out hope for an opportunity to prove myself.

A month later, I was trying to help a colleague with some minor technical problems, but my thoughts were elsewhere. I was thinking of my family's future and what course of action or next steps I should take. My dear Sufi and mentor, Adieb, came to my mind, as did my precious mother who always gave me her words of wisdom for support and guidance. It comforted me thinking of them both, and I resolved to be patient.

The opportunity I was seeking presented itself one evening shortly thereafter, when I overheard some contractors waiting for a meeting with Mr. Götzen. They were bidding on a project to develop eighty-five homes. Sensing a chance to assist, I invited the contractors one at a time into the large meeting room where Mr. Götzen was still sitting at the end of the big table, his head buried in a pile of papers. He must have heard all my conversations and negotiations but pretended he wasn't paying attention. He never looked our way and never stepped in or interrupted. After five long hours (it was already 10 p.m.) I finished with contractor #10 and noticed Mr. Götzen was still there and seemingly inattentive to his surroundings. The room was quiet again. I gathered all the freshly negotiated agreements in a pile, left them on the table and stepped out without a word and headed home. Had I done the right thing? I wasn't sure.

The next morning, Mr. Götzen received me in his office with open arms and a big smile on his face. He ordered coffee for us and asked me to sit down and share the details of what had occurred the previous evening. He was pleased with the results, especially with how I had managed to reduce costs by 20% with those stubborn, over-priced contractors. We celebrated the success, and from that moment, a strong bond of trust formed between us.

SEVERAL MONTHS LATER, I was promoted to be his right-hand man. Around the same time, Mr. Götzen told me about a new housing project in a small town called Hochdahl, about 30 minutes from Düsseldorf. A row of single-family homes was to be built in a beautiful, tree-lined area, and he asked me to oversee the project.

"You should take one of the lots for your family and build your first home in Germany," he suggested.

"It's a wonderful idea, but I don't have credit established with the local banks, nor do I have any kind of down payment. It's just not possible," I replied.

"That shouldn't be a problem," he said confidently. "I have a great relationship with the bank."

The following day, he took me to Deutsche Bank, and we went straight to meet with the director of the branch. After introducing me, Mr. Götzen went on to explain that I wished to build my first house and needed a loan of 500,000 DM, for which he would be the guarantor. I didn't know what to say, and at the same time I was filled with excitement, thinking of my family's well-being. Within one hour, my new account was set up and with a significant opening balance to start the process of building and owning a new home. Mr. Götzen started to feel like a guardian angel as he sat next to me. I had finally found the security that I so desperately needed for my family. I thought back to the beginning of this journey in my mind. First, placing the ad in the newspaper, then meeting Heinrich Götzen and his wife... until today sitting at Deutsche Bank and being able to build our first home in Hochdahl. It felt like life had started all over again, filled with purpose and hope. I had a new job, a new construction project, and soon a place we could call home!

Construction started shortly after my visit with the bank. I oversaw and managed the process and work of all the various contractors. There was much commotion, and it was all so busy and exciting, it seemed with each brick, the excitement grew bigger. Our four-story home was located at the end of a cul-de-sac, tucked in behind tall trees and bushes. This was where we were putting down new roots again, and because the houses were made of concrete and bricks, they were designed to stand for multiple generations. I was already sorting out in my mind the use of each floor and room. The attic would be used as my home office. All the bedrooms and bathrooms would be on the third floor. We decided on mahogany kitchen cabinets and white marble floors from Argentina throughout the entire house. The basement was divided in two separate sections. One side consisted of a Swedish-style wooden sauna with a marble plunge pool, a shower, and wooden chaise-longues for meditation with relaxing music. The second room was our party room, complete with a classic saloon-style bar with a big mirror mounted on the back wall. The shelves were stocked with countless different liquors—just like in a western movie, which I always enjoyed (John Wayne was my favorite actor). The bar top was a solid L-shaped piece of copper. The walls were coated with velvet fabric which made it feel warm and inviting. A disco ball hung from the ceiling - a typical 80's interior accent for the dance section. Over the years, we hosted New Year's parties, birthday parties and celebrations of all sorts in that party room.

The fireplace in the living room which we enjoyed
during cold winter days. Our hunting dog, Amor,
who we all loved so much, enjoyed it too!

ON THE GROUND floor in our living room, we had a French-style traditional fireplace with a mantel made of rose-colored marble. This was the centerpiece of the house where friends, family and guests would be always welcome. It would be a place to share stories, stay warm and build more memories together. As was the case in Persia, our door was always open for family, neighbors, and friends, short or long term. It turned out in the later years that some of Minou's and Kambiz's friends found shelter for weeks and months with us as they worked through various troubles in their homes. The warm Persian hospitality was strongly integrated in our German enclave, and everyone felt loved, welcomed, and secure. It warmed my heart that our family could help whenever needed. The past, and our upbringing were the gateway to the present time and our hardship and experiences kept us human and humble, regardless of income or station. I must thank our role models on both sides, my parents and Gisela's mother who taught us these values with their unconditional love and wisdom.

Our garden was small, but intimate and serene. Gisela spent many hours making it beautiful and lush. I built a cozy terrace where we enjoyed Kaffee & Kuchen together. The stairs from the terrace wound down through the flower beds to a small fishpond and waterfall. The sound of trickling water was relaxing and drew me back to the old days growing up in Persia, as most gardens had a fishpond. In the Persian culture, water symbolizes life, purity, and joy and therefore it is a reminder of all things that exist.

It was such a pleasure for me to come home after a long day on the construction sites with loud equipment, to find peace outside in the garden and watch my loved ones listening to music and sharing their stories with each other. After all, this is all that truly matters in life; family, the memories being built together, a place you call your home, and the bonding that takes place.

Shortly after completing our new home, I took the leap and started my own engineering business, ORBA. Gisela, always supportive, managed the scheduling, administrative tasks, and bookkeeping, ensuring the business ran smoothly. As the company grew, I invited my brother Yaghoub to join and assist with more complex projects. Years later, Kambiz came on board, making it a true family organization. With everyone's and strengths, ORBA quickly blossomed, and we became a tight-knit team, united by both family and business.

My family in Germany. From above left: Mutti, Gisela, Minou, Kambiz, and me.

EPILOGUE

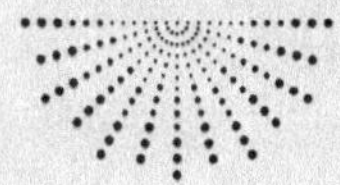

In the never-ending cycle of life, we watched our children follow in our footsteps, as they blossomed and happily settled into the German culture. Minou and Kambiz found peace and a sense of security after being forced out of Persia without warning during the 1978 revolution. As parents, we wish for stability, good health, and prosperity for our children, with the hope for a peaceful tomorrow.

Kambiz and his wife continue to live in Germany, while Gisela and I made yet another big move—this time across the Atlantic to the serene State of Washington in the northwest corner of the United States. Minou and her husband live just down the road from us, and we are blessed to have our two beautiful grandchildren close by, filling our lives with laughter and joy.

My passion for gourmet cooking has flourished here, and I take great pleasure in spoiling my family with international dishes. But it's the treasured Persian recipes passed down through generations that hold a special place in my heart. These meals are not just food; they are stories, evoking memories of our homeland and connecting us to our rich cultural heritage.

Surrounded by the stunning beauty of Washington—the

towering trees, majestic mountains, and meandering rivers framed by fields of vibrant wildflowers—I found inspiration in nature and took up watercolor painting. It has become a favorite hobby, allowing me to capture the essence of the breathtaking landscape that now feels like home. Through cooking and art, I continue to weave together the threads of our past with the vibrant present, always grateful for the life we've built together.

I am grateful, I am content.

May your home be a place where family gathers, friends meet, and love always continues to grow.

God bless.

ACKNOWLEDGMENTS

Experienced in the Azari language, remembered in Farsi, written originally in German, and translated into English, this book would not exist without the support and dedication of my dear friend Libby.